Las Vegas
Little Red Book

A Girl's Guide
to the Perfect
Vegas Getaway

Companion Book

Las Vegas Little Black Book:
A Guy's Guide to the Perfect Vegas Weekend

Las Vegas*

Little Red Book

A Girl's Guide to the Perfect Vegas Getaway

Molly Sullivan

David deMontmollin

Hiram Todd Norman

JUSTIN,
CHARLES
& CO.

Justin, Charles & Co.
Boston, MA

917
.93135
Su
c.1

FIRST U.S. EDITION 2005

ISBN 13: 978-1-932112-48-1
ISBN 10: 1-932112-48-0
Library of Congress Cataloging-in-Publication Data is available.

Published in the United States by
Justin, Charles & Co., Publishers, Boston, Massachusetts
www.justincharlesbooks.com

Distributed by National Book Network, Lanham, Maryland
www.nbnbooks.com

10 9 8 7 6 5 4 3 2 1

PRINTED IN THE UNITED STATES OF AMERICA

Contents

Introduction

★...

Your Weekend: You Deserve a Great Time

If you're heading out to Vegas based on some advice from friends or the lessons learned from a previous trip, you'll probably have a pretty good time. If you head out to Sin City armed with the *Little Red Book,* you'll have a great time.

Good times are regular occurrences in a girl's life; they're shopping with the girls, heading out for a Cosmo after a long week, relaxing over a sinfully delicious meal at a hot restaurant or at your favorite day spa. *Great* times, on the other hand, are much harder to come by. The *Red Book* is here to serve up a great time in Vegas for you and the girls. We'll make it easy for you to create the ultimate girls' weekend: you'll avoid the traps that will soak up your time and eat up your wallet; and you'll leave Las Vegas with a smile on your face and tales to tell for years to come.

This book will provide you with all of the information you need to take the town by the horns and ride it for all it's worth. Every trip can be broken down into a set of key decisions that will make or break your weekend. You need to be savvy, and if you are, good times will follow. You work too hard with too little time off to settle for anything less than getting every ounce of fun out of your much needed Vegas weekend. Going to Vegas with the girls should be a special event; don't wind up at the departure gate saying "Next time we'll know to avoid . . ."

Advice You Can Use

You hear a lot about stories about Las Vegas. Unfortunately, few of them are true. No one will admit how much they spent on a mediocre dinner, how much their hotel room really cost, or how long they had to wait to get into an overcrowded, overpriced nightclub.

Enter the *Little Red Book*. We'll help you tune out the static and hone in on the right frequency, leading you to great places filled with good times and gorgeous men. Don't expect comprehensive reviews, don't expect any information on family friendly activity, don't expect advice on ho-hum destinations; the focus here is on maximizing your fun for you and the girls.

Advice You Can Trust

You don't have much time to spend and you certainly don't have cash to waste chasing mirages in the desert, so why trust the *Little Red Book*? You can trust this book because the authors know from whence they speak. Molly Sullivan has lived the Vegas life you only dream about. Not to brag, but it's true.

As an entertainment reporter for *Hot On! Las Vegas*, Molly spends her days exploring the newest and hottest clubs, restaurants, boutiques, shows, and spas to grace the Strip, and her nights inside the velvet rope interviewing the A-list stars and celebrities who have made Vegas America's most extravagant adult playground. Most other Vegas guides are written by freelance travel writers who blows into town and write reviews. They lack the perspective of a true Vegas insider.

While Las Vegas might be the new Shangri-La, it's Molly's backyard.

You've found the girl who can deliver on your promised "great time."

How to Use this Book

This book is intended to help you during the three phases of your trip: planning, executing, and remembering.

Dreaming Las Vegas — Planning Your Trip

Well in advance of arrival, you need to figure out where you're going to stay and how you're going to spend your nights out on the town. There are also a slew of daytime activities in the new Vegas that are tailor-made for groups of girls, and you need to plan for those in advance too. Spend the time creating a shared vision of your trip with the girls, and make some reservations now.

Viva Las Vegas — Executing the Details

Once you're on the ground, you'll need to get the lay of the land, put the *Red Book* in your purse, and hit the town. We'll tell you where to spend your time and money every step of the way.

Leaving Las Vegas: Remembering Your Trip

Once you leave Las Vegas, you need to be armed with stories for the girls back home. Your experience in Vegas needs to be top-notch, loaded with memories that will last you a lifetime. The *Red Book* will show you how to create memorable experiences and how to tell about them afterward.

The Appendixes: Quick References

The appendixes in the back of the book are reference guides that summarize the information in the book. The first appendix contains six different hour-by-hour itineraries to use for planning your perfect Vegas getaway. The second appendix contains reference lists of places outlined in the book, so you may easily make arrangements and book reservations.

Get to Work / Have Fun

You need to decide right now to take ownership of your trip or risk winding up broke, bitter, and disappointed. A perfect getaway never "just happens." Read on, make plans, and let the fantasy begin!

PART I

Dreaming Las Vegas

✴ Chapter 1 ✴

24 Hours in Sin City

✴···

It's the life you have always dreamed of living. The pace is fast, the people animated, the air charged with an electric current guaranteed to awaken the thrill seeker in all who venture to this desert oasis. This is the Las Vegas I know, and now you too can experience Las Vegas my way . . . the *girl's way,* as I take you on a whirlwind tour of a day in my life as a Las Vegas TV show host, and your concierge to this spectacular jungle of bliss. As a Las Vegas native who lives, works, and plays in Sin City, I've watched the landscape change from a guy's-only playground to the hippest, most exciting vacation spot for girlfriends seeking that memorable, indulgent weekend away from home. But the dizzying array of pleasures awaiting you in Sin City can be overwhelming at best, and to negotiate this terrain of endless temptation you need to know the secrets, the ins and the outs, the hidden gems that will make your getaway the experience of a lifetime. Intrigued?

Come join me. It's time to start my day . . .

9:00 p.m. – On Your Mark. Get Set. Go!

My day starts during your night. I have a Red Carpet gig at PURE inside Caesars Palace. All the A-listers have been invited to what has recently been dubbed the number one club in the nation. PURE, as the name implies, is a breath of fresh air, an indulgent treat for the senses, and *the* place to see and be seen. With its reputation for excitement and its prime location at the center of the Las Vegas Strip, PURE is easily the breakout star on the national nightlife scene.

It's interview time as I line up with my "photog," ready to catch the money shots and exclusive sound bytes. I turn to find myself face to face with Jessica Simpson; when you do Vegas by the *Little Red Book* it's easy to bump into the A-listers. As I secretly wish for Nick Lachey, my call to her is the one she responds to and over she comes. Let the games begin . . .

11:00 p.m. – Beyond the Velvet Rope

I'm off to the private see-and-be-seen party beyond the velvet rope, where only invited guests and credentialed reporters are granted access. Only the trusted few have the opportunity to rub elbows with the glitzy and glamorous where there are no lights, no mics, and no inhibitions. Always looking for the next hot exposé, I ride the secret elevator and find myself escorted into this posh rendezvous. It's a new experience every night.

Even if you don't have a media credential, you can join me with instant VIP access by simply bringing out your Vegas Vixen — sophisticated yet sexy; elegant yet edgy; polite yet assertive; business-savvy yet fun-loving. First, make eye contact with the bouncers and VIP hosts located on the other side of the velvet rope. Next, casually approach the crowded area. Then, listen and try to pick-up one or more of their names. Just as in business networking, names are crucial elements for a successful night on the streets of Sin City. If they don't seem to have an IFB (internal feedback) in their ear to communicate internally, they will more than likely use each other's names to get updates on the night's agenda for their VIPs. So, address one or more of the bouncers and VIP hosts by name and simply ask, "Joe, how have you been?" It's not *what* you say, but *how* you say it. Then, casually mention you're with four other fabulous women, and ask what your chances are for access. Do this with your brightest smile (and of course, a little cleavage never hurt anyone). Confidence is the key to a Vegas Vixen. You will be walking past the velvet rope in no time. We locals like to call it southern Nevada charm!

2:00 a.m. – Beauty Rest

I need my beauty rest. And who doesn't? Take it from a native, pacing is everything in Vegas; it's a twenty-four-hour city, a seductress with a way of making you forget about time by tempting you with one delight after another. It's important to prioritize all those enticing options, and to let the *Little Red Book* help you determine your desert destiny.

I find myself in valet where I generously tip my regular attendant who arranges to keep my Audi close for that fast getaway to my off-Strip condo. Once home, I unwind and recap the events of the evening. I surf for the latest news on *E! Entertainment*, CNN, *FOX News*, the local CBS affiliate news re-broadcast on LV1. I take in the view from my balcony. Located just 15 minutes from the Strip, I can't help but find pleasure in the bright neon lights sparkling in the distance. Vegas is one of the few places in the world where your reality is more exciting than your dreams at night.

5:00 a.m. – Back in Action

It's rise 'n' shine after a few hours of sleep and time to merge into work mode. I slip into business suit attire (which with any luck you will *not* be sporting on your Vegas getaway), fly out the door, grab a smoothie at Jamba Juice, and catch the morning news on the XM Satellite radio in my car while maneuvering through the morning traffic jam with the movers and shakers who make Sin City tick. In Vegas, it's not just *who* you know, but *what* you know — from taking Frank Sinatra Drive to avoid traffic jams on the Strip to the best places to spot celebrities before they hit the pages of *US Weekly* — the *Little Red Book* has your back.

I'm off to downtown and the Fremont Street Experience where I have landed a one-on-one interview with the City of Las Vegas Mayor, Oscar Goodman, personally dubbed "The happiest mayor on earth," and why not, with all the riches of the desert at his finger tips: breathtaking resorts, beautiful people at every turn, sumptuous cuisine prepared by celebrity chefs, glamorous salons and spas, world-class shopping . . . you would be happy, too!

Everyone wants to be in Vegas, which is why our exclusive interviews with the valley's movers and shakers are always a success with our viewers. With only 30 minutes on the air, it's impossible to reveal all of Sin City's hot headlines, which is why you are tuning into the *Little Red Book* for the real juice.

8:00 a.m. – I Report, You Decide

Back at the office I check my e-mails and begin to log the tapes and edit the package from last night's Red Carpet. Next, it's time to become verbose and put my journalistic prowess to work as I pen the scripts for *Hot On! Las Vegas*. Generating the touch of panache that will pique my viewer's Vegas-life curiosity requires research, research, research.

Knowing who to contact is the golden ticket, which is why I seriously treasure my contacts both at work and at play and you will, too. Have your BlackBerry available for the contact information of all the new best friends you may meet here.

11:30 a.m. – Power Lunch

The alarm on my BlackBerry vibrates reminding me that I have a power lunch in fifteen minutes with my girls. Today's outing is at Postrio, inside The Venetian, a one-of-a-kind dining experience brought from San Francisco to Sin City by Wolfgang Puck. Our favorite table is reserved center-left, perfect for watching all the action while catching up with friends. This is the *it* spot on the

Strip to find the celebs and other people in the public eye, some hiding, some shining their own spotlight. The girls and I grew up together in Vegas and know the value of our weekly meet and greets — especially when followed by high-end shopping at The Venetian's Grand Canal Shoppes. After the pineapple sorbet, we make a beeline past the gondoliers serenading a rapturous couple, to our favorite store, bebe. Knowing when to hit the sales at the trendy boutiques is a jackpot in itself, without even hitting the casino tables.

1:00 p.m. – MVP

It is said that when you live in Vegas you are never without friends visiting. It seems that everyone wants to join in on the good life. While back at the office writing additional scripts and confirming logistics for an exclusive interview tonight with Dan Marino, former Quarterback of the Miami Dolphins, my business line rings. It's a friend from college; the girlfriends are gathering for a bachelorette party. It's a date, as I make arrangements for the Hot Pink Suite in the Palms Fantasy Tower; an appointment for an exclusive look at the new bebe collection fresh off the runway at the Forum Shops at Caesars Palace – the only way to ensure my girls are both sexy and sophisticated with styles never before seen on the streets of Sin City; a pool-side cabana at the Hard Rock Hotel to surround ourselves with waterfalls, wagering and wet bodies; a coveted slot for the height of hedonistic indulgence and sizzling, sensuous luxury with the Amp After-Hours experience at the Palms featuring manicures and pedicures with lingerie-clad technicians and a handsome hunk of a butler serving caviar and champagne; dinner reservations at MIX atop of THEhotel at Mandalay Bay; third-row seats for *Zumanity* at New York, New York, including a one-on-one meet and greet with the sultry stars after the cutting edge Cirque show closes its curtains; my usual tables at ghostbar on the 55th floor of the Palms and Tryst Nightclub inside Wynn Las Vegas. Rinse and repeat as necessary . . .

3:30 p.m. – Work It Out

A quick stop at the gym for cardio and weights revives me for the evening ahead. Surrounded by Cirque du Soleil performers, strippers, local headliners, professional athletes and coaches, southern Nevada political figures, and handsome hotel executives — a smile lights-up my face knowing that I live in the best city in the world. Even the ordinary becomes extraordinary in Vegas where a trip to the gym is a form of entertainment, and a romantic walk along the Strip can transport you to the Eiffel Tower in Paris, a fiery volcano on an island paradise, or the pyramids of Egypt.

5:00 p.m. – Glam Time

My favorite part of any day of the week is a visit to Amp Salon located in the Palms Casino Resort. With colorist-to-the-stars and salon owner Michael Boychuck, I am pampered and beautified beyond reality into a "Boychuck Blonde."

I overhear a group of girls making plans for their weekend in Sin City. The southern accent sounds familiar from my days as a Tar Heel, and the Carolina Blue cell phone that suddenly begins ringing UNC's fight song is an instant conversation piece. We begin to reminisce about Franklin Street (UNC's party central) and joke about the scale of the Strip in relation to Chapel Hill's college town options.

Then, it is down to business. I convince my fellow Tar Heel to turn her phone on vibrate as the hustle and bustle of Sin City makes it virtually impossible to identify a call (her girlfriends thank me for saving them the embarrassment). My first question is, "in a city where you can be anyone . . . who will you be? And, where will you be?!"

As I toss their outdated guidebooks in the trash, I immediately take out a notepad and pen from my purse and begin to craft a plan for the newest Vegas Vixens. Listening to their hopes and dreams for the ultimate Vegas getaway, I create a weekend full of glamour and bliss. The co-ed bathrooms at Seamless Ultra Lounge, the Tao Nightclub skyboxes with espresso machines, the topless pool at Mandalay Bay, and the champagne shopping tour have my new best friends bubbling over with excitement. It's never too late to be a Vegas Vixen.

6:30 p.m. – Dolphin in the Desert
I hurry home to put on my game face for the evening's events, including my exclusive one-on-one interview with Dan Marino. My evenings are often filled with work that feels like play. That being said, I have learned that in Vegas it is important to be ready for *anything*.

8:00 p.m. – Knowledge Is Power
An invite to attend a private fund-raising gala to support education throughout southern Nevada proves to be a very worthwhile commitment of my time. Families live in Vegas, too.

The gala moves to Tao at The Venetian. The exquisite Far Eastern décor and signature cocktails tend to lure the hottest guys in Vegas. Sexy, handsome, intelligent, fun men do thrive in Vegas and may just be standing right next to you. With a million sights and sounds fighting for your attention, it is easy to overlook the real hidden gems. Keep your eyes wide open.

As I follow my own advice, I glance towards the Monk Bar and notice the girls from Amp Salon, glowing from the inside out with their new 'dos and matching mani-pedis. I remind them about the story of Ying and Yang and that the signature 20-foot tall Buddha is watching their every move! Cheers!

9:00 p.m. – Bring on Another Day
I have come full-circle. It's back to the Red Carpet, this time at the newest nightclub to burst onto the Vegas scene — JET at the Mirage. First up to the mic is Mark Wahlberg. Who needs Nick

Lachey?! In Vegas, there is something for everyone. *This is Molly Sullivan for Hot On! Las Vegas. That's a wrap!*

We all know Cinderella is supposed to be home by midnight, but in Vegas, time is endless. The experience is what you choose to make it. Vegas is a girl thing. I can show you the way, so that you'll leave with great stories and fond memories. In the words of Bob Dylan, "You don't need a weatherman to tell which way the wind blows." In Sin City, you *do* need an insider to guide you to the hottest spots. Enjoy the ride and I'll see you in Vegas!

Welcome to the world of the *Las Vegas Little Red Book* . . .

✴ Chapter 2 ✴

Vegas Will Surprise You

✴ ....

Years ago, when girls thought of a weekend escape, it was to Manhattan, Beverly Hills, Miami, or that fabulous spa nestled in the Berkshire Mountains. Vegas was the wild, wild west and only catered to a man's world. That all changed when Jan Laverty Jones was elected mayor in 1991. She turned this "boys club" town on its head. Partially because of this lady's touch, Vegas has upgraded its reputation by replacing gaudy lounge shows and prime rib specials with world-class spas, the best shopping this side of Paris and Milan, exquisite cuisine, and plush celeb-filled nightclubs. Intelligent, travel-savvy, fun-loving females who know a great vacation hotspot when they see it have staked a claim in the Vegas of the new millennium. Whether you're in need of a weekend to reconnect with friends, indulge your wildest fantasies, send one of your soon-to-be-married gal pals off in style, or simply rejuvenate your stressed-out body and soul, there's only one destination that can do it all: It's Vegas, Baby! The city that knows what you and your girlfriends want and has the panache to deliver with class.

To understand how a city that has always been about the male ego evolved to become a top girl's getaway, you'll need a quick little crash course on Las Vegas before it became Vegas — a city with nearly 2 million residents and more than 35 million annual guests.

A Little Town Takes Off

This story is too good to stay here: a story of opportunism and
opportunity. Las Vegas was born just over a hundred years ago.
It was a small desert town in the middle of nowhere. By 1999, it
had become one of the fastest growing cities in the United States
and truly was the first city of the twenty-first century. Well-
heeled mobsters, glamorous showgirls, luxurious mega-resorts,
alluring neon displays — Sin City is the world's most famous
monument to reckless abandon and unbridled excess.

People didn't give this tiny desert town much attention until it
caught the eye of a few visionaries who recognized an opportunity that would allow them to lure gamblers to the warmth and
hospitality of the desert. Air conditioning made the dream a reality. Las Vegas has always been about someone taking a gamble,
and Benjamin "Bugsy" Siegel is the man who many credit with
dreaming up Sin City with the building of the Flamingo Hotel. It
sparked Vegas as a travel destination.

Vegas became hot with the high rolling Hollywood moguls who
decided to spend long weekends playing in Vegas rather than relaxing in the traditional haunt of Palm Springs. They came out to
see and be seen. Their women typified 50's Vegas glamour, rub-
bing elbows with the Rat Pack over a few martinis and a steak
dinner, dressed to the nines in rhinestones and furs. Of course,

this didn't last. In an effort to attract a larger gaming audience, new low-price hotel casinos started popping up. Pretty soon every middle-class American couple (think June and Ward Cleaver) could afford Vegas; so, Hollywood decided to move on, leaving a cast of also-rans and has-beens to entertain the masses. There has never been a period in Sin City's post-Bugsy history when the city wasn't booming, and Vegas style was about to shift again: this time into a dazzling fantasyland catering to the needs and whims of the ladies.

 **STRIP TEASE**

The Rat Pack Wasn't Just Fellas: Sinatra's famous gang of hard-partying, Vegas-loving friends, The Rat Pack, wasn't solely comprised of men. Longtime Sinatra friend and collaborator Shirley MacLaine was the only female member of the bunch. MacLaine was one of the guys, joining them in their late night poker games and notorious Vegas antics. Look for her cameo next time you watch the original *Ocean's 11*.

Back in Action

When Steve Wynn opened The Mirage in 1989, everyone was amazed by its unique brand of over-the-top details. Wynn was able to attract the moneyed, party crowd that had avoided Las Vegas for years. Suddenly, Vegas was back. The super casinos — mega-properties comprised of massive gaming floors, first-class dining, shopping, entertainment and spas — brought Vegas back into the forefront of the American leisure psyche. Soon the $29 rooms and $.99 shrimp cocktails were history (well, almost history). Finally, women had something to do other than just gamble and strut by the pool. First-rate entertainment began replacing the worn out acts that had been serving the graying Vegas crowd for years. Vegas once again became the place to stay and play.

Las Vegas reinvented itself as the entertainment capital of the world. Shows and nightclubs, gaming and outdoor activities, were offered to visitors of all ages from around the nation and around the world. In addition to visiting Las Vegas, an increasing number of people started to call Las Vegas home. A period of unparalleled growth began in the 1990s with annual population increases averaging more than six percent.

 **STRIP TEASE**

The Strip is Reborn: The mega-properties of the Strip are all relatively new. The building boom of the 1990s yielded the biggest expansion the Strip and surrounding areas have ever seen. Here is a chronology:

> 1989: The Mirage
> 1990: Excalibur, Rio
> 1993: MGM Grand, Treasure Island, Luxor
> 1995: Hard Rock Hotel
> 1996: Stratosphere, Monte Carlo
> 1997: New York–New York
> 1998: Bellagio
> 1999: Paris, Mandalay Bay, Venetian
> 2000: Alladin
> 2001: Palms

The Vegas Nightclub Revolution

Within the walls of each mega-resort there were plenty of places to roll the dice, but in wasn't until the 1990s that playing in Vegas finally meant more than gambling. When Studio 54 took up shop at the MGM in 1997, Vegas nightlife had at last shed its lounge act image. Management hoped that this 54 could start a sizzling new trend in evening entertainment the way the original Studio 54 had in New York in the '70s. The marketing polls got it right and the new Vegas nightlife was born. Studio 54 set the desert on fire! With its success, the nightclub scene moved east from Los Angeles to Las Vegas. Promoters quickly realized that in Sin City, the sky was the limit. Land was cheap and crowds were huge, allowing venues to be much larger and more profitable than any of the forerunners: L.A., New York, or South Beach. The success of Studio 54 has been replicated in every new property on the Strip, where the concept embraces a high-end nightclub and ultra lounge. The casinos know that a good club lures beauty to the door, and they're hoping that the guys will follow suit.

💋 IT'S GOOD TO BE A GAL

Vegas Perks: Complimentary club admission, free cocktails, all-access VIP passes . . . these are just a few of the perks of being a girl in Sin City. Temples have risen from the desert sands for shopping, dining and entertainment to help keep the girls busy while the guys roll the dice. On one hand, gaming properties know they need to attract women in order to keep their casino packed till the wee hours with men spending all their cash at the gaming tables. On the other hand, they've learned that the new breed of women visiting Vegas have plenty of their own money to spend, and that they need to keep these fun-loving Vegas Vixens happy. Either way you split the deck, luck is indeed a lady!

Vegas Becomes a *Girl's* Destination

The girls have taken over Las Vegas. What used to be a male-dominated getaway now caters to the female traveler. In an effort to keep the girls happy, the restaurant, relaxation and entertainment options have shed their old ways and focused on what the girls want. For example, the classic Las Vegas dining staple — the T-bone steak and baked potato, red-leather-booth steakhouse — has become a Vegas dinosaur. Sure, the steakhouses are still out there (and who doesn't crave a great filet with a bottle of Cabernet from time to time?) but thankfully these male-centric eateries have gone hip and upscale with the rest of the city. The last several years have also seen a boom in celebrity and master chef eateries. The créme de la créme of European and American chefs all own restaurants in Vegas and they all love to cater to groups of girls. Looking for the best sushi you'll ever eat? You'll probably find it in the middle of the desert. Hipster eateries like Nobu at Hard Rock can be the backdrop for an entire evening of entertainment, between lively, star-studded bar scenes and delectable, awe-inspiring creations.

Dining and clubbing are not the only areas where the girls rule. Luxurious spas and mega-shopping abound like glorious islands in a sea of fun and distraction created for every budget, taste, and mood that may strike. So, given this kaleidoscope of pleasures, it's no surprise that Las Vegas has become the bachelorette and girlfriends weekend *center of the universe*. Who said guys should have all the fun? In the last ten years, women have taken over Las Vegas, and that's just the beginning. Vegas, known for both spectacle and splendor on a large scale, has become a pop culture icon in just 100 colorful years.

Celebrities Want in on the Action

Girls, you aren't the only ones who are out to take over the Las Vegas Strip: celebrities want in on the action, too. Before Interstate 15 was built, Las Vegas Boulevard (the Strip) was the primary highway between Los Angeles and Sin City. Today, Hollywood is empty on weekends because the celebs head out to Vegas to indulge in a little gambling, spa pampering, shopping, dining, partying – all the same attractions that lure you to Vegas. Every time you turn on the television, you see "E!" or "Access Hollywood" broadcasting from Sin City. The frequency of celebrities making news has brought Vegas into America's pop culture, turning Vegas into Hollywood's playground. Cruise through the Forum Shops or relax over a martini in Wynn's cocktail lounge, Parasol, and chances are you may see your favorite Hollywood A-listers savoring Vegas' splendor in the very same hotspots where *you've* decided to mix it up.

 TEN VEGAS SURPRISES

Vegas Surprise #1: Girls Have the Upper Hand

Girls, it's time to shift your thinking. Many of us mistakenly view Las Vegas as a guy's destination. And who can blame us? For years, television, movies, even books have presented variations of the same scene over and over: it's a guy's world and

---

⚿⚊⚊ INSIDER'S REPORT

Vegas Neon: Every sign has a story to tell, especially in Sin City. The face of Vegas has changed over the years as many historic hotels have been imploded to make way for the new mega-resorts of today. All that remains of many of those old properties are the neon signs that once adorned them. In 1996, the Las Vegas Neon Museum was created to help preserve that piece of Vegas history. A three-acre lot known as "The Boneyard" serves as a final resting place for hundreds of signs that once lit up Vegas's Glitter Gulch.

Some signs, however, have managed to stand the test of time. One sign in particular has come to be seen as an icon of Las Vegas. The "Welcome to Fabulous Las Vegas, Nevada" sign has remained in its place on the Strip since 1959. It was created by one of Las Vegas's pioneer commercial artists, a woman by the name of Betty Willis. A visit to Vegas wouldn't be complete without a photo next to this famous and fabulous sign. Serving as a gateway to Sin City's extravaganza, it's located on the south-end of the Strip, just south of Mandalay Bay. If you are driving, park on the right side of the road and scurry over a few lanes of traffic to the median, where the sign is located.

---

he makes all the decisions. Enter the assertive, female, corporate executive who is CEO of her billion-dollar franchise business. Thanks, Oprah Winfrey! It's important to note that today more than half the visitors to Vegas are female and that means the girls are running the show.

The real Vegas is a place you can have wrapped around your little finger in a heartbeat. Okay, well, not really a heartbeat, but you can make the city work for you. Case in point, girls, the hottest nightclubs want YOU, and often cater to your every whim. So, while the guys are waiting in the line for hours just to have an opportunity to *buy* their way in the door, you are moved along the line at a rapid pace and feted with generous accoutrements — complimentary champagne, hors d'oeuvres, maybe even the hospitality manager's phone number.

You own this city: as always, the guys are putty in your hands, and you know how to use this information to your advantage. You know that the spas, the shopping, the salons, the restaurants, the nightclubs and the ultra lounges are here just for you. So don't be surprised — Vegas wants your business. Vegas wants you to *be happy* and to *leave happy* so you make Vegas your top travel destination over and over again.

Vegas Surprise #2: There is a Lot More to Do Than Gamble

Vegas used to be all about gambling. Hotels made all their profit from the casino floor, so the gambler was all that mattered. You might be surprised to find out that there's much more to do in Vegas than gamble. Did you know that 50% of the people that visit Vegas don't even gamble? The mega-resorts that dominate the Strip actually make more money from their hotel than they do their casino. Add in the restaurants, shopping, and entertainment, and you start to realize that more emphasis is placed on non-gaming activities than on the casino. Vegas will always be synonymous with gambling, but there is so much more to do here. Why settle for sitting around the smoky casino tables when you can be entertained by an off-Broadway showing of *Phantom of the Opera*, *Spamalot,* or *Mamma Mia.* Check out the latest fashions from Versace, or be pampered at Amp Salon where you can pick up celebrity juice before it hits the newsstands, thanks to your seat next to Paris Hilton. There are so many things to do that your real dilemma is not having time to do everything you want. That's why the smart and savvy Vegas Vixen plans her next trip before she leaves town.

Vegas Surprise #3: There is No One *Perfect Hotel* for You and Your Girlfriends

When it comes to making or breaking your getaway, one of your most important decisions is choosing the right place to lay your head down for that rejuvenating sleep. While Las Vegas has more hotel rooms than any other city in the world, you might be surprised as you do some research that there are actually only a handful of places that will meet all of your

 Strip Tease

Vegas Quick Facts:
- ✿ 1931 first licensed Nevada casino
- ✿ 124,270 hotel rooms
- ✿ 15,000 pillowcases washed daily at the MGM Grand
- ✿ 197,144 slot machines
- ✿ 36.7 million visitors annually
- ✿ 5% of visitors travel to Las Vegas primarily to gamble
- ✿ 3.9 hours per day spent gambling by the average visitor
- ✿ $559 average gambling budget per visit
- ✿ 315 weddings on average per day
- ✿ 37 local golf courses
- ✿ 15,000 miles of lighted neon tubing on the Strip and in Downtown

needs. Your hotel is your *headquarters* for your getaway. It is your launching point, your meeting spot, and your rejuvenation retreat. Although your budget is always important, price is not the only factor to consider when deciding on your girl pad away from home. Any way you look at it; your hotel is the heartbeat of your getaway in Vegas.

Hotels in Las Vegas vary greatly. Take advantage of our insider's knowledge to make sure your hotel choice best suits your Vegas fantasy life. You may not enjoy the dancing waters set to the music of Andrea Bocelli and the ornate grandeur of the Bellagio if your girls are up for the Sunday *Rehab* pool party at the Hard Rock Hotel.

While you can play wherever you like, many of the property amenities are for guests only, and as a guest you will receive preferential treatment. Case in point: most hotel pools are off-limits to non-guests, so even vixen-style sweet-talking won't help you get through those wrought iron gates. Make sure the place you stay gives you lots of options. The right choice in accommodations will be the first big decision of your trip. The *Little Red Book* will give you everything you need to know to make sure you choose the perfect hotel, the one that will provide you and your girlfriends with an experience of a lifetime.

Vegas Surprise #4: The Vegas Wardrobe is Tough to Put Together

While packing for a weekend getaway usually doesn't take too much effort, packing for Vegas isn't like packing for any ordinary weekend. The goal is to have the right outfit for the right venue and the right time of day. Trust me, it's not as easy as you might think! Daytime is casual but trendy, evenings can be sexy and sophisticated, and let's not forget that the temperature can plummet from blistering hot to bone chilling cold in a matter of hours as soon as the sun sets in the West. Then, there's factoring in the appropriate handbags and jewelry, shoes and sleepwear . . . when you visit Vegas, there's no such thing as throwing a few basics in a suitcase and breezing out the door. You have your work cut out for you!

Deciding on your itinerary well in advance of your departure will give you time to carefully consider everything you need to bring. Fortunately, the *Little Red Book* is your Vegas style consultant every step of the way, making sure your party wear is party-worthy, your daywear is chic and easy, and that you feel thoroughly comfortable and confident about the selections you've made. The only thing worse than being in Sin City and opening your suitcase to discover you've packed only silky black thongs and string bikinis, is absurdly over-packing. The *Little Red Book* will make sure you don't fall prey to these *faux pas* and will have you looking your best throughout the entire trip.

Vegas Surprise #5: What Happens Here, Rarely Stays Here

When you book your trip to Las Vegas with your girlfriends, you might be planning to let your hair down and live out your wildest fantasies. While Vegas' slogan is "What Happens Here, Stays Here," expect everyone back home to know exactly what happened in Sin City: the good, the bad, the downright horrifying. People just love to tell Vegas stories.

You will be pleased to know that if you invite the right people, recollections of the night you can't quite recall *can* stay in Sin City. You're here to have fun and unwind a bit; do you really want someone in your group gossiping to everyone back home? What happens here will stay here if you and your girls agree in advance that any potential hook ups, dirty dancing on the nightclub floor, or sloppy kissing of bartenders, valets, and blackjack dealers will be held in strictest confidence and *never*, *ever* shared with the folks back home. You have nothing to worry about with the locals; they've seen much more out-landish behavior than you can conjure up. So, take a moment to talk to your girlfriends about leaving the details in the desert.

Vegas Surprise #6: Nothing is as Close as it Seems

Thinking of dashing over to the hotel next door to borrow a girlfriend's new Marciano halter? Think again. Traveling in Vegas takes effort. Vegas boasts the largest hotels in the world lining the streets of this desert oasis. Although it's difficult to envision unless you've actually visited, just getting from one end of a hotel to the other can be an exercise in frustration. Casinos like Mandalay Bay and MGM Grand are massive complexes, their own little kingdoms. You'll need to give yourself loads of time when traveling from one property to the next. If your friend is staying at the property next door, plan to spend a half hour just getting there.

Some properties, while technically on the Strip, are set way back from the street (Las Vegas Blvd.), so even when you make it out of the front door you still have a hike to get to the Strip. You will notice that each hotel casino has gone to great lengths to entice you and your gold card to stay — and to make it difficult for you to leave its circuitous maze of gaming tables, slots, and bars. Escalators and moving sidewalks are available to conveniently bring you into the property, but if you want out: girlfriend, you're on your own! Bellagio and Caesars Palace, for example, are a good five-minute walk from the front door to the sidewalk.

And, despite how fetching you might look in your Jimmy Choos, hailing a taxi with your bejeweled arm outstretched and one leg nearly grazing the traffic just doesn't happen in Vegas. Although there are thousands of taxis, they can only pick up a fare at specified hotel entrances; it's important for you to know the *rules* to successfully navigate the Strip. Should you decide to walk, but change your mind once you're halfway down the sidewalk (and it's high noon and 100 degrees), you'll have to walk all the way to the taxi stand at the next property in order to catch a cab. On the weekends, expect the wait in the cab line to be so long that your stilettos may begin sinking into the concrete. Plan accordingly by allowing enough time if you want to make your 8:30 p.m. dinner reservation at Spago.

Vegas Surprise #7: Gambling is a Lot More Fun Than You Think

Some girls barely factor gambling in as they plan their trip to Vegas. Why spend hours communing with the masses inside a smoky, noisy casino when you could be lounging by a luxurious pool sipping wine spritzers and flipping through a *Vogue* magazine? Although you might not be a natural gambler, you might be surprised by how much you enjoy it. So, leave your inhibitions at the door and give it a shot.

Start with the easy ones, the slot machines. After a couple minutes, you will be ready to take it to the next level. Work up your nerve to sashay right on over to the table games. This is where the fun is, and there's plenty of it. Once you achieve an understanding of how each game is played, and get acquainted with the tables, you'll find that gambling is actually exhilarating, friendly, exciting, and potentially quite lucrative. You'll make new friends, have great stories to tell, and maybe even win what it takes to buy that new collection from Louis Vuitton you spotted earlier while power shopping.

Vegas Surprise #8: Relaxing at a Great Spa Can Be Hard Work

Vegas has embraced the luxe life with a vengeance. In the last few years, spas and salons have sprouted up at every turn. Although each major property on the Strip boasts the ultimate pampering experience — and any Vegas spa service will be far superior to anything you've experienced at the strip mall in your home town — not all spas are created equal. You might be surprised just how hard it is to find a spa and salon that will actually deliver the transforming, mind and body-altering experience, you and your girlfriends deserve.

Despite the lure of revitalizing seaweed wraps and aromatherapy massages — set against a backdrop of Fung Shui décor and the tranquil sounds of light summer rain — many of Vegas' state-of-the-art spas claiming complete dedication to your well-being, are actually overpriced, understaffed — and worst of all — overcrowded, Do you really want to spend a month's car payment just to be crammed into a glorified gymnasium-style steam room where the beauty technicians shuttle you about like cattle? Of course not. The *Little Red Book* will help you find the perfect place to spend your hard earned cash on a truly restorative spa experience, not on a sloppy makeover in a spruced up Great Cuts.

Vegas Surprise #9: A Good Man is Hard to Find

Mister Right may be waiting for you in Vegas, but you might be surprised just how hard he is to find. There will always be guys vying to spend time with you and your friends, but exercise caution, because many of them aren't the kind of guys you'd give the time of day to, let alone party with.

Tens of thousands of guys roll into Vegas each weekend; finding the one that's right for you requires being at the right place at the right time. Looking for a successful business-type who made a fortune in the stock market, owns homes in Los Angeles and the Caribbean, and dresses in head-to-toe Armani? We'll steer you in the right direction. Hoping for a hip, sexy guitarist who's played with the rock 'n roll legends, and knows the music scene better than any *Rolling Stone* reporter? No problem. Hankering for a guy who is easy to talk to, up for casual fun, and eager to party and dance the night away? Piece of cake. Anything is possible in Vegas, so be sure to carry the *Little Red Book* in your purse, and get ready to roll out the red carpet for your bachelorette party!

Vegas Surprise #10: The Desert Isn't Always Hot

When you think of Vegas weather, you probably think of scorching days by the pool clad in your itsy-bitsy bikini, and balmy nights dressed in just a slip of a sundress, a light sweater thrown casually over your shoulders. It's the desert, after all, so it must be hot all the time.

You'll be surprised when you find out how cold Vegas can get. Though it *is* situated in the Mojave Desert, Vegas latitude is equal to Atlanta's. This is not the tropics, girls. The pools close November through March, and October and April can be surprisingly brisk and windy. In the desert, when the sun isn't shining, the temperature can drop dramatically. An 80-degree day could easily be a 50-degree night. Don't get stuck in a skirt and baby tee at sundown. Prepare for the elements so you're not freezing and finding it too cold to enjoy every minute of your getaway.

Let's Get Started

Now that the *Little Red Book* has clued you into some of the surprises that await you in Sin City, let's get your bags packed, your itinerary set, and your visit to paradise started. There's a world of glorious decadence to energize you in this neon city in the desert, so get ready to have some serious fun. Vegas is waiting for you.

✴ Chapter 3 ✴

Getting the Word Out (Planning Your Party)

✴ ....

Yes, Vegas is *the* place to be; but first, you have to get here.

Far too many fabulous women arrive in Sin City ready to paint the town red, only to end up trapped in a downward spiral of vacation mediocrity. Bad trips *can and do* happen to great people, but if you do a little work in advance, you'll avoid a scenario like this:

It's Friday afternoon, and you've been in a festive mood all day, strutting around the office in your casual Friday jeans and crisp button-down shirt knowing that in just a few hours you'll be racing out of the office to catch your flight to paradise. Your bag has been packed for days, filled with everything from the little black cocktail dress to the *little, little* sheer black and strappy mini-dress you bought especially for this trip. You and the girls have decided to keep things loose — get to the hotel, read up on which restaurant or club to hit, and — since you were smart enough to pack the entire contents of your closet — quickly change into the perfect outfit for that evening. Next stop Las Vegas!

The plane touches down, and not a moment too soon, as you slip past the guy from across the aisle, with his invitation for you and your friends to "swing on by" The Horseshoe where he and his buds will be "partying it up" in their high roller suite. (It shouldn't be too hard to find them, just follow the combined aromas of Drakkar Noir and Jack Daniels). You grab the girls and head to the luggage carousel where you wait for a good half hour, your patience slowly eroding as you watch the continuous loop on the big overhead screens boasting the best buffets, the best shows, the best nightclubs, the "best of Vegas." With *everything* "the best," how will you choose what to do during your 48 — soon to be 45 — hours of pleasure? The bags finally arrive — time to whisk into a cab and venture into the night. But what's this? A cab line stretching far away into the night. You were looking forward to tasting that first Cosmo; now all you taste is disappointment.

An hour and twenty minutes later you finally make it to your hotel, ready to restore your sense of adventure, which is sagging like Joan Rivers's facelift. Suddenly you realize the line snaking out from the reception area through the main lobby is meant for . . . you! Yes, you, and it's another fifty minutes before you fall exhausted into your room, and it's at that precise moment that your cell phone rings. It's your friend Serena from Chicago, who should have arrived hours ago but now says she's going to be late — as in not getting to Vegas until tomorrow morning — a major disappointment. Meanwhile, your friends crack open the mini bar and uncork the bottle of Chardonnay. Out come the $6 gummy bears. Next, it's the half-size bottle of bad Merlot and the mini-canister of Pringles. It's fine, you tell yourself. We all need to chill-out after the airport fiasco and we're having such a great time catching up, and the beds are so very, very comfy. But after an hour of communing, the mini bar is empty, the room is on its way to being trashed, and throwing on a pair of sweats sounds far more appealing than freshening up and changing into your miniskirt and heels. So, room service it is. After all, who needs world-class sushi from Nobu or a five-star Cosmopolitan from PURE when there are soggy room-service club sandwiches and cold French fries to be had? Who needs an evening of dancing and carousing and gambling amidst the gliteratti, when you can lounge in the room and flip through the Pay-per-view? Everyone is talked-out, burned-out, and dying to call it an early night. Some excitement — you might as well be at an airport Ramada Inn.

By the time morning rolls around and you're still lolling about at 10:45 waiting for your turn to shower, you realize it's time for a serious attitude shift. Is it too late? How did your vacation go awry? What happened to savoring an early breakfast of omelets and Bloody Mary's while obsessing over the adorable new chachkahs you bought with your winnings, or evaluating the guys you met on the dance floor?

Girls, don't let this happen to you!

Las Vegas will work for you when you take charge of your get-away. That means being in control and planning far enough in advance to make the right decisions for your group so everyone comes home thoroughly satisfied. Time is precious. Money is even more precious. You can't afford to waste either.

PLANNING YOUR TRIP

By following just a few simple rules, doing some research, delegating duties, and taking formal responsibility for your trip, you can rule the Strip as the Vegas-savvy Goddess you truly are. Or, at least you'll have a much, much better girls' getaway to Sin City.

Take Ownership

One of the biggest mistakes you can make when planning a trip to Vegas is not having a "go to" girl willing to take charge. *But*, you think, *no one wants to be drill sergeant, barking out orders and handing out agendas. Au contraire*: spending a little time researching the hottest spots in Vegas will get you in the vacation mood, and give you a big advantage as you begin to negotiate the exotic culture of Sin City. Besides, someone has to be in charge, so it might as well be you, the one smart and savvy enough to have picked up this book! So, sharpen your pencil, turn on your BlackBerry, call on your inner organization Diva, and get ready to have fun. Is it up to you to make sure everyone has a good time? No. But it is up to you to make sure that *you* have fun, and that everyone else can bask in the glory of your impeccable planning. Don't let your trip just *happen* to you. Be the one to issue the directives. You'll have the vacation you've dreamed of and your girls will thank you. Here's how:

Your Reasons for Going

As you begin to plan your trip, take some time to think about why you're heading to Sin City. This way you'll be sure that your itinerary and your vision of Vegas are a perfect match.

✧ Celebrate in Sin

It's your birthday: C-E-L-E-B-R-A-T-E and make your getaway an experience you'll always remember. Whether you are turning 21, 30, 40, or more, Sin City is the best place to celebrate your new digits with an all-out birthday bash. It doesn't even have to be a milestone. Turning 29? Do it up right!

✧ Party in Sin

Vegas is the bachelorette party center of the universe, with all the glamour and decadence you need to wow your friend before sending her down the aisle. In Vegas, all bachelorette parties are memorable and even the most unique ones are easy to coordinate.

✧ Pamper in Sin

Revitalize your mind, body and soul by spending an hour, half a day, even a full day being catered to by the best-of-the-best at one of Sin City's world-class spas. Then, flaunt that inner glow — and outer Vegas Vixen — by hitting the tables, high-end stores, and dance floor with an energy and confidence you never knew you possessed!

Reunite in Sin

Vegas is a perfect place to reconnect with all those high school friends, sorority sisters, former teammates or career acquaintances you miss but have been too busy to keep up with. You can howl for hours about the bad boys you left in the dust years ago; brag (or complain) about your husband and kids, or catch up on the great new direction your careers are heading. Call your girls to book a flight to Las Vegas and let the sinfully sweet reunion begin.

Escape in Sin

Vegas is an escape from the real world. Despite a brief experiment in the 90s with family oriented theme parks and hotel attractions (featuring small children huddled asleep under slot machines at 2 a.m.), Vegas has been — and always will be — an adult playground. With romantic restaurants, adult entertainment, and nightlife that doesn't even get warmed up until well past midnight, it's time to leave your cares — and your lovely kids and husband — at home, and hightail it to Sin City.

Network in Sin

Vegas is the No. 1 destination in the world for conventions and business networking meetings. Everyone wants an excuse to stay and play in Sin City, but be prepared: Vegas could actually provide you with an opportunity to improve your career as well, with contacts you'll make long after the workday ends. Every city has its local watering holes, but only Vegas boasts the country's hottest evening entertainment venues . . . perfect for passing around your business card and networking, Vegas-style!

❖ Untie in Sin

Don't get all tied up in knots because the relationship didn't exactly become the fairy tale you had hoped for. And, whatever you do, don't call Dr. Phil! Instead, immerse yourself in the fun and fantasy of Sin City and kick off a new chapter in your life. Whether you plan to do it solo or to celebrate ditching Mr Wrong with some friends, a getaway to Vegas will give you plenty to smile about.

Putting Your Group Together

Now that you have a reason for going to Sin City, it's time to select who will make it onto your wild weekend guest list. As you begin gathering your girls, remember to consider the following tips. Oh, and by the way ladies in this case, size does matter!

Group Size

The size of your group can make a huge difference to whether your trip flies, or flops like a bad first date. Your first inclination may be to pull together every friend from a particular time in your life: all the women you worked with back in Chicago, or all the suite-mates who lived with you in the college dorm. Our response to this impulse is a simple, *no*. Keep it small, manageable, discreet, but at the same time don't revert to making it a cozy getaway for just you and your closest friend. Unfortunately, any group too large or small could make for a weekend you'll end up wishing you could forget.

❖ *Too Large : More than Eight*

Any number over eight is just too large. Getting more than eight girls to commit to a fun itinerary and stick with it for an entire weekend is more than you want to deal with. Aside from dissenters and the possible formation of a vacation mutiny, there will inevitably be at least one or two friends you hardly get a chance to schmooze with. And of course, there are the endless questions: Is the sushi raw? Do black and brown match? Is there an intermission? Does this make me look fat? Have you seen my cell phone? Enough said!

The larger your group, the greater the likelihood that someone will want to spin off in a separate direction and take a couple of playmates with them. The point is to spend time *together* in a fun setting. Although everyone can do whatever they like, whenever they like, in this 24-hour playground, if some of your friends spiral off in their own direction the purpose for your getaway may be defeated.

⌨ Insider's Report

Traveling in Big Groups: Traveling with a large group is a challenge. Whenever you leave the hotel, you need to take several cabs. If you want to go the limo route, you won't be able to fit everyone in one vehicle without spending some serious cash for a stretch Hummer. If you have a large group, plan most of your activities in your hotel or a hotel next door because walking is the easiest way to shuttle the group around.

✣ Too Small : 2–4

At the other end of the spectrum lies the mistake of traveling with a group that's too small. A weekend can seem endless once you've exhausted discussing the job, the boyfriend, the kids, and there's nobody else to infuse the conversation with a fresh set of problems and perspectives. You don't want to lose a friend because you spent every waking hour with her. While it's easier to get reservations for a small group, the point of your getaway is to share the time with a number of diverse, unique, and interesting personalities. Good times are in direct proportion to the number of girlfriends sharing the experience.

❖ *Just Right : 5–8*

The right size group for a girl's getaway is five to eight friends, a number that's bound to provide diversity in the form of your funny friend, your party friend, your outrageous friend, your quiet friend . . . and you. With a healthy mix of people, conversation will flow, the vibe won't go stale, and a good time will be had by all.

 Divide and Conquer

There are many ways to use a group to your advantage to make the trip more affordable and fun:

- ❖ Split the cost of a large suite
- ❖ Cover more mall shopping territory in a limited amount of time
- ❖ Spread out to all corners of a nightclub to meet the best guys
- ❖ Keep a place in the long buffet line while others gamble
- ❖ Fan out to find the hot slots in the casino
- ❖ Save a table at the bar while others are getting ready
- ❖ Eat at more expensive restaurants by splitting the main course

---

Who Makes the Cut?

Although it sounds harsh, we all know it's true: if you mess up and invite one luckless, miserable friend your whole weekend could be shot. If you sense a red flag, trust your instincts and pass on anyone who causes you to think twice. Your invite list should include those tried and true friends you always love being with. Stick with the safe bets.

Plan Your Play — Play Your Plan

For convenience sake we've organized the *Little Red Book* into simple categories for your use and amusement. Here are the primary elements you need to integrate into your trip plan:

1. Travel — travel smart, frugally, and together
2. Accommodations — stay at a place that meets the needs of your group
3. Dining — make smart, stylish dining choices that leave the group satisfied
4. Gaming — gamble the right games at the right time without going broke
5. Daytime Entertainment — explore the relaxing side of Vegas during the sunlight hours
6. Nighttime Entertainment — find places that will keep your group enjoying the party
7. Shows — choose the right show for your group
8. Party Time — experience the sexier side of Vegas

In the following chapters the *Little Red Book* will help you determine the best fit for all of the above. Don't assume that you'll be able to get consensus on every single aspect of your getaway — it you don't, it's *okay*. With the *Little Red Book*, you can't go wrong.

Over-Planning

As you start to piece together an itinerary for your getaway, you'll quickly realize there is simply too much to do in Vegas. Trying to pack it all in during one weekend is a recipe for disaster. Instead, focus on the broad strokes. One of the biggest mistakes groups of girls make is to over-plan down to the most minute detail and leave no room for flexibility (a much needed virtue when shopping spills into cocktail hour which spills into dinner, which spills into all night clubbing, which spills into breakfast . . .). The *Little Red Book* will help you put together a perfectly balanced trip to Vegas that will get the adrenaline surging without sending you into cardiac arrest.

> ### ⌇⟶ INSIDER'S REPORT
>
> **The Friend Who Just Broke Up:** While this girl desperately needs a weekend to get away from it all, you don't want it to be on *your* getaway. What you will end up with is a girl who rambles on endlessly about how she is better off, yet breaks down in tears at the slightest provocation, ends up drinking too much and drunk-dialing her old boyfriend every chance she gets. Trust us, this is not a field of critical care you want to deal with on your girls' getaway to Vegas.

It's important to consider everyone's opinions while coordinating the group itinerary, but you need to establish a cutoff time of at least three weeks out to assure that the building blocks of your trip are solidly in place: where to stay (leave a generous amount of lead time), where to go for that pricey gourmet meal, which spa to luxuriate in, and what nights you'll need transportation. None of these are decisions you can make on the fly. Get some input, establish cutoff dates and make decisions. Don't second-guess yourself and don't let one of your friends change your plans at the eleventh hour.

One byproduct of over-planning is an itinerary so rigorous and rigid that it becomes work just sticking to it. This is a getaway to Vegas, not a crash diet. Here's an example of an itinerary that packs in a lot of activity yet leaves plenty of time to have fun and get acquainted with your new favorite vacation destination.

SAMPLE ITINERARY
Friday:
    6:00 p.m. — Brandi, Allie, Laurie, Alicia, and Gracie arrive in Las Vegas.

6:30 p.m. — Limo to the Palms. Brandi, Allie and Laurie check into a suite. Alicia and Gracie check into an adjoining room. Freshen up and congregate in the suite for a celebratory champagne toast.

8:00 p.m. — Dine at N9NE with the A-listers in town for the weekend.

10:00 p.m. — Ride the elevator to the top of the Palms, take in the view, and enjoy a drink at ghostbar

12:30 a.m. — Dance the night away at PURE Nightclub.

3:30 a.m. — Quick breakfast (lunch, or dinner) at the 24 Seven Café

4:30 a.m. — Beauty rest.

Saturday:
9:00 a.m. — Morning pick-me-up at Skin's pool café while working on your desert glow.

⌥→ INSIDER'S REPORT

Don't Buy a VIP Package as a Shortcut: There are plenty of companies offering to put together a great Vegas package for you and your friends. While they sound attractive, they do not offer the best: and don't you and your friends deserve the best? Why depend on a company that offers the same tour packages to everyone? You know what your girls want, so don't leave the driving to someone else. Don't settle for a one-size-fits-all girls' getaway weekend; create a vacation that will provide you and your friends with just the right dash of action, relaxation and naughtiness.

11:00 a.m. — Shopping at the Forum Shops at Caesars Palace. Carefully choose that perfect Vegas Vixen outfit for tonight.

1:00 p.m. — Shopping continues at the Fashion Show Mall, stopping for "photo ops" with Caesars Palace's Roman gods, The Mirage's volcano, Treasure Island's Siren's Cove, The Venetian's Grand Canal.

3:00 p.m. — High Tea across the street at Parasol Lounge at The Wynn.

3:30 p.m. — Try your luck at the slots and blackjack tables.

4:30 p.m. — Taxi back to the Palms to beautify for the night.

6:00 p.m. — Meet up at the Palms Island Bar in the center of the action for the first cocktail of the evening.

7:00 p.m. — Tickets to Cirque du Soleil's *Zumanity* at New York–New York.

9:30 p.m. — Dinner at Tao Restaurant, preceded by a cocktail at the lounge while you wait for Buddha to clear a table.

11:30 p.m. — Upstairs to Tao Nightclub for some good karma.

3:30 a.m. — Indulge in the sexier side of nightlife at Seamless Adult Ultra Lounge.

6:00 a.m. — Beauty rest.

Sunday:
11:00 a.m. — Room service delivers coffee and fruit to the suite.

12:00 a.m. — Check into Rehab, the Sunday pool party at the Hard Rock Hotel.

2:00 p.m. — Pamper yourself with the Palms Custom Massage.

3:30 p.m. — Late Check out of room.

4:00 p.m. — Taxi to airport.

6:00 p.m. — Farewell to paradise.

⊶ INSIDER'S REPORT

Don't Sleep Your Vacation Away: Sure, it's a vacation, but don't wait for a written invitation to experience Vegas. We all know the myth that casinos pump oxygen through the ventilation system into the gaming area to keep you energized and gambling. Whether this is fact or fiction, there is too much to experience in Vegas to sleep the day or night away . . . that's what the trip back home is for! If you still feel the need to be energized, try the Oxygen Bar for a bit of rejuvenation.

Understanding the Logistics of Vegas

It's very important to understand the quirky nuances of Las Vegas before locking down your itinerary. Traveling from point A to point B on the Strip is rarely as simple as it seems. Traffic can be brutal both on the street and *on the sidewalk*: think Times Square immediately after a Broadway show has let out, and that's the entire length of the Strip, night *and* day! You can't simply dash from a Swedish massage at Mandalay Bay to a shoppingfest at the Forum Shops and expect to arrive in ten minutes — sorry babe, it's just not happening, so remember to allow plenty of time between activities as you put your plan into place. If you think you can circumvent this requirement by jumping in a taxi whenever you need to, think again. In Vegas, taxis cannot stop for you on the Strip! You can only get one at a casino property cab stand, and those lines can stretch endlessly. Make life easier on everyone by choosing a place to go dancing that's close to the bar where you'll be enjoying your first tasty adult beverage of the evening.

⚷— INSIDER'S REPORT

Hot Holidays for Celeb Magnets: Every weekend brings Hollywood to Vegas, but the holidays especially bring out the stars. The city is alive with excitement and a sexy energy fills the air. Hot holidays in Vegas are New Years Eve, Super Bowl, Valentine's Day, St. Patrick's Day, Spring Break, NASCAR, Memorial Day, 4th of July, Labor Day, Thanksgiving, and the NFR Rodeo.

GETTING READY FOR SIN CITY

You've invited your group and set your itinerary. Flights are booked, show tickets have been purchased, and dinner reservations made. You have the architecture of your vacation in place; now it's time for a little window dressing to guarantee a getaway that sparkles in your memory for years to come.

Packing Smart

Packing for Vegas can be a challenge. During your 48 hours in paradise you'll be lounging poolside one minute, sipping High Tea the next, then power shopping, dining and dancing until the night is through. If most of these activities require different attire, how do you avoid overloading your luggage with every dress and tank top you own, not to mention pumps, sandals, mules, flats . . . you get the picture. The goal is to think through what you really need, and to pack smart!

The most important rule of thumb is to pack everything in a carry-on and *do not* check your bag. Baggage claim at McCarran Airport is a nightmare no matter what time of the day or night you arrive, which means you should bring a well-edited clothing selection. Think about your itinerary and plan accordingly. Capris, flowy skirts, jeans, and khakis work great for daytime. Wear the same base and bring a change of top for day two. A bathing suit, sarong-style cover-up, and jewel-studded sandals are a must despite the time of year, but don't go overboard: one bathing suit will suffice. Since evening is when it all heats up, bring a different outfit for each night: minidress, skirt, and halter, narrow cut pants with a sleeveless shell — you have most of this hiding somewhere in your closet! And despite the temptation to throw a few extra stilettos in your bag: exercise some self-control and leave them at home!

8—⊤ INSIDER'S REPORT

Luggage — Leave Room for Shopping Finds: Be sure to leave space in your luggage. The shopping in Vegas is *to die for*. You may even have to buy an extra piece of luggage to hold your new purchases on the trip home; if not, be sure to leave a few extra cubic feet of cargo space for those thongs, pumps, margarita glasses, and "My Mom went to Vegas and all I got was this stupid T-Shirt" shirts.

Shoes — The Most Important Decision You Can Make In Vegas
Here's what happens on a typical girls' Vegas getaway: One girlfriend can't wait to wear the "Vegas shoes" she bought months before in a boutique in Beverly Hills. You know the kind — shoes that only fit in Vegas, shoes that anywhere else scream the word "stripper." These "Vegas shoes" steal the show, but not in the way she hoped they would. The girl walks so slowly and her feet throb with such pain that the group can barely make a move without hearing her whine about her aching feet. Instead of hit-

ting the Vegas hot spots, the group spends the evening sitting at a casino center bar because the girlfriend is simply unable to journey on into the night.

Seriously, shoes can make or break your Vegas weekend. You don't want to be one of those girls walking the streets at 3 a.m. with your Jimmy Choos in hand and nothing on your freshly pedicured feet. On the other hand, Vegas at night is so *not* the time for sensible walking shoes. Bring shoes that strike the balance between comfort and style.

Shoe Tips
- Don't buy shoes that day and expect to wear them — and be comfortable in them — that night
- Bring Band-aids for blisters
- Bring a pair of cute, comfortable shoes for walking around during the day
- Bring a pair of heels in your daytime bag so you can change shoes on the fly

---

♈ VEGAS VIXEN

Bring a Small Handbag for Evening: You can't be lugging a king-size Louis Vuitton to the clubs; lipgloss, ID, cell, Visa, and cash are all you need. Keep your bag small and attached to your person. You need to be ready to be a Vegas Vixen at a moment's notice!

Five Sure-Things To Bring
1. <u>Swimsuit</u>: Even if you visit during the winter months, the world-class spas also offer indoor pools, steam rooms, and saunas to help rejuvenate you.

2. <u>Moisturizer</u>: The desert air is dreadfully dry and the sun will make your skin crack after only a few hours. You need to keep your skin moist with a healthy shine.

3. <u>Comfortable Walking Shoes</u>: Just in case you didn't get it before, you need a great pair of walking shoes. By shopping, sightseeing, and exploring Vegas, you'll be walking throughout the day. Make sure to save your feet for later on that night.

4. <u>Business Cards</u>: You never know who you might run into in Vegas: a new friend, a new job opportunity, or maybe even a new boyfriend!

5. <u>Your Common Sense</u>: Vegas is a crazy town and you could find yourself in an uncomfortable situation. Don't leave your common sense at home.

INSIDER'S REPORT

Coordinating Blow Dryers, Curling Irons, Shampoo, Conditioner, Lotions, and Hair Spray Between the Girls: You don't all need to bring everything. Talk to each other before you pack so you can share. Many hotels supply complimentary toiletries. Call ahead to find out what amenities are included in your hotel, and make sure you split up bringing the rest between your group.

Five Things to Leave Behind
1. <u>Slutty "Only in Vegas" Clothes</u>: You can and definitely should be a little more risqué in Vegas, but if you're thinking of bringing that outfit that has been sitting in your closet for months because it's just too outrageous, don't. If you don't feel comfortable wearing it in your hometown, then you shouldn't feel comfortable wearing it in Vegas.

2. <u>Five Pairs of High Heels</u>: You know you aren't going to wear them all. Choose two pairs that fit your nighttime outfits and leave the others at home.

3. <u>Laptop</u>: You're on vacation. Make the most of it and don't get caught up in a time-sucking web of work emails.

4. <u>Coupons from Your Last Vegas Trip</u>: Please! Vegas evolves overnight and those 2-for-1 entry coupons you saved from last year are history.

5. <u>Inhibitions</u>: Your Vegas getaway is a time for you to let loose and have fun. Not only is it okay to get a little crazy in Vegas, it's highly recommended!

Tipping In Sin City

Las Vegas has perfected the art of the gratuity. There's plenty of grease being served up here, and it's not just at the buffets. Don't wind up high and dry when it's time to tip. You'll be handing out dollar bills like crazy in Sin City, so make sure you have at least $10 in singles when you board the plane.

Tipping in Sin City Is a Cinch

♣ Wait Staff: 15 to 20 percent of the bill before tax

♣ Buffet: $2 per person

♣ Valet: $3 to $5 per car

♣ Casino Cocktail Server: $1 to $2 per drink

♣ Taxi Driver: 15 percent of fare

♣ Housekeeper: $3 to $5 per day

- ⚜ Bellhop: $2 to $4 per bag

- ⚜ Concierge: $5 to $30 per appointment arranged, depending on service

- ⚜ Dealer: Amount of your average bet, twice an hour

- ⚜ Front Desk: For room upgrade only — $20 to $50 depending on how well they come through

Safety

Keep one eye on the neon as you throw caution to the desert wind, but don't become so safety obsessed that it ruins your weekend. You can't have fun when you're walking around scared and timid.

Vegas is the safest travel destination in the world. Every casino has more security than a mid-size metropolitan police department. On top of that, there's this little thing called the "Eye in the Sky." What's that, you ask? They are strategically placed cameras located in every nook and cranny throughout the casino. With cameras everywhere it's less likely that someone creepy will actually do something creepy. Finally, remember there is safety in numbers. With 300,000 people visiting Vegas at any given time, you and your girls are never alone.

Common Sense Safety Tips

- ⚜ Always be aware of your immediate environment. Take a moment to look around and familiarize yourself with your surroundings once you enter a new building or area.

- ⚜ Only use commonly used bathrooms — not ones that are off the beaten path.

❧ When you open a tab on a credit card, don't announce it to the world. You'll become everyone's new best friend and the whole bar will be charging drinks to your MasterCard.

❧ Don't accept drinks from anyone other than the bartender. If you set your drink down and don't keep an eye on it, be sure to order a fresh one; you never know if somebody slipped something in. Sad but true.

❧ Only share a cab with someone you trust. It's tight quarters in there.

❧ Make sure your hotel room door closes and locks when you enter and exit the room. Whenever you're inside, use the chain or safety deadbolt.

❧ Use the safe in the room to keep your valuables and cash in.

❧ Be aware of who is in the elevator with you. If they seem creepy, get off on a different floor than your own and then get back on.

⌐→ INSIDER'S REPORT

When in Doubt, Look Up to the Desert Sky for Guidance:
You can always judge your whereabouts by the Stratosphere Tower, visible on the Vegas skyline from wherever you are. If you are moving away from the tower, (and depending on where you want to go) you might just be getting long-hauled by cabbies!

From Takeoff to Landing

When you get to the airport you'll notice the departure gate for Las Vegas is unlike that for any other destination. Just the fact that they're going to Vegas makes people much friendlier than they are at, say, the Tulsa gate. Everyone is heading out to the desert with a dream. Like being in a small town in Europe and running into a fellow American, there's an immediate sense of camaraderie.

Network in the Sky

Chances are you and your girlfriends will be scattered throughout the cabin on your flight out. When the drinks cart rolls around, surprise your girls by ordering everyone a Chardonnay, then strike up a little conversation with the folks next to you by asking where they're staying. Drop a few pearls of wisdom from the *Little Red Book* so that they think you're a real insider.

⌐— INSIDER'S REPORT

Don't Indulge in the Classic Vegas Airplane Drink with the Rowdy Group of Guys!: It's a good bet you will be offered *beaucoup* drinks by guys on your flight to Vegas, but remember, the real action starts once your plane taxis to the gate and you see your first slot machine. Limit your in-flight consumption to that surprise glass of wine you get for the girls. Why sip on a Jack and Coke with the overgrown frat guys, when in just one hour you can be sipping on a Cosmo next to the hottest guy you've ever laid eyes on? Don't spend your Vegas vacation with a headache and puffy eyes! Drink lots of water on the flight and in between escapades!

Roll Into Town in Style

Once your plane touches down, walk by the baggage claim (you don't have anything to pick up, because you only packed a carry-on). You'll see throngs of hotel limo drivers standing around with placards for guests they're picking up. This sight is usually a downer since everyone in your group knows they're not high rollers, and therefore unworthy of such preferential treatment. Together you skulk on over to the endless cab line to hang with the masses. Wrong!

Here's where you pull Vegas Vixen rank and really kick off your trip in style. Call ahead and ask a local limo service for an airport pickup. You'll have a driver waiting to whisk you and the girls off to your hotel in grand style. The benefits of this are pretty simple. It will cost you about $45 for the limo. Compare that to getting multiple cabs (the most you can fit into one cab is four) and waiting in an interminably long line.

The key to making this a real event is to not give any of your girls a clue to your intentions. Trust me: if you call ahead and get everything set without breathing a word, they'll be knocked out when they see the limo guy holding a placard with your names. You'll be at your hotel making your first toast while all the other groups of girls are wilting in McCarran hell.

Airport Hotel Check-In

Several of the Strip properties have check-in desks at the airport. Be sure to call ahead to see if your hotel offers this helpful, time-saving service. If it does, use it. Even if there's a line at the airport, you'll be saving yourself from a much longer line at your hotel. You can get your keys and head off to an ultra lounge straight from the airport, and when you make it back to your room, your bags will be there waiting.

⊶ INSIDER'S REPORT

Have Your Group Dressed and Ready to Go Out Before They Get on the Plane: Your time in Vegas is short and when your plane hits the ground you want to be off and running. Be sure everyone knows to be dressed for a night on the town. You don't want to be sitting around the hotel room primping for hours on your first night in Vegas!

On Your Mark, Set and Go

You are finally in Vegas at the beginning of a grand adventure. If this is your first time, expect to be overwhelmed. If it's not your first time, there is always something new to explore. Remember, the *Little Red Book* is your guide — keep it by your side and it won't let you down. If you do end up wasting a little money on a mediocre meal or an overpriced pair of sandals, don't feel too badly. We've all been there before, we didn't get all of our advice for free, and more than a few tips were learned the hard way.

If you plan ahead whenever possible, your special getaway will certainly be a good one — even a fabulous one. Keep an eye on your girls, stick with the plan, and the fabulous times will flow. There are plenty of adventures awaiting you, and you owe it to yourself to soak the pleasure out of each and every one of them.

PART II

Viva Las Vegas

Chapter 4

Accommodations: You Are Where You Stay

★ ....

Sin City not only has the *most* hotel rooms in the world, it's also home to 17 of the top 20 *largest* hotels in the world, meaning there's no excuse for not choosing a stunning, service-oriented, ever-improving resort as your launching pad, beauty base, and the heart and soul of your Vegas getaway. In a city built on making visitors deliriously happy, your choice of accommodation is the single most important decision you make.

In case you doubt the essential truth of that, consider the following poor choice (a rookie nightmare easily avoided by savvy Vegas Vixens like yourselves): You and your girl friends grab your luggage (after waiting), hop in a cab (after waiting), and head to your hotel (where you wait some more). While researching hotels, everyone told you, "As long as you stay on the Strip, you're totally fine. It really doesn't matter *where* your hotel is since the *real* action happens outside of your room." This sounded like decent advice so you booked a moderately priced hotel on the Strip (offering up to $100 in Vegas coupons), and figured that with the money saved, you could splurge on an afternoon of shopping followed by a facial at a top rated spa. As your cab cruises toward your hotel, you begin to realize that there's a huge difference between being *on* the Strip and being *centrally located on* the

Strip. It's obvious that your hotel is so far removed from the action that you might as well be staying out in the suburbs. The rooms are cheap, but tiny; even worse, in this holdover from old Vegas, they are unrenovated, tacky, musty, and offer no amenities. Want to relax in the spa? It's barely a locker room. Lounge by the pool? It's a postage stamp of green water in the shadow of taller, better hotels. Guys may take pride in being able to do 48 hours in Sin City at a bargain basement dive out in the provinces, but a cramped hotel room still sporting dark wood paneling and rust colored shag carpet, located on the wrong section of the Strip, is simply not an option for us girls.

This we know: Opting to save a little on the cost of your room by staying in a mediocre location with hideous décor, sparse amenities, or one too many roommates will make you head straight to the bar (if you can find it) for m*ucho* tequilas.

WHAT TO LOOK FOR: 8 Key Considerations

The best way to avoid the frustration that comes with choosing the wrong hotel is to know exactly what you're looking for and to plan accordingly.

Each group of girls has their own unique needs. The lobby may be hung with museum quality paintings, but if you are not art aficionados, the masterpieces will pass you by at a record speed. A hotel may rank four diamonds, but if the cocktail lounge is always packed with men old enough to be your dad, then what's the point — unless you're into that kind of thing, of course! When it comes to choosing a hotel, consider the following:

1. Image: You *Are* Where You Stay

Because every hotel attracts a different type of guest, you should choose a place that's caters to *your* kind of people.

Some properties attract flashy high rollers while others cater to lovers. If you chose to stay at a place where most of the guests are long-time couples up for a romantic interlude, and you're out prowling for players in your little black dress, expect to spend lots of quality alone time.

Remember: You *are* where you stay. The first question fellow Vegas visitors will ask you is, "Where are you staying?" Once you get home it will be, "Where did you stay?" Beware the two-star bargain advertised each week on hotels.com as a $99 Weekend Getaway Special. Very few good Vegas stories begin with the line, "We stayed at the Riviera . . ."

2. Location, Location, Location

Desert Mirage
Nothing in Las Vegas is more deceiving than the distance from one property to the next. "Right next door" can mean a half-mile walk door-to-door. (Can we stress this enough?) You will save yourself endless walking by choosing a hotel that's in the heart of the type of action you crave. Hotels are also often priced according to their location. Go figure!

You Can't Get There from Here
One argument for not paying to stay in the center of the action is that you can always take a cab. True . . . if you can find one. Taxis will not stop for you on the Strip, and although every hotel has a taxi stand, a busy weekend evening can mean at least a half hour wait. Finally, expect to be sitting comfortably in the backseat for some time, as traffic is often brutal on and around the Strip.

♣ Hot Zone:
The Hot Zone is the center of the action, and offers the best options for dining, clubbing, shopping and partying, all of which are "relatively" close to each other.

♣ Pretty Cool Zone:

The Pretty Cool Zone provides access to a large variety of options, but requires more effort and resourcefulness on your part in the way of taxis, limos, or power walking. Put your Nikes on!

♣ Ice Cold Zone:

Get a car, because walking is pretty much out of the question. This is no indictment of the properties within the Ice Cold Zone because many of them are first-class luxury resorts. Unfortunately, their location leaves you no choice but to rent a car, cab it, or hire a limo if you choose to leave the property (which you are bound to do at some point to shake things up and experience some handsome new "scenery!").

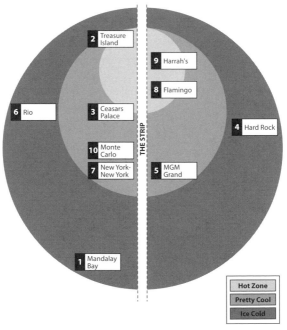

This map will help show you where the action is on the Strip.

3. Nightlife

A great hotel needs nightlife to launch your party and keep things energized. All the HOT properties on the Strip have a top rated nightclub, ultra lounge and bar. Choose a place to stay where stepping out of your door means stepping into a hot Vegas party.

4. Dining

Sustenance is everything. Whether it's a leisurely bowl of fresh fruit on the terrace with a view of the Eiffel Tower and Statue of Liberty in the same glance (only Vegas has Paris and New York in the same city block) or gourmet dining at a five-star restaurant with a celebrity chef catering to you and your girls tableside, this is the stuff memories are made of. Inconvenience should not be a word in your vocabulary, especially if you've planned your get-away as a sampling of epicurean delights. Choose a hotel offering a range of casual to high-end restaurants, or one where the seductive aroma of seared scallops and gourmet tomato basil pizza is only a short walk away.

5. Shopping

Girls, roll up your sleeves and be prepared for a shopping high! The shopping in Vegas is some of the best you've ever experienced! You will be thrilled to know that every major Strip property has its own version of high-end shopping. Since you'll plan to do at least a little (okay, a lot) of shopping, it's best to stay at a place that won't require you to lug your new acquisitions halfway to Timbuktu just to get them back to your room. Any property worth its salt should have enough boutiques to set your credit card on fire.

6. The Pool: Fun in the Sun

Your "It" Hotel must have a lavish pool with private cabanas and lush, tranquil gardens for relaxing and pampering your senses. If fun in the sun is what your group is all about, then spend your afternoon (or a few restorative hours) sipping a Piña Colada poolside, listening to the house DJ (that's right, in Vegas the hot pools have a DJ) and checking out the guys. It is important to note that the hotel pool is for hotel guests only. If you don't stay there, you can't play there. Rare exceptions, such as the Hard Rock Hotel's Sunday Rehab, and the Caesars Palace Venus Pool Club, will be detailed later.

Note *Vegas pools are closed from November to March, so don't worry about this one during those winter months.*

7. The Spa: Your Oasis of Relaxation

Spa culture has taken hold of Las Vegas. If your vision of a Vegas spa looks like a 1950s Rat Pack steam room, then baby, just look at us now! Most Strip properties have spas that hover in the 20,000 to 30,000 square foot range and they're loaded with cutting-edge services and over-the-top luxury. Pamper yourself before a night on the town by selecting a facial, body treatment, or massage (or perhaps one of each). While many hotels have a spa, as with all things Vegas, there are only a select few that could really make into Condé Nast *Traveller* magazine. The hipper the resort, the hipper the spa. Why? Because the only way the hip stay hip is due to a seemingly effortless — yet entirely rigorous — regime of relaxation and pampering!

8. Rooms

Although you'll probably spend a nominal amount of time in your hotel room, if you open the door to face a thread-worn bedspread and '80's mauve and teal décor, the disappointment will hit you like a cold weak latté. Remember: The opulent lobby is only a façade; a top-of-the-line hotel is worthless if the room is shabby, dated, or dirty — and your impulse is to run out and get a tetanus shot.

CHOOSE WISELY

Rank the eight criteria based on importance to your group. Remember, if you plan to visit Vegas anytime between November and March, the pool is really a non-issue. Below are the *Little Red*

Hotel	Image	Location	Nightlife	Dining	Shopping	Pool	Spa	Rooms	TOTALS
Palms	10	7	10	10	6	10	10	10	73
Hard Rock	10	7	10	10	6	10	9	10	72
Wynn	10	8	9	9	9	9	8	10	72
Caesars Palace	9	10	9	9	10	9	8	7	71
Venetian	9	9	10	9	10	7	8	9	71
Mandalay Bay	9	7	9	10	9	10	8	8	70
Bellagio	9	9	9	9	8	9	9	8	70
MGM Grand	8	8	8	8	7	8	7	7	61
Mirage	8	9	8	7	6	7	7	7	59
Planet Hollywood	8	8	7	7	9	6	6	7	58

Book's Top 10 hotels for groups of girls. Use the chart to determine which one is right for you.

 ## THE *LITTLE RED BOOK*'S LUCKY 7 FOR GROUPS OF GIRLS

1. Palms: Hollywood in the Desert

This property *is* the new Vegas. Ever since MTV set "The Real World: Las Vegas" here, this off-Strip property has been white hot. A-listers flock to Palms, Playboy celebrates at Palms, and Victoria's Secret Angels tour to Palms, all for its contemporary sexy ambiance. With legendary nightlife and outrageous themed suites designed with an edge and a sense of humor (care to try out your very own stripper pole?), Palms is smoking — the hippest place where the hottest celebrities stay and play.

Image

Amazing. Celebs love Palms since they roll out the red carpet for Hollywood. Tell your friends you stayed here and assume they'll ask about the stars you spent the weekend with. And although you'll be surrounded by young, sexy, gorgeous, fun-loving "It Girls" — *your* only pre-requisite for staying at Palms is the fun-loving part!

Location

The only downfall is that it's located just off the Strip, making taxis an absolute must; they can be hard to get so be prepared to wait. The upside is that you'll be surrounded by the beautiful, the Botoxed and the bulimic, giving you plenty to look at, and making the wait as painless as possible.

Nightlife

Palms certainly knows how to party. Rain Nightclub is one of the hottest dance clubs in the country, and the sleek and stylized ghostbar is where the beautiful people come to sip and

STRIP TEASE

George and Gavin Maloof, Las Vegas' Most Eligible Bachelors: What separates George and Gavin Maloof of Palms fame from other hotel head honchos? Sure, their cells ring non-stop (the *are* Sin City's most eligible bachelors), but they make an effort to return *every* phone call, are easily accessible to all their treasured guests, and continue to soar with their hands-on approach. Mayor Oscar Goodman once referred to it as the "Maloof touch," as everything they touch seems to turn to gold. Customer service has always been the name of the Maloof's game, which is evident throughout the property, making it the most sought after resort in Vegas.

be seen. The Playboy Club and Moon Nightclub in the Fantasy Tower are more intimate, select nightspots. Avoiding the club scene and just hanging out at the center bar, the Island Lounge, and the new cutting-edge, high-limit gaming lounge, Mint, is a blast since the hotel offers fabulous people watching and an infectious energy. If you stay here, you'll have little reason to leave the premises at night.

Dining Options

N9NE Steakhouse is one of Vegas' hippest restaurants and features a festive champagne and caviar bar. Dramatic floor-to-ceiling views and a delicious French gourmet meal make Alize an elegant option. Nove offers a high-end Italian menu in a hip atmosphere. Little Buddha is great if you're up for sushi, and the 24-hour café serves an excellent late night menu for girls on the go.

Shopping

While shopping at Palms is fairly limited, it does offer some pretty unique options. Looking for a sexy swimsuit for the day or a hot outfit for the night? Palms' gift shop is anything but your typical hotel-style CVS, and features trendy designers straight from Rodeo Drive. You'll be way too sexy for your girls if you purchase a trinket at the new Playboy boutique, the only place in Vegas you can buy the new Playboy line.

Pool

The just-opened Palms Pool & Bungalows features three pools, a climate controlled gaming area, four bars, and two waterfalls. So, while you work on your desert glow, you can also sip trendy cocktails with the beautiful people, nosh on mouth-watering cuisine, and groove to live entertainment. The adjacent three-acre adult poolside playground sports 27 amenity-packed VIP cabanas, and three ultra-luxe 2-story bungalows with sleeping quarters. Yes, we said adult playground: no kids! Rent one of these, and you and your vixens will suddenly be the center of your own hipper-than-thou party for around twenty of your new best friends.

Spa

A superior spa! The best thing about Palms Spa is that it caters to the needs of real women. A cardio-area overlooking the pool filled with bikini-clad nymphettes and hard-bodied Mark Wahlberg look-alikes provides pure entertainment and that added degree of motivation. If you are in need of a massage, try the Southwest Stone Therapy, a thoroughly relaxing treatment where smooth stones are heated with water and placed on various points of your body. They'll have to peel you off of the massage table!

Rooms

What makes Palms unique is that *everyone* is treated like a celebrity, regardless of their tax bracket. Even the most basic "deluxe room" is equipped with the amenities of a junior suite (minus the space). All rooms ooze sophisticated elegance and are minimally decorated with clean sleek lines. The beds are some of the most comfortable and inviting you'll find in Vegas, with thick fluffy duvets and firm mattresses . . . what happens there is up to you! Superior rooms and suites are located in the all-new Fantasy Tower, where the rooms are built with extra sound insulation, and there always seems to be a mini block party going on during the weekends. While we recommend your group of four or more girls to book the level of suite that best fits your budget, whichever route you go at the Palms, you'll feel like a celebrity princess.

 **LUXE LAS VEGAS**

The Fantasy Suites: Located on the Fantasy Tower's 25th and 26th floors, the Fantasy Suites take the themed hotel room to exotic extremes. The Kingpin Suite is a retro-style party room with two full-size bowling lanes, and the Erotic Suite features an eight-foot round, rotating bed, and a "show shower" equipped with special lighting and a dancer pole. Wait, it gets better! Other Fantasy Suites include the Celebrity, Director's, Hot Pink, Crib, and g-Suite. Built with extra sound insulation, each Fantasy Suite doubles as a meeting and entertainment venue. Booked together, they can accommodate up to 600 guests on two floors for a private "Block Party." The Hardwood Suite is the only hotel room in the world with an indoor basketball court, and the two luxury Playpen Suites come complete with the infamous stripper poles.

2. Hard Rock Hotel: The Chic Boutique

Outrageous costumes and memorabilia give Hard Rock its laid back, hip and ultra cool vibe. Light fixtures are recycled drum cymbals. Leather jackets from Aerosmith and U2 are incorporated into the décor. Then there are Madonna's panties — the perfect design accessory. The hotel is petite by Vegas' standards, giving it a more intimate boutique feel. If the massive palaces on the Strip overwhelm you, then this temple of hedonistic pleasure and decadence is your baby.

Image

Girls just wanna have fun! Thankfully, Hard Rock's reputation is nothing like that of their cheesy restaurant chain. Expect your fellow guests to be under 40, have some money (or at least pretend to for the weekend), and be focused on having a really good time.

Location

Fair. You can manage to make it on foot to MGM, but it's probably not something you want to do more than once during your trip. Located one mile from McCarran International Airport and 3 blocks from the Strip, the location is the property's biggest drawback.

Nightlife

"The Joint," a live music venue with a 1,400-person capacity features hot music acts every week. After hours, head downstairs to Body English, a sultry nightclub where the dance floor is packed and the guys rock hard under the shimmering brilliance of a $250,000 Baccarat crystal chandelier. If you stay at the hotel, plan to spend at least one of your evenings here. Why venture to the Strip, when you have the guys, the cocktails and the ultimate vibe right at your freshly manicured fingertips?

Dining

Mr. Lucky's 24/7 is your rockin' 24-hour restaurant specializing in casual coffee shop-style food with the best people watching you could ever ask for. Nobu is a temple of trendy Japanese cuisine; plan ahead and make a reservation. Pink Taco is a hip Mexican eatery with the best margaritas this side of the border. AJ's is a sophisticated Steakhouse with it's very own piano player, and Simon Kitchen + Bar takes a hip twist on classic American fare with great dishes by Kerry Simon, one of the top young chefs in the country. Not a bad mix; you'll find it hard to leave!

Shopping

Just because it's a boutique hotel, doesn't mean there are actually boutiques. The first-ever Hard Rock Hotel retail store offers those same Hard Rock T-shirts you've seen for years at the mall or Disney World — avoid like the plague. Love Jones, a sexy lingerie store, features everything for the girly girl to the undercover dominatrix. Try their "Room Service," where a full menu of lingerie items can be delivered directly to your room to spontaneously enhance your boudoir activities. Check out the guys at Cuba Libre, savoring some of the finest cigars in the world: then saunter in and crash their party like a *Cigar Aficiando* cover girl.

Pool

The Beach Club and Pool at Hard Rock more than make up for the weakness on the shopping front since every day feels like a party. Swim in the lagoon where the rockin' music plays underwater, and try your hand at swim-up blackjack alongside the Palapa Bar & Grill. Recovery never felt — or looked — as good as it does at the pool every summer Sunday from noon to sundown. Take it from past "patients" (including us): This "beach club" party is the best way to rejuvenate your abused mind, body and soul after you've pushed them to the edge by following the *Little Red Book*. Rent one of the 39 über-hip cabanas that resemble plush hotel suites (our favorite is the Love Den), but be prepared to shell out some serious cash — $100 a day during the week, $200 on weekends.

Spa

The Rock Spa is small, but it's all you need. Feel like rock 'n' roll royalty for a day and choose between four different massage treatments from "the quick fix" for 25 minutes, to the "hot stone therapy" which can last up to 80 minutes and features smooth heated stones and aromatherapy oils. For an extra $25, you can be decadently massaged in the comfort of your own room or by the pool. End the day of beauty at Brannon Hair Salon, a Hard Rock Institution. Reinvent yourself *a la* Madonna, or get the same style services you get back home — but with that rocker chick twist!

Rooms

The resort has 645 hip and trendy guest rooms including over 50 suites, all plushly appointed with velveteen fabrics, 310 thread-count linens, a Bose stereo system, and French doors that open to the outside. Ask for a pool-side room so you can observe the action from above like a true voyeur.

⛷➝ INSIDER'S REPORT

Hard Rock High-Roller: "The Penthouse" is designed like an English rock star's pad. The 5,000 square foot, three-bedroom suite features the world's first bowling alley inside a hotel room. The experience also includes a 24-hour on-call butler, a professional pool table, a 6-person hot tub with two plasma TVs, mirrored ceilings, and plasma flat screen TVs throughout. "The Penthouse" starts at $10,000 per night. Mere pocket change for the likes of all those stylish rockers who continue to smoke the joint!

3. Wynn Las Vegas: Opulence Abounds

If you want to splurge on your accommodations, this is *the* place to do it: opulence, attention to detail, impeccable service, and . . . nature. When Steve Wynn returned to the Strip in 2005 he did it in a big way. The sleek, 50-story, curved hotel is all about fusing natural and man-made elements. A $130 million man-made mountain with a 4,000 light lighting panel rises from the Strip right outside the property, and sunlight and water flows throughout the hotel's interior. From inside the resort, you can enjoy the mountain, dancing fountains, 90-foot waterfalls, and a 3-acre, man-made lake. It may sound like a nature reserve *sans* the moose and muskrats, but trust us: Wynn Las Vegas is all elegance and sophistication.

Image

If you want to stay and play among the highest of the high rollers, this is the place to do it. The upscale image and price tags attached tend to attract a fun-loving and sophisticated crowd.

Location

Location is fantastic, right in the hot zone. You have some great dining and nightlife options at other resorts just a short walk away, and the Fashion Show Mall is connected by a walkway.

Nightlife

Tryst has just the type of crowd you'd expect to find at the Wynn: financially successful. Although the nightclub is upscale and elegant, it's the furthest thing from stodgy — how up tight can you be dancing on water under a 90-foot waterfall!? Just steps away, Lure, the seductively inviting ultra lounge, is known for some of the best cocktails and champagne on the Strip.

 **STRIP TEASE:**

Be a Good Girl: Don't expect to get away with anything at Wynn Las Vegas. The resort is home to eight bomb detection dogs — the most on the Strip!

Dining

Wynn has eighteen restaurants and bars including six that are home to renowned celebrity chefs. And don't think you'll be slumming at any chain restaurants; this property is all about sophisticated palates and interesting cuisine that pushes the culinary limits, so if your vixens are only about Cheesecake Factory or Stage Deli, you'd best move on to Caesars. Wynn makes all their own breads right on premises — over 70 different kinds to be exact — so bring on the carbs and work them off while dancing or power shopping.

Shopping

Staying at Wynn is a shopper's dream. Wynn Esplanade includes some of the very highest-end retailers: We're talking Chanel and Dior, so pocket change just won't cut it if you're looking to bring home a little souvenir. If the haute couture price tags start to depress you, there's always the more mainstream Fashion Show Mall, located across the street from the hotel anchored by Neiman Marcus and Nordstrom. Here you can buy the real thing or a designer knock-off that's fashion-forward enough to help you stand your ground amidst the "winters in St. Barts, summers on the French Riviera" crowd.

Pool

While the pool area is large and lush, it is not as impressive as the pools at some of the other facilities. And despite the cabana amenities — your very own cabana host, iPods loaded with your favorite genre of music, ice towels, 30-inch flat screen TV with remote, ceiling fan, sofa, two interior chairs, misting system, two lounge chairs, and the lovely in-cabana massage — the older clientele makes the experience reminiscent of hanging out by the pool at your grandparents' condo in Boca.

Spa

The ultimate spa experience! Not all massages or facials are created equal; each is carefully customized for your personal needs. Imagine a trained beauty technician spending more time analyzing your skin type and relaxation needs than Lindsay Lohan spends changing her hairstyle and image! This is the spa where you should spend a half day with your girls undergoing the Crème de la Mer Ultimate Experience, or their signature treatment, the Good Luck Ritual, an 80-minute, Asian inspired massage. You'll feel like a true VIP, and leave feeling guilty that your normal regime has been such a dated cycle of wash, tone, and moisturize. On the other hand, their reliance on silk robes and massage tablecloths is a common complaint. The silk is quite clingy and lacks the warmth of Egyptian cotton.

Room

Imagine flipping through an *Elle Décor* and pausing to drool over the most gorgeous New York apartment you've ever seen. That would be your room at the Wynn. It's as luxurious and sophisticated as an upper East Side apartment with 180-degree room views of the rest of the pack, a yummy color scheme of Chocolate Cherry, Carnelian & Cream and Crème Brûlée, and sleek, over-sized bathrooms — fully equipped and enormous enough to take on all five of your buzzing hair dryers and make-up artistry at once. And if that isn't perfection enough, then paradise can be found after an evening of heavy partying, as you melt into your pillowtop signature Wynn bed with its 320-thread count European linens. So, as much as you may want to go with that hot guy you spent the evening with, take it from us . . . a room at Wynn Las Vegas is better than sex.

Wynn's Golf Course: The second collaboration of Tom Fazio, Steve Wynn, and Mother Nature has resulted in 18 unforgettable holes right outside Wynn's back door — one of only two courses on the Strip, but the only one attached to a resort. The course is by invitation only, which means that you have to be a pretty good gambler at Wynn to play it. Or, if you offer enough money to play, they will "invite" you and your lucky swing. Wynn also has 36 fairway villas that look onto the golf course . . . so exclusive they aren't featured in the resort line-up!

4. Caesars Palace: Feel Like a Goddess

Caesars is legendary, which until recently meant *old*. In the last few years, however, Caesars has undergone an overwhelming series of expansions and upgrades including the new Coliseum that Celine Dion and Elton John call their second home . . . but don't let a little thing like that scare you away. Caesars is all about opulence: oversized, overstuffed, over-the-top grandeur featuring marble staircases, statues of the Grecian gods, ornate fountains, and elegant, intimate indoor and garden settings for that special day.

Image

The crowd is fairly upscale with a healthy mix of yuppie urbanites and old school Vegas gamblers. Of course there are also some of the uninspired masses that continue to make Celine one of the hottest tickets in town.

Location

Right in the heart of the Hot Zone, with easy access by foot and taxi to many different venues. On the downside, it's big and the layout is confusing, so give yourself some time to learn your way around or you could be walking in circles.

Nightlife

Decisions, decisions! PURE nightclub, named the "No. 1 Hippest Hotspot in the Nation" by E! Entertainment Television, is two stories of stylish late-night indulgence. Adjacent to PURE is The Pussycat Dolls Lounge where you can gawk at the dolls' sexy dance numbers and even catch a spontaneous "celeb doll" burlesque performance. The Seahorse Lounge offers an elegant respite with plush seating around a 1,700-gallon aquarium. Cleopatra's Barge is a cheesy floating cocktail lounge that is a replica of the regal ships that sailed the Nile in ancient Egypt. Shadow is an adrenaline rush with its world champion flair bartenders putting on a show of juggling bottles and back-flips as they concoct your libation. And, relaxing at the bar in the heart of the open-air Roman Plaza will make you feel like you've stepped out of the pages of *Town & Country*. Every single one of these Caesars nightspots are wonderful venues, so decide if it's going to be an evening of down and dirty partying, or suggestive dalliances amidst the rich and famous, then pull out your Vegas Vixen and get to work!

📷 STARGAZING IN THE DESERT

Roman Games: Caesars Palace is renowned for hosting international-caliber sports contests. Such sports legends as Jimmy Connors, John McEnroe, Boris Becker, Bjorn Borg, Andre Agassi, Pete Sampras, Thomas Hearns, Sugar Ray Leonard, Muhammad Ali, George Foreman, Mike Tyson, Oscar De La Hoya, Mary Lou Retton, Bart Conner, Wayne Gretzky, Katarina Witt, and Mario Andretti have showcased their championship style to win riches and honors in Caesars events.

Dining

Your baseline default option is the bright and serviceable Café Lago coffee shop, newly remodeled and located in the back part of the casino near the pool, with an extensive à la carte menu and quality buffet. For more serious dining courtesy of today's hottest celebrity chefs, try the two famous Wolfgang Puck restaurants — Spago and Chinois — more for the happening scene (hot guys and celebs) rather than the overrated food. Both are booked weeks in advance so make your reservations early. Bradley Ogden, the namesake restaurant of the Bay-area chef known for farm-to-table American cuisine, never disappoints but is located only a few steps away from the entrance to Celine Dion's show, meaning you'll be dining to the tune of fans humming the Ti*tanic t*heme song. Famed TV chef Bobby Flay chose Vegas to open Mesa Grill, his first restaurant beyond New York City. Try the shrimp and roasted corn tamale, a burst of savory southwestern flavors that will get you feeling hot and sultry. Ole!

Shopping

As if over 100 of the best high-end retailers all under one roof isn't enough to give you a retail rush! Just strolling through the ancient Roman streetscape housing the Forum Shops, can make you feel awash in a sensual glow, filled with a burning love and passion for . . . those fabulous Kate Spade leopard-print shoes that you just can't live without! And In case you get lost for hours debating between leopard or zebra, the barrel-vaulted ceiling is crowned with a faux sky and computerized lighting that simulates the sun's movement from sunrise to sunset in hourly cycles — quite handy when you need a gentle reminder that it's already 5:00 p.m. and the girls are waiting for you at the Seahorse Lounge for cocktail number one. In a word, the shopping at Caesars is divine, so pay down your credit cards, and get ready to do some serious damage.

Pool

The pool area is one of the nicest in Vegas. It's a glorious place to spend an afternoon of Roman Goddess pampering with its four large heated swimming pools, two outdoor whirlpool spas, lavish gardens, and dramatic fountains and statuary. All the pools and spas are inlaid with marble and granite, and rimmed in intricate mosaics. If you feel energetic enough to do a few laps, the Venus Pool (long and narrow) is a three-foot-by-six-inch deep lap pool and allows European-style topless bathing — not something you'd experience at your community pool amidst the whining toddlers, so unclasp that bikini top and slather on the SPF 45! You can even spoil yourself with frozen towel service, body massages, and Evian spritzers. Keep an eye out for the Grape Goddesses, who will offer you chilled fruit as you soak up the desert sun. Girl, Venus has nothing on you!

Spa

Although the Spa at Caesars doesn't compare in size and scope with the likes of Canyon Ranch, it does cover the basics quite well, and offers the wonderful body-soothing, mind-energizing Roman Bathing Ritual. It works like this: Private men's and women's areas feature a circuit of baths in three distinct temperatures and water pressure intensities. First, immerse yourself in a tepid mineral pool with carefully orchestrated jets. Then, dive into the frigid waters of the cold plunge pool. Immediately, dip into the spa's hottest pool, which forces your body into a state of utter surrender. You'll feel weak and almost ready to pass out — in dire need of water, protein, a place to collapse . . . but hey, it's all good! The steam room infuses fresh aromatic herbs into the misty air, and shaved ice cascades down a fountain in the Arctic ice room — perfect for cooling the body and exfoliating the skin of the modern goddess.

Rooms

The rooms at Caesars are nice; just make sure you avoid the Centurian Tower, which earns its name, as the rooms feel like they're a hundred years old. A much better selection is the new all-suite Augustus Tower where the guest rooms are mini-palaces with nine-foot ceilings and floor plans that begin at 650 square feet — (approximately 50 percent larger than typical fine hotel accommodations in major U.S. cities). Blissful bedding of premium linens, duvets, neck roll pillows, merino wool throws, and luxurious bathrooms appointed with spa tubs and dual vanities topped with individual flat-screen televisions, help create the perfect launching pad for your Vegas Bacchanal.

STRIP TEASE

Oscar-Worthy: Caesars two-story Fantasy Suite was featured in the Oscar-winning Best Picture, *Rain Man*.

5. The Venetian: Style and Size

The Venetian is big. Very big. Third-largest-hotel-in-the-world big. You might think that its overwhelming size could make it feel barn-like and impersonal, but surprisingly, that's not the case. This faux Italian villa-themed property (probably larger than the actual city of Venice) exudes genuine charm, although some of its attempts to appear authentic come off as downright cheesy — anyone up for a gondola ride? If you're looking for real culture, be sure to check out the Guggenheim Heritage Museum right on the premises. The overall quality and location of The Venetian make it one of the most popular destinations for groups of women, but it's also massive and to some may feel too much like Disney's version of "Italy" at Epcot Center.

Image

The Venetian is fairly upscale, but generic. You'll find that you and your girls are probably one of about two hundred groups of women or bachelorettes calling The Venetian home for the weekend.

Nightlife

We love TAO Las Vegas, the multi-faceted and multi-story "Asian City" with its happening restaurant, ultra lounge and nightclub. Expect a healthy dose of décor drama to bring out your exotic side: waterfalls, a 20-foot tall hand-carved wooden Buddha, rich silks and polished woods, and an Infinity Pool with Japanese carp. The drinks are seductive potions, the men gorgeous, the setting sensuous, the karma just right. Feng shui, indeed!

Dining

The star here is Tao Restaurant. Just glancing at Chef Sam Hazen's Pan-Asian menu is enough to bring on an anxiety attack, as you vacillate between the best Peking Duck in town, his famous Wasabi Crusted Filet Mignon, Kobe Beef Shabu Shabu, Chilean Sea Bass Satays, and a full authentic sushi bar. We say go for them all, and share like one big, ecstatically happy family.

Shopping

The Grand Canal Shoppes are a pleasant place to stroll. The faux sky above makes it always feel like the sun is shining in the clear blue sky; it's amazing just how much this illusion can improve your mood! The shops are mostly top chains, including our patron saint of shoes, Jimmy Choo. Although you won't find much more than what's housed at an upscale mall in your hometown, if you didn't pack well and you're in a pinch for a reasonably priced outfit, this might be your best option. Be forewarned that a lively cast of Carnivale characters and street performers will serenade you as you stroll past The Grand Canal, and the living statues located in St. Mark's Square and the Oculus will entertain without saying a word.

We find their artistry charming, so put your cynical, Disney-bashing streak aside and give yourself over to a sensory over-load shopping experience.

Pool

There are three pools at The Venetian and when the sun is out they're delightful, although there tend to be lots of families and kids milling about. There are also some parts of each day when you could be stuck completely in the shade of the hotel — so while you won't have to pack the SPF 45, you could come back sporting a tan that makes people think Ireland not Italy. Avoid the cabanas: They're nicely equipped with elec-tronic toys, stocked fridge, and a "cabana boy" dedicated to fulfilling your every whim (Hello, Mrs. Robinson!), but cer-tainly aren't worth their $350 weekend price tag.

Spa

The Canyon Ranch SpaClub is the best in town. Women will stay at The Venetian and deal with the theme-park atmos-phere just to luxuriate in this serene and elegant temple of pampering that features more than 100 services and 62 treat-ment rooms. Gather your girls and make those beauty treat-ment appointments at the same time you book your hotel, since you'll be competing with every tourist and in-the-know local for expert massages, scrubs and wraps. SpaClub also of-fers a complete fitness facility with state-of-the-art classes to help you work off those 3:00 a.m. hash browns and Bloody Marys, and a wellness center with physical therapists, nutri-tionists, exercise physiologists, and personal trainers to help maintain your status as a healthy, red-blooded American female. The chic lobby of the Canyon Ranch SpaClub features a full-service salon owned and operated by the legendary Michael Boychuck of Amp Salon at Palms. This is the place to splurge. It will make your weekend, and after all, girls — you're worth it!

Rooms

Each room is a petite suite that includes two beds and a living room area with sofa, and boasts an average of 700 square feet (approximately twice the size of the typical Las Vegas room). The rooms are just as gorgeous and sophisticated as those at Wynn, but decorated with a traditional — rather than modern — design sensibility. You'll feel inclined to short circuit your evening to fall into the canopy draped, king size beds with their fluffy duvets, and to prance around in the snazzy slippers that can be found waiting at the side of the bed for your shopping and dancing-abused feet. If your bank account can handle a little extra stress, The Venezia hotel tower is comprised of "luxury suites" (as if the suites described above aren't luxurious enough) with more space and marble than you'll know what to do with, your own mini-business center, access to a lavish pool deck, wedding chapel, and exclusive Concierge Level private lounge providing round the clock cocktails and snacks. As Las Vegas' only hotel (as of this writing) featuring a Concierge Level, this "hotel within a hotel" will be like your own personal sugar daddy, at your beck and call to assist with dinner and transportation reservations . . . anything your little heart desires.

🎥 STARGAZING IN THE DESERT

Celebrities are in Vegas every week. . . . Where the stars like to stay:

> Paris Hilton — Venetian
> Britney Spears — Palms
> George Clooney — Red Rock
> Toby Maguire — Bellagio

---

6. Mandalay Bay: Paradise Found

Tropically themed, with more palm trees than a Caribbean island, a lagoon, mystical architecture, and cascading waterfalls, Mandalay is actually comprised of three hotels: the reasonably priced Mandalay Bay; the swankier THEhotel; and the exclusive Four Seasons, featuring its own entrance, parking, check-in, dining, pool, spa, and convention area. This is a hotel "complex," meaning it includes: a massive convention center; 12,000-seat sports and entertainment facility used for superstar concerts, major sporting events, and television specials; a 1,600-seat Broadway-style theatre; Shark Reef at Mandalay Bay, a total sensory experience featuring 2,000 dangerous and unusual aquatic animals; and of course, shopping and dining.

Image

With three hotel options, Mandalay can be a bit of a mixed bag. That said, it has a consistently classy clientele. As Mandalay Bay is a hot spot for bachelor and bachelorette parties, the crowd tends to skew under 40.

Location

Terrible. Getting anywhere from Mandalay is work. Cabs are a must, and despite what you may hear about the "very convenient monorail," it will only take you to its sister properties Luxor and Excalibur. From there you need to make it across the street (not an easy task seeing that it requires negotiating the labyrinth of Excalibur) and over to MGM to get on the real Vegas monorail (which runs behind the Strip — rather than on it — in any case). Exhausted just reading this? Give it up and prepare to take cabs, and lots of them!

Nightlife

Nightlife includes three winners in rumjungle, Foundation Room, and MIX, located on the 64th floor of THEhotel with one of the best views of the Strip. When we're in the mood for quality Vegas entertainment minus the cheese factor, we make a bee-line for the House of Blues concert hall for an eclectic mix of quality live music from artists such as Bob Dylan, B.B. King, Guns N' Roses, and LeAnn Rimes. Three lounges feature live entertainment nightly, including the Island Lounge with a late night menu featuring caviar and smoked salmon. Crack the champagne for a nutritious, perfectly balanced midnight snack.

Dining

Red Square is a popular option — be sure to order a vodka cocktail. Other great choices include Border Grill and China Grill. There are also plenty of places to grab a fast bite that's a far cry from fast food.

Shopping

Mandalay Bay and THEhotel offer original boutiques not normally seen around the Strip. If you're in the market for a sexy new bathing suit, Pearl Moon is a must, featuring trendy designer swimwear and sun accessories.

Pool

This is the powerhouse of pools, an 11-acre tropical water environment that's more water park than pool, and like most water parks, is flooded with families. It's a great experience if you go during the week when most kids are in school and most parents are here for a convention, but otherwise, you'd better grab a daiquiri for your ride down the lazy river, so you feel less like you're trapped in a G-rated family entertainment center. The vibe shifts dramatically at the far end of the pool area in the exclusive topless pool Moorea Beach Club — girlfriend, you're not in Kansas anymore! Although initially you might not be interested in an *au natural* experience, Moorea Beach is the best place for you and your vixens to go to avoid screaming kids and packs of sleazy guys (most guys feel awkward around women at a topless beach, so they don't tend to stay too long), and eliminate those seemly tan lines.

👄 IT'S GOOD TO BE A GIRL

Untie That Bikini Top and Waltz Right in: Women who are guests of Mandalay Bay get into Moorea free or for a nominal fee, while men are charged from $35 to $45 per guy for the pleasure of your company.

Spa

This is a perfectly nice tropical themed spa that doesn't leave a stone unturned, although it's only half the size of Canyon Ranch. Don't miss the fantastic massaging shampoo at the Robert Cromeans Salon that simultaneously relaxes and invigorates.

Room

The standard deluxe rooms at Mandalay Bay are lovely retreats where every detail reflects a tropical Caribbean theme — all that's missing is the Bob Marley soundtrack! The bathrooms steal the show with separate soaking tub and shower, and imported stone floors and surfaces. The Four Seasons Hotel is located on the top floors of Mandalay Bay and features elegantly understated rooms with lovely details like plush carpet and crown moldings. THEhotel at Mandalay Bay is a separate tower consisting entirely of suites decorated in a sleek, high-tech style with plasma TVs. As a bonus, THEhotel is stocked with plenty of hot guys willing to spend their cash at every turn.

⚷— INSIDER'S REPORT

Use a Credit Card for a Free Vegas Vacation: The MGM MIRAGE Rewards Visa issued by Bank One lets card members earn Reward Points for everyday purchases and double Reward Points for purchases made at participating MGM MIRAGE resorts and casinos. Reward Points are redeemed through Bank One for certificates used for MGM MIRAGE products and services including rooms, food and beverage, entertainment, retail and spa services at participating MGM MIRAGE resorts. This can save a savvy vixen *beaucoup* cash every trip, *if* you're willing to stay at an MGM Mirage property every time you come to town.

---

7. Bellagio: An Upscale Original

Bellagio is about all things good for the girl's soul — fine dining, lush gardens, art, fashion — all infused with the elegance and romance of classic Italy. When it opened, Bellagio raised the bar for upscale Vegas, and for the first time attracted visitors interested in activities other than just gaming. Its museum-worthy art collection, conservatory so fragrant you could swear it's pumped full of Jean Patou, and dancing fountains that rise, fall and spray in time to classical music and dramatic lighting, have made Bellagio a household name.

Image
You appreciate beautiful and elegant surroundings, and prefer

items of enduring class and quality to trendy Eurotrash that will be out of style before you make it to your gate home.

Location
Perfect. This resort is in the center of the action.

Nightlife
The Fontana Bar is at center stage on Bellagio's casino level where you can enjoy live entertainment and expansive views of the lake. Caramel Bar & Lounge is a great choice for enjoying a cocktail before dinner or after an evening show or just as a late-night destination — especially since there's rarely a line to get in. At the Petrossian Bar you can quaff afternoon tea or the finest champagnes, and top it off with Petrossian caviar and smoked salmon. Light is the big draw after dark. The club is upscale and sophisticated like the rest of the resort.

Dining
Celebrity chefs at every turn, but the standout is Picasso for which Julian Serano of San Francisco's Masa won Nevada's first James Beard award. The restaurant is an upscale original where guests can dine indoors surrounded by works of Pablo Picasso (yes, the real thing!) or enjoy a cocktail on the outdoor patio along the water's edge. Picasso served as the location where George Clooney surprised Julia Roberts in *Ocean's 11* so it gets extra points for star power. For the chocoholic, Jean-Philippe Patisserie, the first truly European-style pastry

shop in Vegas, features a 27-foot chocolate fountain, circulating nearly two tons of melted dark, milk and white chocolate. Talk about heaven!

Shopping

Although the haute couture of Armani, Chanel, Karl Lagerfeld, Herms, and Prada are only found in stand-alone stores in the most exclusive urban neighborhoods, Bellagio has managed to bring them together under one roof for your shopping convenience and pleasure. Via Bellagio, with its collections by Fendi, Yves Saint Laurent, Gucci, and Tiffany & Co. may be smaller than other upscale venues around the valley . . . but sometimes it's all about quality, not quantity.

Pool

Bellisima! Bellagio has two huge pools, with beautifully inset mosaic bottoms, surrounded by columns, statuary and cool palm trees. In addition, vixens can lounge around — but not swim in — any of three gorgeous fountains. There is no topless area at the Bellagio pools, as befits its status as a destination for families as much as it is for groups of girls. This is a sedate, serene, mellow pool scene: if you want a wild party, you're better off at the pool at Hard Rock, Palms, or Caesars. Hanging out in this glam display of European sophistication and charm is the closest you can get to a five star trip to Sardinia without a passport.

Spa

The luxurious new Spa & Salon Bellagio offers a fusion of exotic and traditional treatments from around the world. So many guests come to Bellagio with the spa in mind they built an entire tower of new rooms above it (the Spa Tower) so spa guests wouldn't have to traipse across the gaming floor in their bathrobes on their way back to the rooms. The salon has a special bridal/bachelorette area for those wanting a pamper party, and festive special packages including the Girlfriends'

Polynesian Package — grab your favorite gal pal and plunge your feet and hands into a bath of floating tropical flowers! If you're not looking for the full-tilt spa experience, try a luminous pearl manicure incorporating crushed pearl powder that leaves your hands silky smooth. A massive fitness center with all the bells and whistles overlooks the pool and Mediterranean gardens. When you're done working out, slip into the serene Meditation Room, surrounded by water walls and glowing candles — an ideal place to read, meditate or obsess over the hot guy you met the night before.

Rooms

At Bellagio, all room interiors are created equal. When the new Spa Tower (constructed over the Spa & Salon Bellagio) opened in December 2004, every non-Tower room was remodeled to offer the same spectacular and elegant design as those in the Spa Tower. As an added bonus, special attention was paid to the bathroom design: Italian marble floors and surfaces along with plush robes and soaking tubs will make you feel enveloped in a cloud of comfort and luxury. When booking, request the Strip-side rooms in the regular tower for the best views of the Bellagio fountains.

⌐—• INSIDER'S REPORT

Shower Here, Sink There: Having a sink that's separate from the shower area can be a real plus when it comes to getting ready for your night out. If one of your girls showers while the other does her makeup or dries her hair, you'll be breezing out the door for your first cocktail long before the sun sets. The shower/sink split is a must!

On the Cusp — Three Runners-Up

These three hotels are worth considering when you can't get into the top seven. Although they shouldn't be considered top-tier choices, each has its own special charm.

8. MGM Grand: Large and In Charge

They don't call MGM Grand, the "City of Entertainment" for nothing. If you are a sports fanatic, or just like to be around the buzz, The MGM Grand Sports Book is the first in the industry to offer a unique second-level view from exclusive Skyboxes. The resort is home to top productions like Ka and La Femme, and a one-of-a-kind lion habitat showcases up to six adult lions daily, including those that are direct descendants of MGM Studios' famous signature marquee lion. Siegfried and Roy: eat your hearts out!

STRIP TEASE

Don't Stay at a Hotel That Is Due to be Blown Up in the Next Year: You might think it is a great deal: Stay at Barbary Coast Hotel & Casino because the rates are rock bottom, since the hotel will be torn down in six months. Wrong. When a hotel is set for demolition, the company is not planning to put another dollar into its maintenance. So, the pressure in your showerhead's bad? Get used to it. On top of that, they leave only the bottom of the barrel employees to run the place. So, don't expect a wake up call because the receptionist just might still be nursing a hangover from the boilermakers last night at the local saloon.

Image

The sheer size and range of options at MGM Grand make its image pretty bland. It's a nice resort, but lacks any discernable identity.

Location

The location is fabulous; unfortunately, it is set so far back from the Strip, and takes so much effort to get there, you'll need to take a breather once you make it.

 **STRIP TEASE**

Babs in Grandland: Barbra Streisand, in her first concert in more than 20 years, opened the Grand Garden Arena on Dec. 31, 1993, a 16,800-seat special events center home to mega concerts, championship boxing, nationally televised award shows, and premier sporting and special events.

Nightlife
MGM introduced the modern nightlife scene to Vegas with Studio 54; it didn't end there. The über-hip ultra lounge Tabú continues to draw the movers and shakers.

Dining
MGM Grand offers some good culinary choices, from the ultra-exclusive Joël Robuchon at the Mansion, featuring traditional French cuisine in a setting reminiscent of Paris in the 1930s, to more reasonable options like Wolfgang Puck Bar & Grill and Emeril's New Orleans Fish House.

Shopping
The shops at Studio Walk are pretty unimpressive. If shopping is high on your list, cut your losses and move on to the Forum or Grand Canal Shoppes.

Pool
Just like everything else at MGM, the pool is grand. This massive aquatic playground is comprised of five swimming pools, three large whirlpools, a relaxing lazy river, lush tropical landscaping, bridges, fountains and waterfalls. Some days it can feel like Camp Kid, but it's adults only in the Director Pool, so grab a cocktail and head on over.

Spa
With more than 30 treatment rooms, saunas, steam rooms, whirlpools and relaxation lounges, the Grand Spa covers all

the bases. Cristophe (no last name needed), who has been tending to the tresses of rock and celebrity royalty from Beverly Hills to New York City for decades, recently opened his first Vegas salon at the Grand Spa.

Room

Although generally nice, the rooms lack some of the more custom amenities of other Strip properties. If you stay at the MGM Grand, make sure you're in the new boutique-style West Wing, featuring king-size beds with pillow-top mattresses and body pillows, and flat screen televisions. The bathrooms, with sleek styling and marble floors, are designed with over-sized showers and TVs in the mirror, so you won't miss out on your favorite programs while getting ready for the day or evening. The West Wing Bar provides the perfect place to hang out, meet before an evening of dining and entertainment or wind down with a nightcap — not too shabby!

👄 IT IS GOOD TO BE A GIRL

The Hooters Casino Hotel: Want to be the center of attention? Stay at Hooters and you'll be the main event. This newly opened small hotel mostly caters to the single men in their twenties and thirties, so you and your group of Vegas Vixens will never have to buy your own drinks!

9. Mirage: The First Mega Resort

Mirage is a classic (only in Vegas can something become a classic in less than twenty years). This property needed a little sprucing, and after a major overhaul the mega resort is ready to defend its leading-edge position as a Polynesian paradise. The entrance garden of towering waterfalls cascades over rockscapes 50 feet to the lagoon below. In case you can't make your way back home after a night of partying and need a landmark to help orient you, a facsimile of a live volcano erupts each evening, spewing smoke and fire 100 feet above the water as you pass through the lagoon entrance into the hotel. Yes, only in Vegas!

⚷— INSIDER'S REPORT

Mirage's Dolphin Habitat: The Dolphin Habitat serves as the home for a family of Atlantic bottlenose dolphins. The Mirage now offers the experience of a lifetime for those who love dolphins — tourist to dolphin trainer in just a few hours. The recently launched "Trainer for a Day" program provides guests with the unforgettable experience of working side by side with animal experts in the daily care and training of dolphins. As someone who proudly sports a dolphin tattoo on my shoulder from my days as a competitive swimmer, I can guarantee this is one experience you don't want to miss!

Image

While it recently underwent a hipper transformation, most of the folks back home probably still consider Mirage as Wynn or Bellagio's less fortunate, out-of-date stepsister. The fact that you're in the know about this newly renovated gem gives you a leg up.

Location

Located in the heart of the Strip, with plenty of options just a short walk away.

Nightlife

Mirage has worked to make over its somewhat dated image with ultra modern nightclub, JET. This sleek, contemporary, multi-level environment features the best sound design technology available, and consistently draws a good crowd of hot, young partyers.

Dining

Nothing outstanding, but there are plenty of reasonably priced options to choose from. Try the laid-back eatery STACK with its American bistro menu, or the Cravings buffet which is similar to an international bazaar or market. At Carnegie Deli, you can savor New York City's finest home-cured pastrami and corned beef without wrestling with the congestion of Times Square.

Shopping

The Street of Shops at Mirage features the latest fashions from DKNY, Moschino, and La Perla, as well as the work of up-and-coming designers. There aren't a huge number of shops, so you're probably better off spending your shopping time at the mall a block and a half away.

Pool

Mirage's lush tropical pool area is not the largest pool in Vegas, but it gets the job done. Paradise Café received a complete makeover, and provides a scenic view of the pool area. Order a drink and melt into the new soft rattan seating.

Spa

The Spa at Mirage set the standard for the Strip. Unfortunately, other properties have only continued to raise the bar. Although the spa is perfectly lovely, surrounded by trees, foliage and hanging vines that create an environment of pure relaxation and serenity, you won't get that once-in-a-lifetime feel that you'll find at some of the other more lavish spas on the Strip.

Room

You won't be disappointed with the newly renovated rooms at Mirage, but they won't knock your socks off either. Special touches include custom-made wall coverings, draperies and carpeting, and imported Spanish and Indonesian marble in the entries and bathrooms.

10. Aladdin's Planet Hollywood: Aladdin Goes Hollywood

With its new façade incorporating video screens and message boards à la Times Square, improved access to the Strip, and expanded casino and shopping, the new Planet Hollywood Resort and Casino, formerly known as Aladdin, offers you a real slice of Hollywood.

Image

Since Aladdin's Planet Hollywood is the newest kid on the block, staying here says you're hip, in the know, and have done your research!

Location

The resort has the pre-eminent location on the Strip.

Nightlife

Great nightclubs and ultra lounges, most of them transplants from Los Angeles and South Beach.

Dining

Very respectable but not transcendent. You have your standard buffet, steakhouse, and café that offers a variety of Planet Hollywood menu items.

Shopping

Miracle Mile Shops: It's a new name and a new look for The Shops in Desert Passage at the Aladdin. We're talking nothing too high-end here, just funky, trendy men's and women's clothes, accessories, and home décor — think Quicksilver and Urban Outfitters. The question is: does the name also allude to the "miracles" that can happen in the adjoining casino?

Pool
Two sixth-floor outdoor terrace swimming pools overlook the Strip, separating the serious sunbathers from the splashers. The pools are designed to face north and south, just so you can avoid that desert sunburn.

Spa
Elemis Spa, with its exotic Moroccan décor, is perfectly adequate but not a destination in itself. In other words, it's no Canyon Ranch! What it does have, however, is the é Alpha 2010 Relaxation Capsule, a 25 minute miracle treatment that yields the results of 3 full hours of total rest: great for stress, jet lag and sleep deprivation due to your enthusiastic participation in activities found within the pages of the *Little Red Book!*

Room
Each of the Aladdin's guest rooms are oversized and include marble bathrooms with huge bathtubs big enough for two. With six different room options, you are sure to find a room fit for you and your girls. The strategic location of the elevator banks ensures that you will always be within seven doors of your room, eliminating the long walks associated with other Las Vegas hotels. You can also earn and redeem Starpoints at over 750 Westin, Sheraton, Four Points by Sheraton, W, St. Regis, and Luxury Collection Hotels worldwide.

Note: Properties That Didn't Make the Cut
You've probably noticed that several well-known, very good properties aren't on the Top 10. Places like Paris, Monte Carlo, Luxor, and Harrah's are great places to stay; however, they are not ideal for groups of girls. All of these places come

up short on the *Little Red Book* matrix of girl's criteria. So, while the Lucky 7 list is not definitively the 7 best hotels in Las Vegas, it is absolutely the 7 best hotels for groups of girls.

🔑 INSIDERS REPORT

Lucky Swimwear: Just because it's approaching 120 degrees in the desert sun doesn't mean you can stroll into a fine-dining restaurant or even the casino in just your bikini and flip-flops without some sort of cover-up. Vegas casinos are casual, but just play it safe and cover the goods with either a trendy tank, shorts, or breezy dress. But then again, this *is* Vegas — so if you do want to try your luck in your bikini, swim on up to the blackjack tables at the Hard Rock Hotel or indulge in Wynn's Cabana Bar & Casino.

No Place Has It All

One mistake that many Vegas newcomers make is trying to find the one place that has it all. No single property has everything you're looking for. We have yet to find a Strip hotel that leaves you with no reason to go off property. While it's important to take where you stay seriously, know that there is no be-all and end-all. Remember: there are clubs, spas, restaurants, and attractions to fulfill your every fantasy. This is Vegas — explore the riches and experience the pleasure, just make sure your lodgings meet your needs.

Venturing Away from the Lucky 7

If you choose to stay at a place that isn't on the Lucky 7, you may live to regret it. There are lots of other great places to stay in Vegas, but none of them will satisfy the needs of you and your girls. Remember: If you decide to stay elsewhere, do your homework and use the 8 keys for finding a good hotel as your guidelines. Ignore them and watch the clouds roll in.

How to Get the Best Room Rates

✢ Start on the property's Web site. Many hotels will give their best rate on line because it costs them less money to book someone electronically.

✢ Call the central reservation numbers and ask for the price of a suite. You'll stand a fair chance at being upgraded from a regular room to a suite at check-in. However, if you're not a Vegas regular you might want to spend the extra cash and book a suite just to be sure.

✢ The largest Vegas destination Web site is VEGAS.com and they have an amazing track record of low prices and in-depth research tools. They are located in Vegas, making them the only *other* true insiders that you can trust for everything Vegas.

✢ Ask if there are any packages that are out there for the dates that you want to stay.

✢ Never accept the central reservation number's first price. Always ask if there's something less expensive. Central reservation agents are trained at profit making, so they'll start with their highest rate, but will do what it takes to earn your business. There's usually a lower back up rate they can offer, and remember they get paid on commission, so they won't give up too easily

✢ Even if you find yourself at the front desk without a room, call the central reservation number from your cell phone. The front desk will only offer the highest price possible.

Book a Suite

When it comes to booking your room, a suite is the best option. A suite will allow you to fit more girls into one space in style, and by dividing the price by four or five, you may even come out ahead. A suite can serve as a meeting area, and as a comfortable place for hanging out while everyone is washing, drying, coiffing, and spritzing. It's far more civilized to sit on a couch while gossiping with the girls than it is being perched on the edge of a bed. You only live once; go for it and get a suite! Just remember that in Vegas, "suite" is a relative term.

⌥━ INSIDER'S REPORT

Use Your Alumni Network for a Vegas Deal: You would be surprised how many former colleagues and classmates work and play in Vegas. Chances are if you start asking around, you will find that either one of your old college friends either works in Vegas or has a good friend that does. People that work in Vegas can sometimes hook you up with a discounted room rate or a suite upgrade, or even drop your name on a nightlife guest list. It never hurts to ask: It's all about karma . . . and networking.

Types of Suites
There are several different grades of suites. Although every hotel uses different naming conventions, suites generally fall into the following four categories.

Executive or Petite Suites
Slightly larger than a standard hotel room, these suite types feature a couch, coffee table and sitting area that is part of the room. At some hotels such as The Venetian and THEhotel, all rooms are at this level, and the hotels bill themselves as "all suite" establishments. However, make no mistake: If you're looking for a major suite this won't live up to your expectations. Another example of this grade is the Caesars' Petite Suites. <u>Sleeps</u>: 3.

One-Bedroom Suites

This level of suite features a living room with sitting area that is entirely separate from the bedroom: essentially, it's a one-bedroom apartment. Examples of this grade are MGM's Hollywood Suite and Hard Rock's Deluxe Suite. <u>Sleeps</u>: 4.

Two-Bedroom Suites

A separate living room with two adjoining king-size bedrooms. The living room usually features a bar and a dining table. An example of this grade is MGM's Marquis Suite. <u>Sleeps</u>: 5.

Sweet Suites

This level refers to any suite that goes above and beyond the size and grandeur of a two-bedroom suite. These suites are usually reserved for the casino high rollers, making them difficult to reserve; the standard two-bedroom suite is usually the most lavish option you'll be offered. Although sweet suites are over-the-top impressive, remember that you came to Vegas to have fun, so don't get hung up over accommodations that are off-limits. Besides, when they are available, they cost *beaucoup* bucks, and that's money better spent on bedecking and bejeweling yourself! Examples of this grade are Hard Rock's Penthouse Suite and Caesars' Duplex Suite. <u>Sleeps</u>: 8

<u>Note</u>: Most suites come with king-size beds. It's very rare to find a suite where the bedrooms contain two queens rather than one king bed, so be sure to ask about the number of beds when booking. For executive and one-bedroom suites, book the connecting room since it usually has two double or queen beds.

PUT YOUR HOTEL TO WORK

You've chosen your hotel, now it's time to put it to work. Here's how to get the most out of your hotel.

Your Grand Arrival

The Hotel Entrance

Make sure you arrive at the right door. Vegas hotels have several different entrances, and there is nothing worse than having a taxi driver drop you off at an entrance only to have to schlep your bags through the casino to find hotel registration. Always specify that you want to be dropped off at the hotel entrance.

Carry Your Bags

If you follow the *Little Red Book*'s advice, you'll only have a carry-on bag that you can easily bring to the room yourself. Getting your bags sent up to the room can take forever, especially if you're checking in on a Friday. Save yourself the time and skip the bell service.

The Side Valet

Most hotels have a side valet. They're tucked away at the side of the hotel and allow you to enter and exit with greater ease. You'll spare yourself the agony of watching your precious evening melt away, if you park your car with these guys rather than with the main valet.

What to Remember at Check-In

❖ If it's an option, you might want to check in at the airport. Some hotels offer this service, and it's a great way to avoid a huge line once you get to your hotel. Let them give you your keys and take your bags, while you begin your adventure. It is an easy way to milk an extra hour of fun out of your evening.

❖ Always ask how much a suite upgrade will cost. If it's around $40 or less, then definitely splurge: just make sure that you know the type of suite you're being upgraded to. You don't want to pay extra for a glorified standard room.

❖ Ask for a room key for each girl in the group. There's nothing worse than being locked out of your room at 5 a.m. because your girlfriend is sound asleep inside and can't hear you banging on the door and leaving voice mails on her cell phone.

♣ Make sure to ask if there is a "fun book" for guests. These books have coupons in them for free table bets and discounted food. You may end up tossing it in the trash, but it's worth a look.

Tip Well at Check-In

Flashing a tip to the person at the registration desk can pay off. Here are a few things you can ask them to do for you:

♣ Ask to be put in the "new tower." This is Vegas: Every hotel has a new tower, and at a property like Caesars Palace, the difference between the new and the old tower is night and day. The rooms in the old tower are often smaller; they're products of the old days, when hotel management didn't want you to be so comfortable in your room that you wouldn't be out on the floor gambling.

♣ Ask to be near the elevator: if you aren't, you'll regret it. Remember, we're talking about the largest hotels on earth; walking from the elevator to your room can sometimes require a hardy Sherpa guide.

♣ Ask for either a Strip view or pool view. If you spend more than five minutes in your room (and despite your best intentions, you will be in your room for more than five minutes), you'll want to have something pleasant to look at. You didn't fly all the way out Vegas just to stare at a giant air-conditioning unit or a banquet facility. Although less desirable than the Strip view, the pool view is practical since you can look down in the morning to see if it's too crowded to join the poolside action.

♣ Ask for the largest standard room available, especially if you don't get the suite upgrade. Many hotels have different sizes of standard rooms.

Remember Me: Get the Concierge on Your Side

The best friend an unprepared traveler can have is an attentive concierge. A good concierge can put you in the heart of the action, as they have a fairly elaborate network of access to restaurants, clubs, shows, and events.

Although you might have made every effort possible to plan ahead, you may find yourself salivating over a brand new restaurant, or dying to see a sold-out show. Or, perhaps that 10:00 a.m. facial seems a little too ambitious and 2:00 p.m. is really your preferred time to beautify. A concierge wrapped around your little finger just might do the trick.

What to Do

When you check in, walk over to the concierge's desk, introduce yourself, and slip him $50. Flash your warm, radiant Vegas Vixen smile and say, "Keep me on top of things." This way, he will be inclined to go the extra mile should you have a special request.

What You Can Expect

If you have a reservation at the right restaurant at the wrong time, ask if he can pull a few strings. If you're looking for tickets to a show at the last minute, see if he has access to the box office. Don't count on your concierge to produce a dozen tickets to O, but he should be able to provide some options. If you think $50 is too much to part with, think again. That $50 can be the difference between an okay meal at a ho-hum restaurant, and a table at a celeb-studded hotspot that would have required weeks of advance notice for a reservation. He can also get you a rental car at the hotel so you don't have to take a shuttle to the car rental place or pay the airport tax fee.

BYOB

Looking to do a little pre-party as you're getting ready? Don't make the mistake of raiding the over-priced minibar. Instead, stock up in the afternoon. They sell mini-bottles in most of the hotel convenience stores; think ahead and pick up your provisions before you call it an afternoon. Then crank up the tunes and pour a round of drinks before you doll yourself up for the night. If you avoid that pesky minibar you'll save yourself some serious cash. As a matter of fact, perhaps you should reward your fiscal responsibility by purchasing a new pair of shoes. Just a thought.

 STRIP TEASE

Best Bathrooms in Sin City to Sip, Splurge, and Score: *Sip:* Why pay for a booth with a view at MIX, when you can sip your martini in the first-class bathroom?

Splurge: At Wynn, you will be surrounded by gold, gold, and more gold.

Score: Score with a short-line at Hard Rock, not with a guy! Just an elevator ride up, and you can beat the line in the club and make a pit stop in style. Just remember to get stamped so you can breeze back in and score the real deal.

Chapter 5

Dining: An Epicurean Experience

✷ ....

Your cell phone rings. A quick check of the caller ID, and your stomach starts doing little back flips. Could it be the dashing, utterly intriguing guy you *almost* hooked up with the night before? Hardly. It's . . . Wolfgang! When in Vegas, nothing makes the adrenaline surge like scoring a coveted "two-month-wait" dinner reservation at one of the hottest restaurants in town. Vegas has come a long way since its old-school days of prime rib and shrimp cocktail specials, but that doesn't mean dinner is drama-free. With nearly every top chef from around the world hanging a shingle in Sin City, you and your girls are left with the most taxing of problems: which delicious dining experience to choose. Although the stars of The *Food* and *Fine Living* Networks make their living showcasing their creative prowess in the desert, you shouldn't assume that just because a restaurant boasts a designer label it will automatically provide the type of dining experience you're looking for.

Food *may be* the centerpiece of a great dining experience, but if the atmosphere is elegant and serene when you want casual and lively, or the location has you schlepping from one end of the Strip to the other during peak party hours, a huge percentage of your precious Vegas evening could end up as lackluster as a bad business lunch — only longer and more expensive. Fortunately, we'll give you the true scoop on dining in the desert so you can make the right decisions for you and your girls.

Dining in Vegas is Hot!

Over the past few years, dining has emerged as one of the key ingredients for creating an incredible "all out" Vegas getaway – and we're not just talking "fine dining!" Skillfully prepared food — be it *steak au poivre* or chicken salad on toast, complemented by the perfect ambiance — is one of life's great pleasures. And, since Vegas is all about pleasure in its many shapes and forms, it only makes sense that Vegas has become a true epicurean center.

🍽 *Little Red Book*'s Lucky 7 Celebrity Chefs:

Las Vegas has attracted the best of the best chefs from around the world. But, of the hundreds to choose from, who are truly tops? Here are 7 who stand out in the crowd.

1. Emeril Legasse

<u>Restuarants</u>: Emeril's New Orleans Fish House at MGM Grand, Delmonico Steakhouse at Venetian.

<u>Why</u>: Emeril didn't become the best known chef in America by accident. In addition to being a good showman ("BAM!") he knows his way around the kitchen, providing Las Vegas with some Cajun kick.

2. Wolfgang Puck

<u>Restaurants</u>: Spago and Chinois, both at Caesars, Postrio at Venetian, Trattoria del Lupo at Mandalay Bay.

<u>Why</u>: Quality dining made its way to the desert when Puck brought his Hollywood eatery, Spago, to Las Vegas in 1992. His signature designer pizzas (caviar and goat cheese) and new twists on German classics are legendary.

3. Nobu Matsuhisa

<u>Restaurant</u>: Nobu at Hard Rock

<u>Why</u>: Matsuhisa has taken dishes from his native Japan and fused them with South American touches. Get a taste of his black cod in miso and you'll know why A-list celebs are still lining up for a table at TriBeCa's Nobu New York and here in Vegas.

4. Joël Robuchon
<u>Restaurants</u>: Joël Robuchon at The Mansion, L'Atelier de Joël Robuchon at MGM Grand.

<u>Why</u>: He was awarded "Chef of the Century" by the *Guide Gault Millau*, France's top restaurant guide. Of course such a talent doesn't come cheaply. At the intimate Mansion restaurant the 16-course tasting menu will set you back about $350. Thankfully, you can get a cheaper taste at L' Atelier.

5. Thomas Keller
<u>Restaurant</u>: Bouchon at Venetian

<u>Why</u>: Keller is beloved by wine country diners who wait several months for a reservation at his California eatery. The French Laundry. Declared "America's Best Chef" by *Time* magazine in 2001, Bouchon's boss has the goods.

6. Alain Ducasse
<u>Restaurant</u>: Mix at THEhotel

<u>Why</u>: This celebrated chef knows how to pick a location. Mix sits high atop THEhotel and serves up some great food. Ducasse is a legend in his native France where he used to be the head chef at Monte Carlo's famous Hotel de Paris.

7. Todd English:
<u>Restaurant</u>: Olives at Bellagio

<u>Why</u>: The star of *Cooking with Todd English* is a wunderkind.

He opened the original Olives at the tender age of 29. The Bellagio branch is one of the jewels of the Las Vegas dining scene.

Dining Defines the Resort

How can you have a five-star resort without five-star dining to match? A successful, high profile restaurant helps brand a resort as a top, full-service facility. While it costs tens of millions of dollars to remodel a resort, it costs substantially less to attract a successful restaurateur. Luring the rock stars of food to set up shop at a resort keeps the property on the cutting edge, and ensures that the on-site restaurants will generate the kind of buzz that makes even the most cool, collected Vegas Vixen hyperventilate with anticipation.

Dining In Vegas is Different than Back Home

Don't relegate dining to a basic need you have to "get through" before moving on to the evening's real main course. Remember: unlike at home where meals are sandwiched between endless responsibilities, dining in Vegas is a form of entertainment unto itself, and deserves the same amount of care and planning you would lavish on choosing a hotel or show. Here are some Vegas basics to consider when planning your dining adventure.

Dinner Should be an Experience

Your most memorable meals will be your dinners in the desert. Make them a focal point of the evening by ensuring they're filled with delicious and complex tastes that make you swoon with delight, a sumptuous ambiance you can melt right into, and a dash of theatrics just to keep things interesting. Pair the dining experience with an after dinner cocktail at an ultra lounge and you have the perfect beginning to a perfect Vegas night.

Light Lunches

Don't bog your day down with a huge meal at lunch. Lunch should be quick and consist of a fresh salad or a sandwich. But, just because it's fast and light doesn't mean you have to settle for food-court quality fare. With great coffee shops and cafés offering freshly baked breads, and salads chock full of grilled seafood, veggies and imported cheeses, your midday pick-me-up should be a deliciously satisfying respite from a day of serious shopping . . . or relaxation.

Snacks are Important

You'll be burning calories galore walking around Vegas, so be sure to bring along healthy snacks (almonds, raisins, granola bars, bottled water) to keep the blood sugar flowing. We all know how even the sweetest girlfriend can quickly turn into queen bitch when she's hungry and tired. Don't let this happen to your group! Make sure everyone has something to nibble on and you'll all be happy campers.

Late Night Cravings

Part of the Vegas experience is to enjoy a breakfast-style meal after a night of drinking, dancing, and clubbing like a true party girl. Dining late extends the night, so you can trade stories and compare notes about that hot guy from L.A., Phoenix, Austin, or Chicago, all while savoring yummy eggs Benedict and hash browns. If you don't congregate for one last meal, it's straight to bed without any post-club decompression time. Boring.

⚷━ INSIDER'S REPORT

Plan Ahead: It's worth noting that just like everything else in town, the hot restaurants fill up early. Don't settle for what's available. Make your reservations as soon as you book your hotel rooms. Remember, you can always cancel, so reserve first and ask questions later. Of course, give the restaurants advance notice if you won't be dining there. Otherwise you're just courting bad Vegas karma.

★ DINING OPTIONS ABOUND

While you *will* have reservations for your dinners, you'll be eating outside the glitz and glamour of the celeb-filled restaurant scene at least twice a day. Many of the standard Vegas restaurants go way beyond the merely serviceable and provide mouth watering options for breakfast, lunch, and late night munchies.

The Standard Vegas Restaurants

❖ The Buffet: The Vegas original. You haven't eaten at a buffet until you've been to Vegas. You might be surprised how much you and your girls love the buffet for its quality and versatility; a great option for a couple of meals during your getaway.

❖ The 24 Hour Café: Usually the only restaurant that's open late enough to satisfy the wee hours of the morning hunger pangs — and absorb the effects of one too many cocktails. Cafés also serve great breakfast selections.

❖ The New Steak and Seafood: Every casino has a traditional steakhouse that serves prime cuts of beef and a high-end selection of seafood. Fortunately, the smoke-filled, stodgy, male-only vibe is out and a bright new era of the contemporary, hip, unisex steakhouse is in.

❖ International Edibles: There's a world of international delights to explore in the form of Thai, Japanese, Italian, Mexican, Tex-Mex, Indian, Chinese, fusion — any ethnicity or combination you can imagine. Some are casual, fun and funky, others elegant and high-end.

❖ The Grab and Go: For those times when it's all about the quick fix, and you're just looking for enough fuel to keep moving toward the next adventure.

🍽 THE BUFFET

When you think "buffet," do you think carving station, frozen peas and carrots, red Jell-O in parfait glasses with dollops of Cool Whip? Of course you do. The buffet is a cheesy part of kitsch Americana that ranks somewhere near the revolving restaurant and pineapple flambé in its contribution to our culture. With Vegas being the buffet capital of the universe (the early bird diners in Florida ain't got nothing on Sin City), why would you ever considering stepping into one of these glorified cafeterias? Because there are a handful of establishments that will shatter every negative association you may have with the concept of "all u can eat."

Buffets Have You Covered

Your group may balk at dining at a buffet, so learn the advantages of buffet dining and meet their objections like a pro.

- ☙ There's Something for Everyone: Buffets will resolve any food argument you might have between your vegetarians, vegans, gluten-free, allergy afflicted, South Beach dieters, and Weight Watchers point counters. The right buffet is nothing short of a godsend and will have something for everyone including your all-American vixen who is free of food shticks, and ravenous for a delicious high quality meal so she can continue to burn the candle at both ends.

- ☙ Dining Room Quality: Buffets have adapted to the new upscale, female-oriented Vegas by offering a dining experience complete with traditional fare cooked to perfection using quality ingredients, interesting and unusual dishes rarely served *en masse*, and a comfortable, updated dining room with a casual and cheery atmosphere. If you're thinking Old Country Buffet, you're wrong: expect dining room quality.

✧ Time Saver: Most top rated buffets have a line, especially during peak meal time hours . . . but don't get discouraged. Even if you wait for fifteen minutes, chances are you'll end up saving time. Remember: The moment you enter, you begin hunting and gathering. Within five minutes you're sitting back and savoring. There's no waiting for a menu or a server.

☙ INSIDER'S REPORT

Pay Lunch Price for the Dinner Menu: Buffets change their menus throughout the day from breakfast to lunch to dinner. As the menu changes, the price increases. The most significant price increase is from lunch to dinner because seafood options such as crab legs, shrimp, and sushi are added to the menu. Usually at 4 p.m., the buffet begins putting out the new dinner items and the price increases. Use this to your advantage. Pay for lunch at the buffet at 3:45 p.m. By the time you've finished your salad, the *tekka maki* and stuffed flounder will be available. For a group of eight, this could mean a $100 savings!

What Makes a Good Buffet for a Group of Girls?

Not every buffet will make you and your girls feel comfortable and satisfied. Although nearly every resort has a buffet, it's important to know which will fit the bill for a group of discerning girls.

Keys to a Good Buffet

✧ Short Wait: There is always a line at a buffet, but a good one moves quickly. Be wary if you are in line and you begin losing circulation in your feet for standing still longer than five minutes.

✧ Fresh Food: The fresher the better. If the food has been sitting under a heat lamp for hours, it will have that Old

Country Buffet look and taste you can live without. The best buffets have small quantities of food prepared continuously.

❧ Healthy Options: Sushi, salads, and fresh veggies can keep the meal light, so you will still feel satiated — and saintly without feeling bloated.

❧ Pristine Facility: A buffet should bus their tables regularly so empty plates don't sit at the table while you're up prowling for another serving of fresh berry mélange. Serving areas should be cleaned and maintained to perfection, so the presentation resembles the center spread in *Martha Stewart Living: The Buffet Issue.*

❧ Reasonable Pricing: Price is important, but a few dollars shouldn't be your deciding factor on which buffet to choose. Your red flag should be any buffet that starts inching upward toward $30 per person.

⌐ᢇ INSIDER'S REPORT

Have a Vegetarian in the Group?: Most restaurants only have one or two choices for the vegetarians in your group. Since buffets have a wide variety of food, your vegetarians will be thrilled that they won't have to compromise and can chow down with gusto.

The Best Buffets for Groups of Girls

The Buffet at Wynn Las Vegas
Great atmosphere and exceptional food will make you forget you're at a buffet. Although a bit pricey, the quality and variety of food is worth every penny. For dessert, try a red candy apple; it will take you back to summertime during your childhood.

Dishes at Treasure Island

Dishes prepares and serves its menu items in small quantities — not in big troughs for mass feeding. Enjoy lunch or an early dinner before the Sirens of TI pirate show lets out; after the show, throngs of people flock into the casino and swarm the buffet. Make sure to save room for dessert: fresh strawberries dipped in a vat of rich creamy chocolate right before you eyes will set your endorphins soaring.

Cravings at Mirage

This is the buffet that sets the new Vegas standard with multiple stations where chefs prepare individual portions of food "made to order." The Asian station toward the back of the restaurant is the best, and includes a great sushi bar.

The Buffet at Mandalay Bay

Short lines and excellent food make The Buffet a solid choice. Although small by Vegas standards, the wide selection makes it a prefect stop when you can't decide on a cuisine for your next meal. It's not worth traveling across Vegas to visit, but The Buffet is a nice place to dine after shopping at Mandalay Place. For breakfast, they make a first-rate fluffy egg white omelet.

The Carnival World Buffet at Rio

Known for its desserts and freshly baked bread, this buffet is a Vegas legend, meaning it's extremely popular, and you can expect a long wait anytime after 4 p.m. If the line is too long, pass and go to the All American Bar & Grill right next door.

THE 24-HOUR CAFÉ

Every hotel casino in Las Vegas is required to have a restaurant that is open 24 hours a day.

Why You Need Cafés

You probably think of dining at a hotel café as a last resort dining option. While it may not offer a full-tilt dining extravaganza, you'll spend more time at your hotel café than you think due to its sheer convenience.

- ❖ Eat Any Meal at Any Time: Cafés serve up breakfast, lunch, and dinner items 24 hours a day. If you wake up late, you can still start your day with bagels, lox, and cream cheese.

- ❖ Late Night Meals: It's pretty much your only option after 11p.m. Since there aren't any clocks in casinos, the night creeps up on you pretty darn fast, meaning the café is the only place where you can end your day at 3:00 a.m. with bagels, lox, and cream cheese.

- ❖ Convenient Alternative: The café is your de facto place to dine when you're either too tired, hungry, or pressed for time to venture into Vegas madness. It's located in the hotel, just steps away from your hotel room, and is easy, quick, and doesn't require fighting long taxi lines or risking melting your eyeliner as you trudge through the desert heat.

High Tea in the Nevada Desert

Looking for a little respite in the late afternoon? Sit your cosseted posterior down for a spot of tea. You can sip your Earl Gray or cleansing Green while enjoying a great alternative to a late lunch by snacking on dainty cucumber sandwiches and scones at Bellagio, Four Seasons, Wynn, and Caesars Palace. It's very ladylike, and a welcome retreat from the over-stimulating sights and sounds of the Strip. Be sure to call ahead for information as days and times vary.

Keys to a Good 24-Hour Café

❖ A clean and pleasant atmosphere. A place where you will enjoy spending an hour whether you're in a party mood or dogged to the bone from last night's Fuzzy Navel shots.

❖ Timely service. Coffee shops aren't exactly an epicurean experience. They exist to take the edge off . . . quickly.

❖ Good, tasty food in reasonable portions.

The Best 24-Hour Cafés for Groups of Girls

Mr. Lucky's at the Hard Rock Hotel

Mr. Lucky's is the best coffee shop in town. You'll get great food, impeccable service and a fun atmosphere 24 hours a day. The views from the tables are first rate: There's usually no shortage of good-looking guys hanging around! Show your friends you're an insider by ordering the chicken quesadilla: it's served as an appetizer but large enough for two to share as a main course.

Grand Lux at The Venetian

Managed by the Cheesecake Factory group, the Grand Lux is a fun and delicious dining experience. If the wait is too long, walk over to the bar area where you can usually find a highboy table; they'll serve you right there in the bar. If you do get seated in the dining area, request a table on the patio for some serious people watching.

Bellagio Café

Nestled in the corner of the conservatory, Bellagio Café goes all-out with its 24-hour coffee shop. The morning wait is fairly short, made even more civilized by the complementary gourmet coffee. Ask for a seat on the right-hand side of the restaurant where you can soak up the beauty of the conservatory flowers. The top menu item for mid- to late-day dining is the chicken penne pasta.

Peppermill Restaurant

If you're on the north part of the Strip and have a rental car, Peppermill Restaurant is a perfect coffee shop choice. This old-school Vegas favorite has your wings, nachos and quesadillas covered, but the breakfast items get top billing starring a granola and yogurt parfait, and oatmeal with raisins, bananas, and walnuts. Whatever the time of day, you are bound to see many patrons nursing a Peppermill Bloody Mary. These concoctions are justly famous for soothing the soul of late-night casino refugees and early morning party girls alike.

Is your hotel's café not on the list? No worries. Every hotel in the top 10 has a solid coffee shop; these four are just the best of the best.

 Room Service

A Great Breakfast Alternative: A great way to get your day going is having breakfast brought up to your room. You can sip coffee and graze on French toast while you're still waking up and getting ready for your day. If you place your order in the morning, be prepared to wait. The better option is to order breakfast right before you go to sleep, either by calling Room Service, or filling out the breakfast order card to hang on your doorknob. This guarantees delivery at the precise moment you wish to eat, and saves you the frustration of rousting everyone from bed, showering en masse, deciding on a restaurant, getting seated, ordering . . . you catch the drift. Fill out the breakfast card, hang it on your doorknob, and sweet dreams!

THE NEW STEAK AND SEAFOOD RESTAURANT: Not Your Daddy's Surf and Turf

Step aside, guys: Steakhouses are no longer your own precious domain. The testosterone-filled, carnivore-only, glorified men's clubs of yesteryear have evolved into hip, trendy establishments adored by women. Here are a few of the new, contemporary steakhouses that are redefining what steak and seafood in the desert is all about.

Keys to a Good Steak and Seafood Restaurant
- Semiformal, yet comfortably hip ambiance. You want to wear your mini skirt with boots, your black cocktail dress with heels, your slim cigarette pants with matching blazer — and you want to revel in an atmosphere where everyone else looks as put together as you!

- Top-of-the-line menu items, carefully prepared with top-of-the-line ingredients.

- Attentive staff that brings more to the experience than filling up ice water.

⌐ INSIDER'S REPORT

Choose a Restaurant Near Your Next Destination: Pair your dining with your club by choosing a restaurant that will make for a quick transition from dining to dancing. The last thing you want after a great meal is to flail around looking for a cab or to walk 30 minutes and arrive amidst the glitterati feeling annoyed and frazzled.

The Best Steak and Seafood Restaurants for Groups of Girls

N9NE at the Palms
If you're looking for celebs, this is the place. Dress your best because N9NE is hot and trendy, and boasts a true ultra lounge atmosphere. Along with the steaks and seafood, N9NE is also famous for its champagne and caviar bar:

Ladies, this is an unequivocal must! If there's no room at the bar, order "Caviar to the N9NES" for the table: a sample of three caviars with potato cakes. It's just enough to give you a taste of high society.

FIX at Bellagio

Talk about a hip place! Start with a round of Pomegranate Martinis and one of the shared table menu items. The most adventurous of these is simply called "Forks:" smoked salmon and Osetra caviar poppers, each served on a fork standing straight up, and looking more like a contemporary art construction than appetizer. After dinner have a cocktail in the ultra lounge, Carâmel, and then hit the nightclub, Light, and dance the night away.

> ### 👄 VEGAS VIXEN
>
> **Save room for Dessert:** Dessert? You normally don't want the extra calories, but Vegas Vixens know that at these trendy eateries, the desserts are light, original, and utterly yummy. Splurge a little and order at least one for the table — you won't be disappointed.

Delmonico at The Venetian

Top quality steaks and seafood are the specialties at this not overly fancy, Emeril Lagasse eatery. Compared to the others on the list, Delmonico most closely resembles your traditional steakhouse, but with the added panache of the Emeril touch. His menu features only the best cuts of meat and the freshest seafood. Start with the pan-fried Parmesan oyster appetizer, a delicious aphrodisiac that will add a little "oomph" to your post-dinner flirting.

STACK at Mirage

This American-influenced eatery boasts a fairly unusual menu that includes items like "Pigs in a Blanket" (yep, the same ones that had center stage at all those suburban cocktail parties from the '70s) and "Mini Kobe Chili Cheese Dogs." For a little interactive fun at the table, order the "Hot Rocks." Eaten with chop sticks, this dish consists of thinly sliced strips of sirloin that you sear on super heated stone in the middle of the table.

AquaKnox at The Venetian
The best seafood in town served with style! Find a friend (or two) to share the Seafood Plateau: a cornucopia of succulent shellfish such as mussels, oysters, clams and lobster.

⊶ INSIDER'S REPORT

Steakhouses Come With Great Bars Attached: Steakhouses have excellent bars for cocktails and low key socializing. Loaded with comfortable chairs and tables, these hidden gems are more laid back than most resort center bars. Plus, you can always have a light appetizer to hold you over.

🍽 INTERNATIONAL EDIBLES

While there are hundreds of restaurants spanning every cuisine imaginable, an international restaurant must meet certain standards to be worthy of your time and hard-earned cash.

Keys to a Good International Restaurant
❖ Hip atmosphere where you can comfortably hang out with the girls and possibly meet a group of cute guys doing the same.

❖ A trendy lounge adjoining the restaurant for cocktails and appetizers. Many people will chill in these exotic dens of pleasure with no intention of moving on to dinner.

❖ A staff that is professional yet will schmooze and banter

about your hometown, your taste in guys, or your shopping obsessions.

The Best International Restaurants for Groups of Girls
Let your appetite take you around the globe with these great international options.

Mon Ami Gabi at Paris (French)
Wait for a seat on the balcony — first come, first serve, no reservations. The balcony is situated right on the Strip with a prime view of the Bellagio Fountains. If the wait is more than 20 minutes, head up to the Eiffel Tower Restaurant (the entrance is directly across from the Mon Ami Gabi) and have a cocktail while gazing out at one of the most breathtaking views of the city.

Red Square at Mandalay Bay (Russian)
If you think borscht and cabbage rolls when you think of Russian cuisine, then it's time to make a visit to Red Square and sample the delicious steak, seafood and roasted lamb — all based on authentic Russian recipes. Be sure to only drink Russian Vodka martinis. They serve them ice cold and they go down smooth: the perfect beverage to complement your caviar appetizer.

Okada at Wynn (Japanese)
Not only is the sushi incredible, Okada is also a hip joint with a huge bar on the right, and views of the Wynn waterfall in the back. Since Okada is conveniently located directly above Tryst night-

club, you should make reservations at Okada, indulge in their unique Japanese dishes, and head to Tryst for some late night fun.

Nove at the Palms

Sitting atop the Palms Casino Resort's new Fantasy Tower is Nove Italiano, a super-luxe, see-and-be-seen restaurant and lounge that features peerlessly authentic Italian cuisine. As in Italy, past dishes are not over-sauced, and simplicitiy is the prevailing theme. Spaghetti Nove, a decadent seafood pasta, is a signature of the establishment, along with thin crust pizza and Caesar salad prepared tableside.

Tao at Venetian (Asian)

This Asian restaurant/nightclub spans the Far East by offering Chinese, Thai, and Japanese specialties. The food is irresistible and you may find yourself eating more than you wish you had, but don't worry . . . You can dance it off in the Tao nightclub when the dining is done!

Spago at Caesars Palace's Forum Shops (California Style)

While you may not think California Style should be considered "international," Executive Chef Wolfgang Puck was one of the pioneers of this light, healthy, flavorful cuisine recognized the world over. Make sure to order a couple of appetizers to share. The restaurant is large, with the best seats in the main dining room. If you're with just one other girlfriend and grabbing lunch, ask to sit up front; it's an excellent place to watch the shoppers.

⌛ INSIDER'S REPORT

Restaurants Not on the List: There are many excellent restaurants not mentioned here. Does that mean they are not worthy? Of course not . . . but the restaurants listed *are* perfect for groups of girls.

 THE GRAB AND GO

Looking for something healthy that will fill you up without slowing you down?

If you only have a little time on your hands and you would rather spend it shopping or spaing, then quick eateries are your perfect solution.

Keys to a Good Grab and Go Restaurant

❖ Enough choices (some places are glorified hot dog stands).

❖ Food prepared to order: nothing pre-made or frozen in sight.

❖ Easy entry, easy access, easy exit.

❖ Items that are edible while walking without risk of dribbling sauce or olive oil down the front of your halter top. It's not "grab and go" if the food has to be eaten at a table. After all, there's shopping to be done!

The Best Grab and Go Restaurants for Groups of Girls

La Creperie at Paris

Delicious crepes made to order, just like in France. Have them filled with fruit, or if you're feeling the need for a sugar rush, try the dessert crepes with chocolate and caramel.

Jean Philippe Patisserie at Bellagio

The first thing you will notice as you approach the Patisserie (located in the walkway to the left of the conservatory) is a huge chocolate fountain on the right side of the restaurant. But the Patisserie has much more than chocolate and desserts. Sandwiches, salads and many other tasty treats round out the menu.

ZoozaCrakers at Wynn

A cross between a New York deli and a fancy coffee house, this grab and go offers all the deli staples (corned beef, matzoh ball soup) and is open until 11 p.m.

Snacks at Bellagio

Nestled between the Sportsbook and the restaurant FIX, Snacks offers gourmet snacks served in record speed.

Starbucks

While there is nothing special about the Starbucks in Vegas, you can't beat an iced latté in the late afternoon. Starbucks also has an assortment of light snacks. Locations on the Strip are at Hard Rock Hotel, Treasure Island, Fashion Show Mall, Harrah's, MGM Grand, Stratosphere, and Planet Hollywood.

♪ YOUR DIVA DINNER AWAITS

Plan on one fabulous meal during your getaway: We're talking the caviar, the great wine, the entreé you could never find at home, the decadent dessert. Make it your Diva Dinner, and plan to enjoy it at one of the high-end restaurants recommended in the *Las Vegas Little Red Book*. If you're in town for the entire weekend, it usually makes sense to have this meal on Saturday night when you have the whole night stretched out in front of you.

Why Saturday?

Everyone Will be There: Unless everyone travels together, there's invariably one person whose flight doesn't allow her to arrive in time for a fine dining extravaganza on Friday night.

You'll Have Time to Prepare: Why bother going to a glam restaurant that's all about seeing and being seen . . . if you're in no shape to be seen? You'll need time to prepare for your major dinner out, and Saturday will allow you all the time you need.

<u>What's Left?</u>: Let's face it: dining at a five star restaurant is going to be one of the highlights of your trip. Why "get it out of the way" on Friday, when you can savor it on Saturday?

What's Important?

As you're evaluating where to go for your Diva Dinner, it's important to keep a few things in mind.

<u>Great Food</u>: Great food should not be taken for granted. Remember, just because a place has a big name chef on the door doesn't mean the cuisine will be what you're looking for. Most hot spots have a version of their menu available on their Web site. Make sure you choose a place where there's something exciting for everyone in your party.

<u>Good Atmosphere</u>: A good atmosphere can mean sleek and sexy, elegant and sophisticated, or bursting with high-octane energy. It doesn't matter which type of atmosphere you choose, as long as the restaurant has good people, good music and good vibes that work for your group of vixens.

<u>Sizzle Factor</u>: Who wants an extraordinary dinner in ordinary surroundings? Make sure you spend your evening at one of Vegas' hottest places to eat. If you saw the restaurant mentioned in the latest issue of *In Style*, it probably has enough sizzle for you and your girls. Sizzle factor is the most important component in selecting a restaurant for your big dinner out. If you're sitting next to George Clooney, are you really going to remember that the crab and corn chowder had a bit too much cream? Of course, it's a safe bet that wherever *he* dines will exude a healthy dose of sizzle.

Places to Consider for the Diva Dinner
Remember, this is the one meal that warrants dropping a little

cash. While none of these options can be considered cheap, they will all be memorable.

Joël Robuchon at the Mansion: MGM

If you really want to break the bank, celebrity chef Joel Robuchon has your number. To stand a chance of getting a table at this exclusive establishment you'll have to reserve early: like, two months early. It's small so there aren't many reservations to be had. If you are lucky enough to get a table, you'll be rewarded with a high-end (think $300 per person) multi-course extravaganza. This is one three-hour-tour you won't forget.

Mesa Grill: Caesars Palace

TV star-chef Bobby Flay will make your mouth water with his southwestern fare. Chiles and spices accent his signature grilling. What else would you expect from the star of *Boy Meets Grill*?

Nobu: Hard Rock

Nobu is known as a hobnobbers paradise. Everybody who's anybody eats at Nobu, but don't just come on a celebrity hunt or you'll miss the real draw: the food. The sushi and sake alone are enough to secure Nobu's status as an "It Restaurant." Try the tasting menu or go à la carte. Whatever you choose, you really can't go wrong.

Aureole: Mandalay Bay

If you're looking for ambiance, Aureole (the name alone is naughtily evocative) fills the bill. In addition to some good takes on American classics, Aureole has something you won't find any-where else: the three-story glass wine tower. Women suspended on *Mission Impossible* cables move up and down the tower filling bottle requests. It's spectacular, it's a show, and yes, you have to see it to believe it!

After the Diva Dinner

Now that you had a memorable culinary experience, it's time to amp it up a notch. Whatever you do, *do not* go back to the room, at least not yet. This is Vegas, baby! You and your girls are hot, and the night is young.

Chapter 6

Gambling:
Don't Let the Guys Have All theFun

✶ ....

Ah . . . the Vegas casino. Rooms so smoky you need an oxygen mask to enter, cocktail waitresses thrusting surgically enhanced cleavage in your face, and of course, the migraine-inducing clamor of surging crowds, clanging bells, and shouting drunks: best to sidestep this pedestrian, money-sucking circus of the masses and leave the blackjack to the swaggering frat boys, and the slots and Keno to the blue-rinse set fresh off the tour bus from the Native American casinos. Right?

If this is your image of the Vegas casino gestalt, then baby, read on. Fortunately, things are refreshingly different in the gambling capital of the world, where the casinos are exhilarating carnivals of fun and debauchery, filled into the wee hours with all types of people hard at play, including women just like you.

If you don't know much about gambling, you're not alone! Most people are *not* gambling experts. Although there are plenty of books offering surefire gambling systems on winning big at slots or killing 'em at the tables, the *Little Red Book* is here to guide you toward a fun and memorable gambling-bonding experience for you and your girls. While you won't become Annie Duke overnight, we will provide you with an overview of the best gambling options, common mistakes you can easily avoid, and how to play so you can smugly hold your own at any Vegas casino.

👄 IT'S GOOD TO BE A GIRL

Casinos *Really* Want Girls to Gamble: Put a girl at an empty blackjack table and suddenly the guys are swarming, wanting in on the game. It works so well, that casinos used to put gorgeous, paid "shills" in a chair, just to attract men to the table. While they don't pay shills anymore, casinos love it when girls gamble. What does this mean for you? You will be lavished with attention — and extra friendly employees — from the moment you set foot into a casino.

🂱 WHY YOU SHOULD GAMBLE ON THIS TRIP

It's fun, it's thrilling, it's the key to that new Rolex, and it's a great way to meet the hot guys. Gambling should be one of your top agenda items during your Vegas getaway: Here's why . . .

Playing with the Girls

Even if gambling *is* on the roster, sandwiched somewhere between spa pedicure and champagne shopping tour, don't plan on isolating yourself for hours at one of the gaming tables, willing yourself into "the zone." Gambling on a girl's getaway should be all about playing with your group: the excitement of winning a few hands, losing a few hands, and enjoying a few cocktails with your friends.

Meeting Men

When you're playing at a table, you won't be the target of the "hard hit" by annoying random guys. Although the men at the table *will* try to initiate small talk, they'll be focusing intently on the game at hand. Of course, you'll have already determined whether they're contenders or rejects with just one glance, but actually playing with them gives you a chance to do a quick personality check. Does he have a big pile of chips at the table, and appear as if he's having fun? Translated: The guy is smart, savvy, knows what he's doing, and knows how to have a good time.

Does his lip twitch and is there a sheen of sweat collecting on his forehead? Translated: He could be just as nervous in the bedroom . . . run as fast as you can! Digest your findings, and you call the shots. It sure beats sitting around the bar waiting for some loser to ask the age old question, "What's your Sign?"

Storytelling

Everyone needs to come back from Vegas with a gambling story. It's practically required, just so you can answer the question, "How did you do?" If your response is simply, "Didn't gamble a penny," then expect the line, "What did you go to Vegas for?" Gambling can be a huge rush — and a huge heartbreak. Within that drama there are some fabulous stories waiting to be told. We're not saying you should bet the house, but you should at least put a few bucks into play. Otherwise, what did you go to Vegas for?

Win Some Money

Not everyone leaves Vegas a loser. People win huge sums of money every day. You could be next!

⚸→ INSIDER'S REPORT

Don't Gamble Bored: Many groups of girls don't have a gambling plan and end up hanging out at the nickel slots with a disenfranchised group: some gamble, while others sit around watching. Allocate a couple of hours specifically to gambling so your whole group can embrace the experience with gusto. Don't make it the default activity when you can't find something else to do.

🏙 LAS VEGAS, LAND OF DISTRACTION

Everyone in Las Vegas wants your money. It's true: the restaurants, the spas, the bars and, oh, yeah – the casinos. They'll do everything possible to coerce you into parting with your hard-earned cash. What's a girl to do? It's hard to say "no" to everyone, so you need to be strategic about how to spend your fun money — and know a red flag when it's waving right in front of you. Here are just a few ways the casinos try to loosen your purse strings.

Casinos are Designed to Take Your Money

1. Floors:

Looking to remodel your condo? Chances are you won't be rushing to Carpet World to find a pattern identical to the one you saw at a Vegas casino. Zigzags, waves, crazy asymmetrical shapes: The casino floors are designed to make you subconsciously turn away and direct your attention to the gaming tables. Their logic: You're not going to play a table game if you don't see it, so the casino will go to great lengths to make sure your attention is always focused at eye level.

2. Ceilings:

While the Grand Canal Shoppes at the Venetian may boast lovely painted ceilings and frescoes high above the fray, there are no such visual treats at the casino. Again, all the action takes place at — or just above — eye level so nothing diverts your attention from gambling, gambling, gambling.

3. Geographical Points of Reference:

There are no landmarks in a casino: no compasses to get your bearings, no visible exits, no decorative Roman statues to help lead you to your next stiff martini. Every row of slots is identical to the next . . . and the next. As you walk back into the deepest recesses of the casino, you'll be hard pressed to pick out a specific place to meet up with your girls. You can't say, "Meet me at the blackjack tables"; they're everywhere.

4. Straight Lines:

Straight lines aren't just lacking on the floor; they're lacking everywhere. It's impossible to walk in a straight line from one end of the casino to the other. First you'll run into a couple of gaming tables, then a row of slots inexplicably placed in the center of what seemed to be a clear route, and then — lo and behold — there's a raucous little cocktail lounge teeming with revelers! They might as well place a sign in the middle of your path saying, "ha, joke's on you, sucker!"

5. No Clocks, No Windows:
Casinos are clock-free, because, surprise-surprise, the casino wants you to lose yourself in the excitement. You will be shocked at how fast time flies when you're sitting at a blackjack table or slot machine. For the same reason, windows are nonexistent to help lull you into a state of utter oblivion about whether it's day or night.

6. No Coins:
Almost all Vegas casino slot machines now pay out winnings through vouchers rather than coins. This means that rather than clinking into the slot machine tray, money gets reloaded on your credit meter: much easier for gambling away those winnings, my dear. But wait . . . what's that clanging sound you hear? Festive coin sound effects provided courtesy of a speaker imbedded in the slot machines.

7. Penny Machines:
You can't lose huge sums of money playing a slot machine that works on pennies, right? Here's what you don't know: The machines are set up to play tons of pennies at once. For example, a typical penny machine plays 900 credits, meaning it costs $9.00 each time you play! With these types of games, you generally win at almost every pull, but rarely win more than you bet. You may win 450 credits on a 900-credit pull, so that winning high washes over you . . . until you realize you're actually losing big time!

8. Ordering a Drink:
When you place an order with the cocktail server, she's taking

ten other orders along with yours. It takes time for her to walk all the way to the bar service area, it takes time for the bartender to fill ten drink orders, and it takes time for her to walk back to your area and serve several other groups along with yours. You may have wanted to gamble for only a couple of minutes, but may end up giving it "one more try" for 15 minutes and losing $40 waiting for your "free drink."

👄 IT IS GOOD TO BE A GIRL

Have Guys Teach You How to Gamble: Guys love showing a girl they're experts at something. Admit you don't know how to play, and the guys will be sidling up, bestowing their insider knowledge to guide you toward the right decisions. Should you run out of money, a guy will feel so badly that you've lost on his advice, he'll probably replenish your stake so you can continue playing. Obviously, you know better than to count on all of them to know exactly what they're doing. But of course, they're guys, and they'll never admit that!

🎆 WHAT TO PLAY

There are many ways to lose your money at the casino. You'll stumble across all sorts of strange games, including those that will make you feel like you're stuck in an alternate reality. Feel like a game of War? That's right, you can actually bet on the kid's card game. Stick with these recommendations; they're perfect for a fun-loving group of women.

Roulette

Roulette is a good place to start: easy, fun, exciting, no skill required, and the opportunity to win big. Remember *Wheel of Fortune*? Roulette is basically a spinning wheel with a ball and a bunch of numbered colored squares.

How to Play

❉ Start With $20.

❉ Learn the Table: The inside section of the table (closest to the dealer) contains squares numbered 1–36. You may bet five chips on one of these squares, or spread five chips over several. The outer portion of the table (closest to you) has nine larger boxes: 1st dozen, 2nd dozen, and 3rd dozen; 1–18 and 19–36; red, black; odd, even. Place a bet of at least five chips on one or several of these. Rule of thumb: You must have a minimum of five chips on each area you're betting on.

❉ Get Your Own Colored Chips: Give the dealer $20, no more, no less. $20 will give you your own $1 colored chips for use at that table. For instance, you may be playing with purple chips, while the other players may be playing with blue, red, orange or green. That way, everyone keeps track of their bets. If you win, the dealer will pay you in your colored chips, so you can keep playing.

❉ Wait for the Dealer to Spin the Ball: The ball will go around the wheel and land on one of the numbers. Anyone with a chip on that number on the table is a lucky winner!

✤ Collect Your Money: The dealer will pay you with more colored chips; dazzle him with your most vibrant smile and start all over again.

✤ Exchange Your Colored Chips for Casino Chips: When you're done gambling, push your chips toward the dealer and tell him you're done. The dealer will count your colored chips and exchange them for casino chips. This is important, as the colored chips have no value off the roulette table.

Tips on Playing

1. There are No Sucker Bets: Many girls are wary of gambling because they don't want to be lured into a game "that only suckers would play," because the chances of winning are so low. No matter where you place your chips on the roulette table, you have the exact same chance of winning as the pro gambling next to you.

2. You Can Bet More With Five Dollars: On most table games, you must bet at least $5 a hand — sometimes $10 or $25 — depending on how crowded the casino is. In roulette, you can make five $1 bets on the inside, even when the casino is packed. This is a great way to squeeze as much gambling pleasure as possible out of a meager five dollars.

3. Roulette is a Slow Game: Each time a bet is placed, the dealer must allow time for everyone at the table to place their chips (which can take forever if a lot of people are playing), spin the ball on the wheel, wait for the ball to stop on a number, collect all the losing bets, and pay all the winning bets. In comparison to blackjack, where each hand takes about one minute to play, roulette takes about two minutes. That means you can play longer with less money.

4. Play Where You Can Sit: Roulette is no fun if the game is so packed that you have to stand and reach around someone's polyester pantsuit to place a bet. Find a table with some empty seats and park it!

Slots

Slot machines, referred to as "slots," have taken over casinos; there are miles and miles of them in every casino in Vegas. Every-day, more table games are put out to pasture, only to be replaced with these 24-hour moneymakers. They're popular because many people are intimidated by table games and don't want to look incompetent by committing a breach of gaming etiquette in front of a large crowd.

How to Play

❖ Insert Some Dollar Bills into the Slot Machine: Once you enter money into the slot, it will give you credits on a meter. One credit is equal to one unit of currency in the denomination of the slot machine. On a 5-cent machine, each credit is worth 5-cents. On a dollar machine, each credit is worth $1.

❖ Hit the Spin or the Max Bet Button: This will take credits out of your meter and start the game.

❖ Wait and Win: The machine will spin the reels for a few seconds and stop. If the symbols on the reels are one of the winning combinations, you win and credits are added to your meter.

❖ Repeat: Repeat as necessary . . . which will probably be immediately, and indefinitely; slots are addictive.

❖ Hit the "Cash Out" Button: When you're ready to wean yourself from slot obsession, the machine will calculate your credits and print out a cash voucher for the dollar value you are owed.

Tips on Playing

1. Play One of the Progressive Jackpot Games: Megabucks and Wheel of Fortune are two of the most popular games because the top jackpot keeps growing as more people play the game around the State of Nevada. Instead of winning a couple hundred dollars, you could actually win millions! It happens more than you'd think.

2. Avoid the Old Mechanical Reel Games: The new technology of the video reels adds a whole new dimension to the game. The best thing about video reels is the bonus rounds. This is when the game switches to an arcade style mode where you select bags of treasures, for instance, to let you know how much you've won. You get to the bonus round by matching up certain items on the reels. The bonus round is where you can win tons of money.

3. Play Only at Games That Don't Use Coins: Coins are actually outdated in Vegas casinos. The new technology is

called "ticket in-ticket out." You insert bills into the slot machine and when you want to cash out, it prints out a voucher. You can either put the voucher into another slot machine or cash it in at a kiosk or with a casino cashier. The "no coins" policy also has another benefit: You won't dirty your hands or break a nail digging through a bucket of nickels.

4. Slots are Never "Overdue" to Hit: Slots don't have memories. No matter how long it's been since the last big jackpot, each play has an equal chance of winning because the machines are controlled by a random number generator.

5. Play Slots at the End of a Group of Machines: Casinos tend to put the better paying games on the outside banks of machines rimming the aisles. The strategy: if somebody is winning big on a slot machine, they sure as hell want everyone to see the windfall and be swept over by an uncontrollable urge to get in on the action.

6. Be Sure to Get Free Drinks: Don't pass on the free drinks from the roaming cocktail server. Free drinks are the casino's little way of saying "thanks for spending your hard-earned cash right here, and we'll do everything we can to make you so comfortable you'll never leave." That same drink will cost you (or some guy) $10 in the nightclub, so bottoms up, baby!

Video Poker

Video Poker, aka the "crack cocaine of gambling," is similar to the slots, but the player must make decisions on which poker hands to play. Those decisions determine if and how much the player wins. A player can play conservatively and hope for small wins or play aggressively and try to hit the top jackpots.

How to Play

Insert money just like you would with a slot machine: The machine will give you credits. Hit the "play" button: You will receive five playing cards on the screen. You have the option of keeping none, one, two, three, four or all five of the cards. Highlight the cards you want to keep by touching the cards on the screen, and hit the "deal" button. New cards will replace those you chose not to keep. If the five cards you now have make a winning combination, then you're a winner. The better the combination, the more money you win. Here are the winning hands, in order of the smallest to the largest payout. Examples are shown for each hand.

⁂ One Pair (Jacks, Queens, Kings, or Aces)

⁂ Two Pairs (A pair of Aces and a pair of 3s)

⁂ Three of a Kind (Three 5s)

⁂ Straight (4, 5, 6, 7, and 8; they don't have to be the same suit)

❧ Flush (any five cards all of the same suit)

❧ Four of a Kind (Four 6s)

❧ Straight Flush (5, 6, 7, 8, and 9, all of the same suit)

❧ Royal Flush (10, Jack, Queen, King, and Ace, all of
the same suit)

Tips on Playing

1) Play 25 Cent Video Poker: In dollar video poker, your
money evaporates in one second, and in nickel video
poker, you can't win anything big. In quarter video poker,
you'll be playing five quarters— $1.25 per play — and you
have the opportunity to win $1,000 if you hit the jackpot.

2) Play "Jacks or Better" Video Poker: There are several different versions of video poker and most machines allow you
to choose which one you want to play. The most common
types of video poker are "Jacks or Better," "Double Bonus,"
"Double Double Bonus" and "Deuces Wild." Jacks or Better
is basic video poker, which is simple and easy to play. With
the others, the game is a bit more complex and might di-
vert your attention away from your free Margarita.

3) Don't Search the Casino for the Best Video Poker Game:
Unlike slots, all Video Poker games are created equal.
There may be slight variations from game to game in how
much a flush or straight pays out, but it's far better to ex-
pend your precious energy cruising the bars and ultra
lounges, than traversing a maze of players in search of that
game.

4) Play Max Coins, But You Don't Have To: If you play the
maximum coins allowed per game, you will be gambling
five coins at once. With maximum coins, you will receive a

bonus if you hit a royal flush. If you want to spend less money but still stay in the game, it's just fine to play one or two coins at a time.

5) Sometimes You Don't Need Any More Cards: If the first five cards you receive make a straight or a flush, you won't need any more cards. Remember to select all five cards (many anxious people discard winning hands by hitting the deal button before they have selected all the cards), hit deal, and sit back and fantasize about mama's new pair of shoes.

6. Don't Be Afraid to Discard All of Your Cards: Sometimes the five cards you receive won't help you hit a winning combination. Discard all five cards and keep your fingers crossed that the five new cards will be filled with good gambling karma.

⌘╾ INSIDER REPORT

Knowing How to Play Before You Sit Down: Nothing is worse than sitting down to play a game when you haven't got a clue. If you're going to play a game you've never played before, study the basic rules before you begin playing. If you don't, you may end up losing money during the learning curve . . . that is unless you're one of those golden girls blessed with beginners luck – you know the type we all despised in high school? There are plenty of Web sites and books out there to tell you everything you need to know.

Blackjack

This is the most popular table game in the casino. It's a simple game that anyone can learn, and everyone enjoys. If you're playing at the right time of day, your friends can grab a seat beside you for a few hands and together you'll run the table.

How to Play

Blackjack pits each player against the dealer. The object is to amass a total point value that is greater than the dealer's without going over twenty-one. Numbered cards are worth their face value (the nine of hearts is worth nine; the four is worth four, etc.), and face cards are all worth ten points. An ace may be played as either a one or an eleven. If the player's card total goes over twenty-one, the player "busts" and automatically loses, no matter what the dealer's total.

Each player is dealt two cards, face-up. The dealer is dealt two cards, but one of them is dealt face down; this card is referred to as the "hole" card. If the player is dealt an ace and a face card, he has a "blackjack" and automatically wins and gets paid before the dealer plays. For any hand other than "blackjack," the player has options. The player can "hit" and ask for another card, or "stand" and not accept any more cards. If the player has two of the same-valued cards, the player can "split" the cards and play two separate hands. This requires another wager equal to the first wager. With any two cards, a player may also "double down," which is an additional bet that is up to the value of the original bet. The player then receives only one card and may not "hit" again.

Once all players at the table have played their hands, then the dealer plays. The dealer has a standard set of rules. If the dealer's total is sixteen or less, then the dealer must hit. If the dealer's total is seventeen or greater, then the dealer must stand. After the dealer plays, if the player's total is greater than the dealer's, then the player wins. If the hands are a tie, the game is declared a "push" and the original bet is returned to the player. If the dealer's total is greater than the player's, then the player loses.

Tips on Playing

1) Assume the Dealer's Hole Card is a Ten: There are more tens than any other card in the deck, so always assume

the hole card is a ten. If the dealer's up card is a two, three, four, five, or six, then assume the dealer has to hit and therefore has a good chance of busting. If the dealer's up card is a seven, eight, nine, ten, face card or ace, then assume the dealer has a good hand and will stand (if the dealer's up card is an ace and hole card is a face card, the dealer automatically has blackjack, and wins.)

2) Play Your Hand Based on the Dealer's Face Card: Play your hand based on what you think the dealer will (or must) do by the evidence of his up card. If the dealer has a two, three, four, five, or six showing, then hit when your total is eleven or less, and stand when your total is twelve or more. If the dealer has a seven, eight, nine, ten, face card or ace showing, then hit when your total is sixteen or less and stand when your total is seventeen or more.

3) Doubling Down: The simplest strategy is to always double on an eleven and double on a ten if the dealer has nine or less showing. There are more advanced options of doubling down on other numbers, but you will always be safe if you stick with the basics.

4) Splitting: Always split when you have a pair of aces or eights. Other splits can be slightly beneficial with certain cards, but they are not that simple to understand.

5) Buy a Strategy Card: A strategy card will show you the optimum play for every hand in blackjack. Once you know how to play every hand, it's just a matter of luck. Buy a strategy card at the hotel gift shop or download one from the Internet; it'll tell you everything you need to know.

6) Learn the Game Mechanics: The hand signals might seem simple, but many a player has looked like an idiot or, even worse, lost a lot of money simply because he didn't

know the signals. To "hit," scratch your two fingers towards you on the table. To "stay," wave your hand once over the table. To "double down" or "split," place another bet alongside your current bet. The dealer will adjust the cards and continue.

7) Start with the Shoe Games: The shoe games are those that use four or six decks of cards, all shuffled together and dealt from a single feeder, or "shoe." They are simpler to play and think through than single or double deck games because all cards are out front, face-up on the table. It will be easier to keep track of everyone's hand (except, of course, for the dealer's). Once you have been playing for a while, then move on to the single and double deck games, if you desire.

8) Don't Count Cards: Don't confuse yourself on card counting systems. Card counting is very difficult and you will end up losing more hands if you don't do it right, or if you have had a couple of drinks and miss a card or two. The casinos frown on it anyway, and successful card counters eventually get banned from play. While that's assuredly not going to be you, you don't want to risk getting 86'd from the casino, do you?

9) Sit in First or Second Base: If you are new to gambling or your blackjack skills are a bit rusty, you want sit on the right-hand side of the table, preferably in the first base position that is dealt to first. This way, you won't be caught up with all the action of the other players, and if you make a move that causes all the players to lose, they won't be able to directly blame it on you because so many cards had been played since your move. In the far left-hand position, you are last to be dealt to before the dealer. Make the wrong move and the dealer will get a different card than he would have had you played correctly, and

everyone might lose. Do that enough and the other players will blame you for losing — not an experience you will really cherish.

10) Avoid Insurance: Insurance is a side bet that allows the player not to lose their original bet if the dealer has a blackjack. A player may only take insurance when the dealer is showing an ace. Trust us, this is a sucker's bet, as the odds are far in the casino's favor.

11) Avoid Side Bets: Many blackjack games have additional side bet games at the tables. Royal Match and Super 7s are examples, but forget 'em. The odds on these side games are terrible, and they're just trying to get you to bet more. Avoid the temptation and stick to the regular game.

12) Avoid "Feeling the Cards": Sometimes players ignore basic strategy and either hit or stand when they shouldn't because they have a "feeling" about the cards. Blackjack is math: It's a numbers game, and illogical play will change the natural flow of the cards. Your fellow players will not appreciate this when you, and they, lose.

👄 IT IS GOOD TO BE A GAL

Guys Want to Give You Money to Gamble: If you just stand around the high limit room, there's a good chance men will give you money to sit next to them and gamble. Be smart — know when to "go all in" and when to shuffle-up and scram.

Craps

Craps is a very intimidating game. There are four dealers working and up to 16 people playing at the same time: but that is also why it is so much fun! When all 16 people win at the same time, every one celebrates together. You will hear hooting and hollering all the time. Some of the best gambling stories come from shooting craps.

How to Play

A craps game starts out when the pair dice are given to a new player, or "shooter." The shooter places a pass line wager and rolls the dice. The first roll of the dice is called the "come out roll." If the shooter rolls a seven or eleven, then the pass line wins and shooter rolls another come out roll. If the shooter rolls a two, three, or twelve, the pass line loses and the shooter again rolls another come out roll. If a four, five, six, nine or ten is rolled, then that number becomes "the point."

Once the point is established, the shooter keeps rolling until he rolls the point number or a seven. If the shooter rolls the point number, then the shooter "made the point" and the entire process repeats itself with the same shooter with another come out roll. If the shooter "sevens out," then the game is over and the dice move clockwise to the next shooter.

Bets to Make

❖ The Pass Line Bet: This bet is made before the come out roll by placing a bet on the pass line, which is on the outside of the table. You win even money on the bet when the shooter makes the point number. Always bet the table minimum on the pass line bet. If you wish to bet more, increase your odds bet or bet another type of bet.

❖ The Odds Bet: The odds bet is an even money bet that is placed behind your pass line bet. The bet is made only after the point is established. This bet is a 0 percentage bet for the casino. The casino has no advantage when a player makes this bet. The bet wins when the shooter makes the point number. Most tables offer two times odds (2x), meaning that you can bet $10 on the odds bet if you have a $5 pass bet going. Some off-Strip Vegas casinos offer ten times and even hundred times odds. If you don't take the odds, you will look like a novice gambler, and the dealers and everyone at the table will keep telling you to make the odds bet.

❖ The Six and Eight Place Bets: Place bets are side bets on a number that you can put up and take down at any time. While you can bet four, five, six, eight, nine or ten, the only ones that you want to bet are the six or eight. These bets payouts are 7 : 6, so make sure you bet in increments of $6, or you won't get the full payout.

Tips on Playing

1) Play at a Full Table: Craps is a social game, and it's not nearly as much fun if there's no one to talk to. Plus, at a full table it takes a long time for the dealers to pay out all the bets, so you won't be playing as fast. You'll extend the life of your bankroll, chat up the cute guys, and get your share of "free" cocktails.

2) Don't Play the Don't Pass Bet: This bet is the opposite of the pass line bet, except you are betting that a seven will be rolled before the shooter makes the point. Don't pass bettors really piss everyone off; some players are insulted because you are hoping the shooter will lose.

3) Learn Dice Etiquette: You don't want to look like a novice when handling the dice. First, pick up the dice with one hand instead of two. Next, don't bring the dice above the rim of the table. Blowing on the dice is strictly for the movies — if you do it, you'll look like an idiot. Now, use an underhand motion and throw a nice soft arc having the dice first hit the table about three-fourths down on the table. The dice should bounce once, and then bounce off

the backstop of the table and come to a stop on the far side. This isn't Yahtzee; you don't want to put so much oomph into it that the dice ricochets off the table and onto the floor. If this happens, take the sweet innocent girl role and just laugh at yourself. Practice makes perfect, so pick up a pair of dice in the gift shop and throw them in your room. If you're still not comfortable with your throws, just let someone else be the shooter.

4) Make Fun Bets While the Table Is Hot: While the winning percentages are low, there are some bets that are just fun to do. The "hardways" are bets on the four, six, eight or ten that the number will be hit with double dice before a seven, or the number with two other dice is hit. For example, a "hard four" bet is saying that "two and two" will be rolled before any combination of a seven or a "soft four" of a three and one. The "yo" bet is a one-roll bet where you win if an eleven is rolled. Only bet $1 on the yo bet. Get into it and yell it out like the rest of the players.

5) Tip by Placing Bets for the Dealers: The best way to tip is to place a bet for the dealers. Do this by throwing a $5 toward the stickman and yelling "Horn high yo for the boys." The "horn bet" is a one-roll $1 bet on the two, three, eleven, and twelve. The "high yo" means that the extra $1 from the $5 goes on the eleven, making the eleven a $2 bet. While most people don't know what it means, the dealers know and they will be excited. It's a good way to keep the energy up for the table.

Pai Gow Poker

Blackjack is not the only card game in town; switch it up with Pai gow poker. With Pai gow poker, you can play for hours and barely lose any money because 60 percent of all hands end up in a tie between the dealer and the player. Pai gow poker is a great game for friends because you can show each other your cards and give advice on how to play. It's a slower game than blackjack, and is not a big money maker for the casino, so they don't put their top dealers on it. That means a slower pace of play, and thus, more "free" drinks and time to socialize with the girls.

How to Play

Pai gow poker is played like blackjack, where each player is playing against the dealer. The players and the dealer are each dealt seven cards. The player must then make two poker hands of cards, a five-card hand and a two-card hand. The five-card hand must be a better hand than the two-card hand. For example, if a player only has a pair of queens in the seven cards, then the pair must be kept in the five-card hand.

After the players have made their hands, the dealer also makes two hands and all the hands are revealed. To win, the player must win both hands. The player's five-card hand has to beat the dealer's five-card hand and the player's two-card hand has to beat the dealer's two-card hand. If the player loses one hand to the dealer, then the bet is a push. If the player loses both hands to the dealer, than the player loses the bet.

Tips on Playing

1) Play the Hands According to the Rules: Remember, the best value hand is played in the five-card hand; the two-card hand is the second value hand. If you get this wrong, your hand will automatically lose. Be sure to study up on the rules on Pai gow poker before you play.

2) Remember the Vig: The Vig (short for "vigorish") is a percentage that the house takes out on each winning bet you have. If you don't have quarters and half dollars, they will keep a running total of the money you owe, and when you leave the table, you'll have to pay up. Don't leave the table with zero money or you might have to suffer the indignity of being escorted to the ATM machine by security. This *will* happen. They won't let it slide.

3) Ask for Help: Pai gow is the only game where you can lay your cards on the table and ask the dealer what you should do. The dealer will be more than happy to tell you what they would do with that hand. Remember, the dealer wants you to win. People tip when they win.

4) Don't be the Bank: Pai gow poker offers the opportunity for a player to act as the Bank versus other players and the casino. In addition to just playing against the dealer, you'll also be playing against all of the other players at the table. Don't do it unless you like taking on everyone else with little chance of winning.

5) Avoid the Dragon: The dragon is a second hand that a player is allowed to play when the game is not full. Don't play the dragon hand, because it requires you to make an entire other bet. If you want to bet more, just make a larger initial bet on one hand.

Poker

Poker took over the gambling scene a few years ago. With the newfound popularity of televised poker, the nation is going through a poker renaissance. While poker used to be a male sport, women have begun to give the guys a run for their money. After all, it's a game of smarts and strategy, two qualities most women know a little something about!

Poker Rooms

Poker rooms used to be glorified banquet rooms with a few beat-up tables. The new poker rooms of today are extensively decorated, first class operations with many tables. They are open 24 hours a day and are usually packed with a waiting list to play.

⁕ When you walk by poker rooms, you'll always see a crowd of people attempting to watch the action. But, if watching poker on television can put you to sleep — watching it in person can put you into a coma. It's nearly impossible to get a decent view of the cards, which are obstructed by the bodies of players. If you find yourself craning your neck to get a view, it's time to move on.

⁕ Stick with the smaller poker rooms. These rooms usually

have some low limit tables where you can play without losing so much you have to ask your best friend to spot you for a morning latté. Plus, the huge poker rooms of Bellagio or Caesars are filled with serious high rollers, which can be a little intimidating even for us!

Different Types of Poker Game Formats

Casino poker games are a bit different than what you may play during a "girls night out," sitting around a friend's kitchen table, sipping Chardonnay and eating chips. There are two formats to play poker in Vegas: Know which one you're getting into.

- Standard Poker: Games can be found at every poker room at any time. You can come into a game and leave a game at any time. If you want to play, let the poker attendant at the front know that you are looking to join a regular game. He'll either walk you over to a seat or put your name on a list to be called out when a game is available.

- Tournament Poker: Poker Tournaments are held at specific predetermined times; all players start at the same time and buy in for a certain amount (for example, $100 each). Most tournament games are "No Limit," so a player can bet or raise any amount they desire. Your place in the tournament is determined by how long you last in the game: be the first one to run out of chips and you get last place, be the last one with chips and you win first place.

  The amounts that you win for first, second and third place are all pre-set before the tournament begins. No player can come into the game, and players only leave the game when they run out of chips. Sound appealing? Just let the poker attendant know which tournament you want to join. Tournament times are usually posted. You can join tournaments days in advance; you don't have to play the moment that you've signed your name on the dotted line.

Texas Hold 'Em: The Only Version of Poker You Need to Know

Only play Texas Hold 'Em. If there is an Omaha High-Low or Seven Card Stud game with empty seats, pass on it. Texas Hold 'Em is a game that is easy to learn and fun to play, but hard to master. Each player is trying to make the best 5-card poker hand from two player cards and five community cards.

Tips Before You Play

✧ In a Non-Tournament Game, Play at a Low Limit Game: You will find Texas Hold 'Em games in the poker room called $1–2, $2–4, and $3–6. The $–-2 means that the first two rounds of betting have a limit of $1 and the last two rounds of betting have a limit of $2. You may only raise or bet the amount of the limit. The lower the limit, the less you stand to lose.

✧ Play Online Before Playing in a Live Poker Room: While the concept of the game seems simple, the basic strategy of the game is complex. You need to play for a couple hours so you learn the subtle nuances of the game. Recommended Web sites are listed at the end of the chapter.

👄 VEGAS VIXEN

Do you want to be a Poker Diva?: A Poker Diva is a hot woman poker player that uses her girl powers to separate male players from their money. Some of the best women poker players around like Annie Duke, Evelyn Ng, Clonie Gowen, and Jennifer Tilley (yes, the actress) know how to use their looks to confuse and intimidate men. To join them, you need to dress sexy, show some cleavage, and suggestively wink and smile at your male opponents. You will drive their heads (and their loins) spinning, encouraging them to make bad decisions. Believe us: this works.

Going "All In": You have probably heard the "All In" expression before: it has become *the* catch phrase associated with poker. When you go "All In," it means that you are betting every chip you have left. It usually only happens in tournament poker when only two players are left playing a hand (all the other players have folded already).

Other players may either "call" your bet or fold. If they call, then they are matching your bet. If they have less chips than needed to match your bet, they can still call you, but the new bet amount becomes whatever the other player has. So even if you go all in and lose, you still may end up having some chips left.

For example, if you go all in with $1,000 in chips, and another player with $500 in chips "calls" your bet and you end up winning, then you only win $500 from that other player. If you end up losing, you only lose $500 of your $1,000. When a player goes all-in and is called, both players turn over their hole cards. Then, they just sit back and wait for the flop, turn, and river.

How to Play

1) Know Your Dealer: While the players don't actually deal, there is a small token called the "dealer button" that moves around the table player by player in a clockwise position. The person with the dealer button in front of them is the last to get cards for that game.

2) The Blinds: You probably know what an "Ante" is. In Texas Hold 'Em, the Antes are called the "Small Blind" and the "Big Blind." Both blind bets must be made before the game begins. The small blind is a bet that the player to the immediate left of the dealer button must make. It is half of the table starting bet. The Big Blind is a bet that the player two

spots left of the dealer button must make. The bet is equal to the starting bet. For example, in a $2–4 Texas Hold 'Em Game, the small blind would be $1 and the big blind would be $2. Nobody else at the table needs to make an ante bet.

3) The Dealer Deals Two Cards: Dealers give two cards to all the players, face-down. Don't let anyone look at your cards. An initial round of betting starts with the big blind player. That player has the option of raising the initial bet. The betting then moves left around the table. Each player may raise, fold or call the bet. If you lose track of how much the bet is, ask the dealer. They are there to help.

4) The Flop: The dealer deals three cards from the deck to the middle of the table, referred to as the flop. These are community cards. Another round of betting starts, this time with the small blind player.

5) The Turn: The dealer deals one card from the deck for the community. Another round of betting starts with the small blind player.

6) The River: The dealer deals one final card from the deck to the community; there are now five cards face-up. A final round of betting starts and ends. All the players' cards are shown. The best 5-card poker hand wins the pot.

Sports Wagering

Las Vegas is the only place in the country where you can legally bet on sports. Although sports betting has traditionally been more of a guy's activity, plenty of girls have discovered the thrills and allure of watching a competition unfold in real time, knowing they have money riding on the outcome. Even if you don't plan to visit a sportsbook, it doesn't hurt to know the basics in case you happen to be in town during a big football or basketball weekend, and the whole town is buzzing with people betting on the games. You don't want to be left out of the festivities!

Sports wagering also provides hours of heart-racing excitement, since each bet takes about three hours to complete. You can feel your mood soar and crash with every play of the game because your money is riding on it — so lay down a little cash and have some fun.

👄 IT IS GOOD TO BE A GAL

If You See a Guy Win Big, Flock to Him: Guys don't just gamble to win money. They gamble so they can win tons of money and then turn around and blow their winnings on women: believe it! If you've ever been around a guy that just won $10,000, he'll pretty much spend half of it in a couple of hours — Champagne, limos, VIP tables, expensive meals, gifts; the $100 bills are strewn around like confetti. Guys love to flaunt their money so women will notice them. Give in to their weakness: You may just walk away with a nice little "present."

Tips on Playing

1) Stick with the Basics: Don't worry about the five-team parlay, futures, money lines, or even the over/under. Stick with basics: bet the point spreads. A point spread bet is not a bet on whether a team will win, but rather that a team will cover the point differential. For example, a "Broncos minus seven" bet would only win if the Broncos won by more than seven points. If the Broncos won by six points, then the bet would lose. Conversely, on a "Steelers plus seven" bet, the Steelers don't have to win, they just can't lose by more than seven points.

2) Bet in $11 increments: If you win, you get your $11 back plus $10. Any increment other than $11 and you'll end up with change and look like a rookie.

3) Create Drama: Spread your money over four or five games so you're immersed in drama. It's fun to have money on the line while trying to keep up with multiple games simultaneously.

4) Only Bet on Televised Games: Yes, even though there may be 150 televisions in a sportsbook, there are plenty of games that aren't televised. If you bet on these games you'll miss seeing your gambling dollars at work. You shouldn't be betting on Grambling versus Slippery Rock anyway; if it's not television-worthy, it's not worthy of your money.

5 Ask for Drink Vouchers: When you're placing a bet, be sure to ask for drink vouchers from the agent. Casinos are clamping down on giving out comp drinks to non-players, so if you order a drink in the sportsbook and don't have a drink voucher, the cocktail server will charge you.

6) Get a Good Seat: A good seat in a sportsbook can be hard to find. Expect that 75 percent of the seats will have a "Reserved for Race Players" sign, which means they are off-limits. Of the 25 percent remaining, look for seats that have a view that won't be blocked by pedestrian traffic. If you can't find a seat in the sportsbook, there are usually some good views at the adjacent bar.

Other Games

Casinos offer a variety of other games to tempt the players. These games are not your standard "meat and potatoes" casino fare, and the chance you will actually play them while in Vegas is pretty slim, but just in case you feel like trying something completely different, it's helpful to have a baseline level of gaming know–how for those games on the fringe.

1) Let It Ride: You receive three cards and the dealer has two cards. Before you see either of the dealer's cards, you have

the option of pulling back part of your bet. Then, you see the first of the dealer's cards. Again, you have the option of pulling back another part of your bet. Finally, you see the second of the dealer's cards. If the combination of the total five cards (yours and the dealers) is a poker hand of 10s or better, you win. The better the hand, the more you get paid.

2) Three Card Poker: It's a little tricky to play, but the basic concept is this: You receive three cards and the dealer receives three cards. If your three cards beat the dealers three cards, you win.

3) Bingo: If you are down to your last $10 and have an hour to kill, then bingo is the only way to keep gambling. While you won't be enjoying yourself in a completely quiet, smoke-filled room with a bunch of retirees, at least you'll keep on gambling. Well, sort of.

4) Keno: Basically, Keno is a lottery. Pick from 1 to 10 numbers out of 80 and turn in your ticket. The Keno machine will randomly pick 20 out of the 80 numbers. If your numbers hits, you win.

5) The Big 6 Wheel: A big wheel at the front of the casino. It should be called the Big "Sucker" Wheel. Avoid it at all cost, unless you suddenly feel the urge to give your money to the casino with a miniscule chance on winning.

 LUXE LAS VEGAS

What to Buy With Your Jackpot: You just hit Megabucks and are a newly hatched millionaire. What is the first thing you are going to do? Here are some suggestions:

✿ Amp After Hours Experience — $2,500 pedicure
✿ Champagne Shopping Tour — starting at $60/person (does not include your new thongs, shoes, or earrings)
✿ Neiman Marcus private Elton John concert — $1,500,000
✿ Dining experience with chef of the century, Joël Robuchon, at MGM Grand for 16-course sumptuous meal — $300/person
✿ Hard Rock cocktail with a diamond stirrer — $500, gratuity not included!
✿ Fantasy Suite at the Palms — starting at $10,000
✿ World Series of Poker Seat — Sure it's a mere $10,000 buy-in, but last year's payout was 12 million!

🕐 WHEN TO PLAY

Daytime Gambling

Daytime is the best time to gamble on a girl's vacation. Why? Because during the evening the casinos get so crowded that you will not be able to gamble with your friends. During the day, you have a chance to sit at the same table with your friends to play roulette, blackjack, or pai-gow poker.

At night, the table minimums go up. Some of your girlfriends might not be too happy playing blackjack at a minimum of $25 a hand. At those prices, you can guarantee that a few of the girls can't afford to lose for very long without getting upset. And who can blame them? Why throw your money away in large chunks at night when you can have a great time with a small amount of money during the day.

During the day, you and your friends will run an entire table, be able to talk to each other without guys listening in, win together, and drink margaritas on the casino's tab. So, find a table with a lonely dealer who's just sitting there, and take it over. The same table at night will have a line three deep for every seat.

Tips on Daytime Gambling

1) Find a $5 Blackjack Table: There's no reason to sit at a $10; all you will do is double your losses.

2) Go Manual: If you have a choice between a manual shuffle and an automatic shuffler, go with manual. A manual shuffle is when the dealer has to shuffle by hand. Automatic shufflers do one of two things: continuously shuffle the cards, or prepare new decks of cards while the dealer is dealing the current cards. Yes, it's true that card counters can only work with the manual shuffle, but you should look for a manual shuffle for your own reasons. A manual

shuffle is better than an automatic shuffle because it:

- Gives you a natural break to run to the bathroom or tell a story to your friends.

- Extends your playtime, allowing you to drink more on the casino's tab, because you aren't playing (and losing) in the extra five minutes it takes for the dealer to shuffle.

3) Get to Know the Dealer: When the dealer is shuffling, break out a conversation and ask a couple of questions. Dealers can help you out by keeping you from making stupid decisions, which will become especially helpful after you have had a couple of drinks.

Nighttime Gambling

At night, the tables fill up quickly and table minimums go up. Although it's probably a good idea to restrict your play to earlier in the day, there is definitely a buzz of energy in the casino at night. If you're going to play at night, here are a few things to remember.

Tips on Nighttime Gambling

1) Don't Play in Big Groups: If you have a group that is trying to gamble at night, you will spend the majority of time walking around trying to find the mythical empty table. Face it, the place is packed, so if you want to play you'll probably have to gamble in groups of two or three — or, more likely, individually.

2) Bring a Larger Bankroll: Table minimums will be up, so bring more money with you, otherwise you won't be able to withstand the swings. The swings can be steep, so be prepared to suck it up and lay your money down, otherwise you'll get yourself into a hole without the resources to play your way out.

3) Play in the Party Pit: Some casinos such as Harrah's, Imperial Palace, Stardust, Hooters, and Rio offer a table games area that also serves as a form of entertainment. Their pit area is swinging, so withdraw your cash, gather your girls, and have a good time.

☍ VEGAS VIXEN

You Can Tell a Type of Man By His Chip Color: When you're in a casino, it may be hard to size up which men are the successful ones and which are gambling on money borrowed from a credit card cash advance. If the old adage is "the clothes make the man," then in Vegas, it's the color of chips that defines the man. Take a peek at the color of chips he's gambling with: it's a sure fire way to tell what type of man he is.

Chip Colors

- White = $1 — Can't afford to come to Vegas in the first place. His version of a night out is drinking a six-pack with his roommates.
- Red = $5 — Right out of college or a young pup in the work force. Has big dreams ahead of him, one of them is striking it rich and impressing a Vegas Vixen like yourself.
- Green = $25 — In his mid-thirties, and making enough money to pay the bills. He's a player out to impress you with his money.
- Black = $100 — An executive in his forties or early fifties. Cares more about gambling than impressing women; he's probably ridden the divorce train several times after falling prey to vixens such as yourself.
- Purple/Pink = $500 — Owns his own business, and prefers the finer things in life.
- Yellow = $1000 — A rich, older, distinguished gentleman with tons of self-made or inherited money. Anna Nicole Smith would be all over this one.

Late-Night Gambling

In the wee hours of the night/morning, the table minimums go back down and the casinos empty. The late-night crowd is usually a wacky bunch. The real boozers have passed out hours ago; this crowd is filled with the socially inept and downright strange. Though we recommend that you should get some beauty rest or get some food, there are some things you need to look out for when you gamble late at night.

Tips on Late Night Gambling

1) Don't Play Drunk: There is no way to lose your money faster than gambling when you are drunk and tired. At this point you've probably been up for too long and drunk too much to have any chance of playing smart.

2) Don't Play by Yourself: If you look around and notice that you're playing alone at 5 a.m., go to sleep. The dealers don't even look like they want to be there, why should you. If you insist on sticking it out, find a table with at least a few other players so you can have some sort of interaction. Just be prepared to have some sleazy guy coming on to you or chewing your ear off about how he can't leave now because his private Gulf Stream jet is being serviced.

● WHERE TO PLAY

While the games are the same from casino to casino, the action isn't. Not every casino caters equally well to groups of women. The key to picking the right place to play is atmosphere. You need to be somewhere upbeat and fun. Generally speaking, seasoned players tend to be pretty mellow at the tables. Fortunes are won and lost and you wouldn't even know it. You need to pick a place where the crowd is fun, you feel safe and the drinks are plentiful.

The Hard Rock
A hip place to gamble. The dealers are attractive and friendly, and there is no shortage of table games, all around the casino's hot center bar. Plus, it's much nicer to place your bets to a soundtrack of rock 'n' roll, than to the clanging bells and whistles of the slot machines.

MGM Grand
It's massive in size, and has a large variety of slot and video poker machines. Just don't venture too far away from your friends in search of or that hot slot machine, or that hot guy that just walked by: You may never find them again; yes, it is that big.

 PLAY WHERE THE STARS PLAY

Dennis Rodman, Matt Damon, and Ben Affleck play at Hard Rock.

George Clooney and Cindy Crawford play at Red Rock Resort.

Pam Anderson plays at Palms.

Tiger Woods plays at Mandalay Bay.

Toby Maguire and Leonardo DiCaprio play at Bellagio.

Palms
Calm during the day, happening at night. The table games area is basically one big social "meet and greet." Plus, with so many celebrities, you never know whom you might be gambling next to.

Wynn Las Vegas
All class. While you may be only gambling a couple bucks, the sophisticated ambiance makes you feel like you're playing with

hundreds. Wynn is a worldly establishment with top-notch employees who cater to your every whim.

Rio

Rio is a big casino with a lively atmosphere, but the layout makes you feel like you're in a much more intimate establishment. It's a nice change from the vast, cavernous casinos along the Strip, and the cocktail servers who break out into song on mini stages every ten minutes add a touch of cheesy fun.

Hooters

Laid back atmosphere, where every one is friendly. Hooters claims to be the "Cure for the Common Casino," and it is. It is the only casino in town where you can "high five" the dealer, talk on your cell phone at the table game, and order free "Washington Apple" shots along with your free cocktail.

Do Your Homework:

If you're coming to town with the intention of gambling with some of your hard earned money, make sure you know what you're doing.

⚷━ INSIDER'S REPORT

Go Window Shopping for Something Expensive and Set That as Your Goal for Amount of Money to Win: Let's say you saw that new Marc Jacobs purse, but can't think about shelling out $500 for it. Then by all means, let Mr. Jacobs be your goal! We know the sob stories: "I was up $300, and then I gambled it all away." If you're winning, then run — don't walk — out of the casino and into the soothing world of fine leather goods. Don't re-gamble your big winnings!

Five Gambling Books to Read Before Your Trip:
1. *The Complete Idiot's Guide to Gambling Like a Pro* (Stanford Wong & Susan Spector):

2. *How to Win at Gambling* (Avery Cardoza)

3. *The Unofficial Guide to Casino Gambling* (Basil Nestor)

4. *Guerrilla Gambling* (Frank Scoblete)

5. *The Winner's Guide to Casino Gambling* (Edwin Silberstang)

Five Gambling Web Sites to Learn More About the Games:
1. www.thewizardofodds.com

2. www.flopturnriver.com

3. www.gamblingtip.net

4. www.pokerhelper.com

5. www.playwinningpoker.com

Five Gambling Web Sites to Practice Playing:
1. www.bodog.com

2. www.fulltiltpoker.com

3. www.pokerstars.com

4. games.aol.com

5. zone.msn.com

Chapter 7

Daytime: Relax, Recover, and Retail

✳ ....

Sleeping late? Nursing a hangover all day? Catching up on movies in the room? Not in Vegas, baby! Some of the best activities for groups of girls are only available during the daytime, so charge yourself up with a double latté and get ready to have some fun.

POOLS

During the long summer days in Las Vegas, the pool is the daytime center of your hotel. If you don't have any plans for the day, start off at the pool and see what happens from there. Even if you wake up late, the sun will be up and hot, leaving plenty of time to take it in.

While at most resorts the pool is just for lying out and swimming, in Vegas it is much more than that. Here are some options to consider.

❖ Dine Under the Sun: Many pools have a restaurant that opens up on to the pool or a pool café that's serves wraps and sandwiches. Enjoy an early lunch or afternoon snack in the sun. It sure beats the long lines of the crowded buffet.

- Socialize Under the Sun: The pool scene is a huge daytime party where it is easy to meet and flirt with the opposite sex. Not that it is a meat market, but if you want to be noticed and approached, I am sure you know how to do it. And if a little innocent voyeurism is your thing, check out all those six-pack abs!

- Drink Under the Sun: A late afternoon at the pool is the perfect setting for a cocktail. To step it up a notch, attend a poolside concert at the Palms or Mandalay Bay and listen to music under the stars.

- Gamble Under the Sun: A new trend at Vegas hotels is blackjack tables outside, so you can test your luck while admiring the scenery. It is a nice change from a smoky casino. Just watch out, it will cost you. The casinos usually set the poolside table minimums at $25, so the best way to play for a while is to find a guy willing to bankroll your hot streak.

SHOPPING

Vegas has some of the best shopping you'll find anywhere. From only-in-Vegas boutiques to runway high fashion, you will be spending in style and going home looking better than when you came.

Why Shop in Vegas

Like you need a reason to shop?

- You Are on Vacation: Money seems to be easier to spend when you are on vacation. The thrill that comes with being out of your everyday environment often brings on the inspiration needed to buy that little something you've been eyeing for months.

❖ Vegas Has a Huge Variety of Stores: Every store imaginable can be found in Vegas, from the mall-level franchise to the high-end clothier.

❖ It is About the Experience: Although shopping in Vegas is a one-of-a-kind experience, remember, it 's not just about the stores: It's about sharing a heart-thumping shopping extravaganza with your girls.

When to Shop

Vegas stores and malls have ungodly hours, staying open from the morning to sometimes 11 p.m. or midnight. There is never a bad time to shop — but do you really want to waste your precious nighttime hours shopping? Shop by day, play by night.

❖ Morning Shopping: Morning is probably the best time to hit the high traffic shops. If you're looking for special attention, this is the best time to get it. Start hitting the stores around 10 or 11 a.m., before the rest of Vegas wakes up.

❖ Afternoon: Afternoon is the highest traffic time of the day. Malls provide a refrigerated escaped from the blistering desert sun, so many people hit the mall just to stay indoors. If you don't mind crowds, have at it.

❖ Evening: Not the best time to shop, because any Vegas Vixen worth her salt should have other evening plans like hitting the ultra lounges and ravishing the nightclubs. If you see a great looking leather satchel while dashing through the Forum Shops on your way to Spago, don't give in to temptation. Who wants to lug a bag full of purchases around all night, and besides, it will be there in the morning!

⌗➔ INSIDER'S TIP

Don't Take the Free Reading Materials on the Strip: You know those guys who stand on the Strip with fliers for strip clubs and escort services? They're canvassers. After many debates with the city bigwigs, the canvassers appear to have won the right to pass out this essential information. No need for laughs or lectures, just keep walking and continue to enjoy the sights and sounds of Sin City on the Strip.

✓ THE *LITTLE RED BOOK*'S LUCKY 7 PLACES TO SHOP

Advertisements boasting the best shopping can be found everywhere you turn. Ignore them! The *Little Red Book* is here to point you in the right direction.

1. Forum Shops at Caesars: The Romans Would Be Proud

The Forum Shops introduced the concept of high end shopping in Las Vegas, and after a major expansion in 2004, continues to hold its own as one of the city's premiere shopping destinations. Not only is it loaded with over 160 fabulous stores (in the spirit of a Rodeo drive or Madison Avenue), the Shops also house retailers such as FAO Schwarz, and a vamped-up Victoria's Secret with specialty European and "Adults Only" sections.

More people come to the Forum Shops to check out the ornate fountains, Roman statues, and beautifully painted ceiling than actually shop, so although you'll be dodging tons of people strolling around, the stores are — refreshingly — not that busy. When choosing what to wear, avoid a hard, flat shoe like a platform or wedge because the floors are made to look like a street with bumps and cracks making it hard to balance. Forum Shops are open until midnight on weekends and 11 p.m. midweek.

Getting Around

From inside Caesars Palace, walk towards the Cyprus Marketplace Court, a collection of fast food joints; the entrance to the Shops is immediately to your right. A massive fountain called the "Fountain of the Gods" serves as the center of the Shops, with passageways leading off in different directions. Stroll back and forth along the passageways, (ignoring the big aquarium with the dated Atlantis Show and the Festival Fountains) until you find the spiral escalators that take you to the shops in the new addition. Parking is easiest if using the Forum Shops or Caesars' valet, but you can also park at Mirage; the entrance to the Shops is just outside the White Tiger exhibit.

Stores for Women

 Plenty to choose from. Buy a rhinestone-encrusted thong at Victoria Secret's Superstore. Slip into a hot pair of jeans at Diesel. Experiment with dramatic jade-colored creme eye shadows at MAC, Lust over multi-carat diamond studs at Harry Winston, one of only five in the county. With other premium shops such as Juicy Couture, Jimmy Choo, Versace Jeans Couture, Marc Jacobs, Kate Spade, and Coach, you won't have trouble satisfying your fix for top of the line items.

Places for a Bite

Located near the entrance to Caesars, Wolfgang Puck's Spago is a perfect place for a light lunch. Sushi Roku on the third floor of the new addition will satisfy that late afternoon sushi fix. If you have Canadians in your group who can't get the enormous servings and free refills back at home, there's always Cheesecake Factory, located by the aquarium and the Atlantis Show.

2. Grand Canal Shoppes at the Venetian:
Italians Make Better Shoppers

With its replicas of St. Mark's Square, canals, and gondoliers, you'll actually feel like you're walking the streets of Venice — without the insalubrious odor of the *real* Grand Canal. The Grand Canal Shoppes may not have a vast number of stores, but the décor, atmosphere, and collection of couture make it a fabulous place to spend a morning or afternoon.

Getting Around

Located a floor above the casino; if you find yourself face to face with slot machines, you're in the wrong place. To leave the casino floor and get to the mall you have two options: Take the escalator up by the Grand Lux Café, and you'll be in the middle of the mall. Or, take the escalator up by the front hotel entrance; you'll be at the end of the mall near the Strip entrance. If you're staying at TI or Mirage, venture on the overpass across the Strip. It will lead you right into the mall entrance.

Stores For Women

Expect the assortment of chain stores you'd find at "Any Mall U.S.A." But then, as you stroll deeper into the Shops, you'll find more unusual and elite delights, such as Jimmy Choo, Amore, Max Azria, Burberry, Caché, Gandini, Dior, Marshall Rousso, Privilege, and Wolford.

Places for a Bite

The Mexican Taqueria Canoita is a perfect place for a Cadillac Margarita. It's situated right on the canal, which means great people watching. If you're looking for a lighter meal, Tsunami

Asian Grill offers excellent sushi with a hip atmosphere. Postrio, a Wolf Gang Puck restaurant, is located in the St. Mark's Square area of the Shoppes. Ask for a seat on the patio, so you can people watch and enjoy a little musical entertainment from the street performers.

3. Miracle Mile at Planet Hollywood: Marathon Shopping

Miracle Mile, formally known as Desert Passage, boasts one and a half miles of shopping. Did we say, "Wear comfortable shoes?" Although it's a relatively quiet mall by Vegas standards, it still does a fairly brisk business.

Getting Around

Think of one gigantic loop that requires a major trek to get back to the far side. If you drive, park in the valet, which is located in the same parking garage as Planet Hollywood. From the Strip, there's an entrance close to the entrance to the Paris Hotel.

♈ VEGAS VIXEN

Travel in Style on the Pedicabs: Are your feet tired from walking around the mall? Hail a bicycle pedicab that seats two people, costs only $4, and whisks shoppers around the mall. Perfect when both arms are loaded with bags, your feet hurt, and you just had a post shopping cocktail!

Stores For Women

A very large BCBG store is located just off the entrance. For a younger look, try Parallel, a BCBG spin off, located further into the mall. If you're dying for shoes, try Tulips: Just be forewarned, these shoes aren't made for walking; they're the closest you can get to stripper shoes without looking like a 'ho. If you're feeling adventurous, take a spin into Hattitude, a boutique store with a large selection of outrageous hats and wigs. Even if you don't want to buy one it is fun to try them on with your friends — or your Vegas boy toy — and snap a few pictures.

Places for a Bite

Most of the restaurants are in the far back end of the mall, so if you walk in form the Strip, it will be a hike. Aromi d'Italia is located near the parking garage entrance, and has a selection of Italian gelato, coffee, and sandwiches. Directly across from it is Tacone — perfect for a wrap and a protein smoothie. If you're looking for a bonafide sit down for lunch, your best choices are Max's Café for a light salad or sandwich, Blondies Sports Bar for traditional bar food and beer, and Cheeseburger in Paradise for a tropical, lighter version of the all-American Hamburger. For a caffeine boost, try Starbucks located near the entrance to the mall from the casino, and Coffee Bean or Tea Leaf (yummy apricot hot tea) located on the walk from the Strip to the back of the mall.

📷 **STAR GAZING**

Britney Spears loves the Miracle Mile: After dining at Cheeseburger in Paradise, Britney purchased some wigs at Hattitude. She had to "disguise" herself from the paparazzi, of course!

4. The Fashion Show Mall: Everything Under the Sun

Fashion Show Mall is a massive, newly remodeled facility with every chain store you've ever seen in upscale malls throughout America. The two-story building has restaurants bordering the Strip entrance, and large department stores anchoring the sides and end of the mall. This is a shopping venue that will make you feel like you never left home: families in the throes of holiday or back to school shopping, teenagers roaming around aimlessly, mothers pushing strollers and chasing whining toddlers.

Getting Around

Located directly across the Strip from Wynn Las Vegas, Fashion Show Mall is accessible by walkways over the Strip that can get you into the Mall in a flash. If you're coming from Treasure Island, be sure to walk out the main entrance by the "pirate show," and continue up the street to the entrance. As part of it's "suburban, non-Vegas milieu," the Fashion Show Mall actually closes at 8 p.m. everyday, except Sundays when it closes at 6 p.m.

Stores For Women

You can't argue with department store greats such as Saks Fifth Avenue, Dillard's, Neiman Marcus, Robinson's May, Nordstrom's, and Bloomingdale's for covering the basics. On a more intimate scale, emerging designers Karen Zambos and Crimes and Misdemeanors have stores alongside the well-established Chloé and Sonia Rykiel. If interesting and edgy is what you're looking for, check out Talulah G., the choicest fashion boutique in Vegas, frequented by Nicky & Paris Hilton, Naomi Campbell, Mariah Carey, Chloe Sevigny, and Heather Locklear. An amazing in-store tailor makes any on-site alterations a sure fit.

Places for a Bite

Café Ba-Ba-Reeba is an excellent tapas restaurant with outdoor patio. Order a couple of dishes for the table and a pitcher of red sangria. Next door, RA Sushi features a hip indoor setting, an open-air outdoor patio and a fresh sushi menu. If you want to dine while shopping, the gourmet Mariposa restaurant is located in Neiman Marcus. Try the Market Place Café on the top floor of Nordstrom for a more casual dining experience.

5. Mandalay Place

While Mandalay Place is a nice diversion from the casinos, it is not a shopping destination and should only be frequented if you're staying or hanging at Luxor or Mandalay Bay. It simply does not have the number of stores needed to make for a satisfying afternoon of shopping.

Getting Around

Ascend the escalators by the House of Blues restaurant to the main part of the mall. If you're walking from Luxor, look for signs for the Steakhouse; the escalators are just to the left. If you are at New York–New York, it's quicker to take the monorail from Excalibur down to Mandalay Bay and then walk back to Mandalay Place rather than walking through Excalibur and Luxor.

Stores For Women

55 Degrees is a unique wine store. Buy a bottle and they package it in a cool vacuum-sealed tube so you don't risk breaking it on the way back to your room. Looking for a book to cozy up with at the pool? Peruse the goodies at the Reading Room, a boutique bookstore. The hip Samantha Chang boutique is the one and only specialty shop for this famous lingerie

designer. Her entire signature fashion line is showcased, and much of it is exclusive to the store. Other stores to satisfy your shopping jones are Forever Silver, and Max & Co.

Places for a Bite

Mandalay Place features two lunchtime restaurants. Burger Bar may sound like the family hangout at a rodeo, but is actually the experiment of famous chef Hurbert Keller, known for elevating the all-American hamburger to a new level of designer cuisine. Try the turkey burger with cranberry sauce on a sesame seed bun, with a side of sweet potato fries. Giorgio Caffe is a touch of gourmet in a hip casual setting — a perfect spot to sip champagne at the bar or enjoy a light salad or appetizer to tide you over. If you're craving chocolate, the truffles at the Chocolate Swan are simply orgasmic!

6. Wynn Las Vegas Esplanade

The Esplanade is a lovely place to stroll, window shop, and indulge in the fashion forward threads featured in the collection of high-end designer shops.

Getting Around

Shops are located inside the casino, so once you enter the resort, look for signs directing you to the shopping area. Contrary to popular belief, Wynn resort is relatively easy to navigate; even the most geographically challenged will find the shops in just a few minutes.

Stores For Women

The Esplanade is home to a few Vegas exclusives including Oscar de la Renta, Graff jewelers, Jean Paul Gaultier, and the Manhattan shoe god Manolo Blahnik. Be sure to stop by the high-end cosmetics shop, La Flirt for some interactive fun. The store is laid out like a make-up studio with sampling stations so you can experiment with model quality cosmetics and products. Other shops read like a Rolodex of fashion's most predominate names: Dior, Chanel, Cartier, and Louis Vuitton.

Places for a Bite

There are no restaurants inside the shopping area, but the Wynn buffet and café are only a short walk away. If it's late afternoon, stop by Parasol Up lounge for high tea. If you're in the mood for a light snack or a sandwich, stop by Zoozacrackers.

⚷— INSIDER'S REPORT

Buy that perfect swimsuit: Did you forget to pack your swimsuit, sandals, or sunglasses? Not to worry, Vegas has fabulous stores for swimwear. Here are the best in town:

- 👙 Juicy Couture at Forum Shops
- 👙 Capri at Bellagio Shops
- 👙 Amore at Grand Canal Shoppes
- 👙 Everything But Water at Fashion Show Mall
- 👙 Aqua Swimwear at the Fashion Show Mall
- 👙 Bikini Bay at Miracle Mile
- 👙 Sauvage at Mandalay Place
- 👙 Love Jones at Hard Rock Hotel
- 👙 Swim at Mirage

---

7. Via Bellagio: High-End Paradise

The shops at Via Bellagio are for those with major disposable income, those who just won big at blackjack, and those who simply enjoy scoping out the latest and greatest. You can stroll through the high-end shops in a matter of minutes, so if you're at Bellagio, do yourself a favor and enjoy some serious browsing.

Getting Around

One long walkway makes Via Bellagio simple to navigate. From inside Bellagio, the shops begin by the FIX restaurant.

They end at the casino exit on the way to Caesars Palace.

Stores For Women

Talk about chi chi! While there are only a few stores at Via Bellagio, all of them are the highest of the high end: Armani, Chanel, Dior, Fendi, Gucci, Hermès, Prada, and Tiffany & Co. These stores cater to the high rollers, who spend so much money at the casino that they get to shop for free!

Places for a Bite

Olives is located near the shops, and is one of the best lunch places in town. If the weather is nice, ask for a seat on the balcony overlooking the Bellagio Fountains. It may take a while to be seated, so get your name on the list, and hit the shops before you are seated.

⚷— INSIDER'S REPORT

Some Items Are Over Priced for Big Gamblers: You'll be stunned when you check out the prices of the outrageously overpriced merchandise found at the high-end shops located in the casinos. These stores aren't expecting someone to actually pay cash for these items. They're hoping that the spouse of a high rolling gambler will select an item from their store as a "perk" in exchange for all the dollars spent in the casino. Since the customer isn't actually "paying" for it, she could care less about the price, and the casino ends up reimbursing the store for the item.

Individual Stores of Note

These stores are not part of the shopping malls, but are fabulous places to shop.

Love Jones at Hard Rock

Featuring trendy burlesque-style lingerie, as well as a great selection of swimwear, sexy accessories, and erotic books. To find a really good deal, ask an employee to open the curtain to the small room in the back. While this area looks like an "employees only" stock room, it is actually where they house all the luscious on-sale items.

Blue at the Mirage
Located on the way to the Danny Gans theatre, Blue is a small designer boutique carrying trendy items usually found only in L.A., such as 575 denim jeans. The service is excellent and you'll be sure to find something guaranteed to make everyone back home jealous.

Gamblers General Store in Downtown Vegas
Your man loves to play poker. All men do. Pick him up a poker set at the Gamblers General Store in downtown Vegas. It has a huge selection of everything and anything having to do with gaming. He'll love you for it.

The Attic in Downtown Vegas
You may recognize this über-hip, unconventional vintage clothing & antique store from a Visa commercial and a *Vogue* magazine feature. Gather your girls, enjoy a pre-spree cocktail or two, and cab-it over to this funky downtown boutique. Racks and racks of vintage fashions, a variety of wild retro furniture, and a decent selection of funky new clothes and accessories will have you all buzzing around the place and laughing the entire time. Try on some costumes and take a group picture with the Attic's resident diva, London actress and model, Lisa.

Entry is $1 per person, and don't expect dime-store prices as it's not an Amvets thrift store. Getting there is easy but the return cab will need to be called in advance.

Souvenir Shops Along the Strip

From Elvis thongs to one of a kind Frank Sinatra collector items, no trip to Vegas is complete without buying a campy, overly glitzy souvenir. The Strip is souvenir central and since most souvenir shops are created equal, you can do your damage at the one directly in your path. Don't Go Home Empty Handed!

You need to buy a great little trinket to trigger all those wonderful memories of your trip to Vegas, plus a couple of tchotchkes to give your friends back home.

EXPLORING THE LAS VEGAS STRIP

When it comes to views, Manhattan has Central Park, Paris has the Eiffel Tower and Vegas has the Strip (which has the Eiffel Tower too). Vegas newbies need to venture out onto the Strip to see what it's all about. No trip to Sin City would be complete without a sightseeing stroll down Las Vegas Boulevard. But instead of endless walking trying to see the sights, add some adventure to it and make it an afternoon. You need to do the *Margarita March*!

The Margarita March

This walking tour is more of a drunken stroll than an actual march. It is cruising up the Las Vegas Strip with a frozen libation in hand, sipping away as you see the sights. It all starts down at the largest hotel in the United States.

Start: Fat Tuesday's at MGM Grand

Fat Tuesday's is located in the bowels of the MGM Grand. Take the escalator just off the main lobby down to the parking garage and look for Fat Tuesday's at the bottom of the escalator. Or, if you are coming from the Monorail, you will pass it on your way to the lobby. Buy a 16-ounce slushy margarita in a plastic to-go cup. Once your group has drinks in hand, hug the left-hand side of the lobby and proceed into the casino. After you pass Tabú, MGM's ultra lounge, take a hard left and keep walking. In about two minutes, on your left, you'll see the lion habitat, a large glass enclosure featuring two (sleeping) lions. Take a quick peak at the lions as you enter the large, circular room. Don't go up the escalators; instead, stay on the main floor and cross around the Centrifuge Bar to a Strip exit. Once you're outside, take a right on the sidewalk and move forward. Get past MGM and get ready for a refill at your next stop.

Stop 1: La Salsa Cantina

La Salsa Cantina is a cheesy Mexican fast food/bar on the Strip. This isn't a place to hang out, but it serves as a good refill station. This is the one place where The *Little Red Book* recommends buying a yard of margarita, because here you actually get your money's worth. The next leg of your journey will take you through a dead part of the Strip where you won't see anyone that will make you feel embarrassed about drinking from a cheesy, three-foot-tall mug. Once you leave La Salsa Cantina, walk past GameWorks, the M&M Factory, the Coca-Cola bottle, Fatburger, a couple dingy souvenir shops, and a few mini-marts.

Stop 2: Hawaiian Market Place

As you pass the last mini-mart, you'll see the Hawaiian Marketplace on your right. The Hawaiian Marketplace is a covered outdoor "village" sandwiched between the Polo Towers and the Harley-Davidson Café. Inside the Hawaiian Marketplace is your next stop: A Tiki Hut that sells frozen drinks. Take a look around the marketplace, occasionally, you will find a troupe of Hawaiian hula dancers performing in the market's center. Just be careful as you watch, because they will drag you out there to learn the dance yourself.

In the Tiki Hut, the *Little Red Book* recommends going with a pina colada instead because it contains a pineapple wedge that might help to counteract the negative effects of all that booze you've been chugging down. Okay, it probably won't, but at least you're consuming something that's healthy-ish.

Continue up the Strip, passing the Harley-Davidson café, and the Aladdin/Planet Hollywood Property. Before you get to Paris, cross over to the Strip to the Bellagio and continue up that side of the street. If you are there at the beginning or middle of the hour, then you will see the fantastic Bellagio fountain show. Watch in awe and snap a few photos for back home. If the show has not started yet, turn around and admire the Eiffel Tower, which is a half-size replica of the real deal in Paris.

Now, continue your walk up the street and take the pedestrian cross over towards Caesars Palace. This will be your longest walk between pit stops, so be sure to leave the Hawaiian Marketplace with a full drink

Stop 3: The Daiquiri Bar at the Caesars's Spanish Steps
When you come over the cross walk, continue straight towards Caesars Palace and you will enter the Spanish Steps, an outdoor plaza leading up the main Caesars Palace entrance. In the middle is a circular daiquiri bar that serves big frozen drinks. It is in the shade, so sit for a second at the bar and rest. It won't hurt to flirt with the bartender to try to get an extra shot in your drink.

When you are ready, head back towards the Strip and take the crossover to the Barbary Coast. But don't go in, walk up the street past the Flamingo to your next stop.

Stop 4: The Margarita Bar in Front of Margaritaville

At the end of the next casino, the Flamingo, is Jimmy Buffet's Margaritaville Café. Don't bother heading into the main bar: Margaritaville doesn't get hopping until later at night. Instead, head to the frozen margarita bar just beyond the main entrance. Refill here and head out to the small terrace and enjoy your drink.

Stop 5: Beacher's Rockhouse

Located at the entrance to Beacher's Rockhouse at Imperial Palace, the Daiquiri Bar is a nice pit stop. Be sure to flash tip money as they're pouring your drink to get a little extra booze in your blend. Once you've filled up, grab a seat at the Rockhouse. This is small bar that gets totally crazy at night. But right now, it is a great spot to people watch. Everyone who enters the Imperial Palace has to pass through.

Upon leaving the Rockhouse, continue up the Strip. You'll pass Harrah's, Casino Royale, and The Venetian toward your destination, TI. At The Venetian, cross over the Strip to TI.

End: Sirens Outdoor Drink Stand at TI

You've made it; this is your destination. Walk past the valet entrance to the TI center entrance (next to the ships). As you approach, you'll see a stand with attractive women doling out the last of your margaritas. The drinks here aren't the strongest, but at this point you really shouldn't need much more help.

If it's late in the afternoon, you might be just in time for the first show of the night. The show *Sirens of TI* is free, and the first performance is at 7 p.m. In this outdoor adventure, a group of beautiful sirens lure a band of evil pirates from their cove, to a watery grave. Yes, this is a must-see in Vegas, but make sure you stay within arm's length of the bar, because standing around in a crowd waiting for the pirates to arrive is really boring.

By the way, did you notice that you've seen some of the interesting sights along the Strip? Between Tabú, the Eiffel Tower, the outdoor canal at The Venetian, and the Bellagio Fountains, you've seen a lot of neat places. So raise your glass, and thank the Lord you took pictures! With all you've been drinking, do you think you're going to remember all this?

⌁━☀ INSIDER'S REPORT

Take Plenty of Group Photos: To remember your trip, you need some shots of your group in front of distinct Vegas sites, not just photos of drunk, red-eyed babes taken at the night-clubs. There are many great places to take pictures along the Strip. Don't be embarrassed to stop and snap a few, or to ask random passersby to shoot your group; everyone walking past you is also a visitor to Vegas, and will be taking their fair share of photos.

Things to Remember When Venturing Out

✢ It *is* the Desert: It's dry in the desert! Stock up on lip balm, sunscreen, lotion and H_2O! There are plenty of places to get water along the way, and you should probably stop at most of them.

✢ Plan to be on Your Feet: Wear shoes that are fashionable but *comfortable*, and spare yourself the blisters. Wherever you decide to go during the day (unless it's to the spa for a full roster of treatments), you'll be doing a lot of walking.

✢ If it's Important, Bring it With You: In Vegas, a simple diversion can turn into an exclusive VIP party, so you need to be prepared at all times. Bring your money, phone, etc. whenever you venture away from the hotel. You will almost certainly not make it back to your room as often as you plan.

❖ Give Yourself Time to Get Back: Be careful of how far you wander, if you don't have a lot of time to spare. Don't wind up so far down the Strip, that you don't have enough time to primp and preen while getting ready for dinner.

⧗ SPAS

If you've never been to a world-class spa, then baby, you've come to the right place; time to wipe away any image of your local day spa! Vegas spas are like temples for the body: imported tiles line the floors, fluffy Egyptian cotton towels and robes keep you cozy and cosseted, and the fragrance of fresh cut flowers fills the air. Book your reservations early, leave all of your cares at the door (something you should have done the moment your plane touched down . . . if you haven't, this is your last warning), and let yourself go.

Do I Have Enough Time to Go a Spa?

We know what you are thinking: With everything there is to do in Vegas, can I really devote a couple of hours to relaxing in a spa? Sure you can. Checking in to a spa is a planned activity that beats milling around the casino looking for something to do. Even if you plan to be out until 4 a.m., book a spa appointment for 10 a.m. the next day. Two hours of pampering will make you feel better than if you slept those two extra hours.

Reasons to Go to a Spa

Your Body Needs to Relax and Rejuvenate from Excessive Partying
Smoke from the casino, dehydration, and lack of sleep can really take a toll on the body. The spa is the prefect place to rejuvenate so you're ready for another round of partying Vegas-style. If you book your spa appointment on the last day of your trip, you can start your rehab process early.

It is a Fun Group Activity
Some of the best girl gossip can be found at the spa; the hot steam must loosen loins, *and* lips. Just remember that if you're with a larger group you'll spend more time than you thought hanging out in the spa, sipping herbal tea and gabbing.

You are on Vacation and You Deserve It!
A spa is a luxury, go for it!

Tips on Spas

Go Exotic
Forget the standard massage. Try something unusual like a massage treatment incorporating exotic body wraps, hot rock therapy, or aromatherapy. Save your standard Swedish for the local day spa back home, in between laundry and carpooling.

Get There Early
You don't want to be running late and stressing out on your way to the spa. Give yourself ample time to check in, rest and relax before your treatment.

Use the Entire Facility
It's not just about the treatment: take a steam, revel in a long, hot shower, schmooze with the girls in the hot tub, snack on fresh oranges and mangos. Many spas have their own exclusive private pools and cabanas just for the spa clients, so take in some sun and order lunch and a fruit smoothie poolside. Before you leave, use all the complimentary shampoos, lotions and oils to feel smooth, sleek and sexy.

No Need for Cash
Bring a credit card, and leave your purse in the room. The cost of most treatments already includes service charge and gratuity. If not, the spa will have a list of recommended tipping for each treatment. There's no need to tip above the included gratuity or recommended amount, but as with all things, if the service was beyond anything you've ever experienced, it's always nice to let the staff know by adding a little extra. Don't worry about stuffing loose cash into the pocket of your robe to tip your masseuse in-person; the specialists know you'll take care of them when you pay the bill.

Best Spas for Women

All of the *Red Book's* "top 10 hotels for women," house amazing spas that will leave you satiated and satisfied. If you end up staying at a non-*Red Book*-endorsed property and want the spa experience, choose from these spa greats.

Palms Spa

The place to be during the day at Palms. Go with a deep tissue massage and add on a 25-minute body treatment themed after you favorite cocktails: Mojoito, Cosmopolitan, and Margarita.

Rock Spa at the Hard Rock

Rock Spa is small, but social; the workout facility is a singles meet and greet. Go for one of their packaged "journeys": set packages that include a body treatment, facial, massage and foot massage. The journey takes 3 hours, but is so pleasurable you'll be practically crying when it's over. Because the spa is located down the long hallway leading from the garage to the casino, you needn't set foot in the casino to arrive in paradise.

Canyon Ranch Spa Club at The Venetian

With a massive 40 foot climbing wall at the entrance to the facility, Canyon Ranch is the most impressive looking spa in Vegas. Even if you're not getting a treatment, stop by to have a light healthy vegetarian lunch at the Canyon Ranch Café. If you're not staying at The Venetian, finding the entrance to the spa can be a little tricky: From the Grand Canal Shoppes, take the private elevator located next to the Canyon Ranch Living Essentials boutique, and voila . . . heaven!

Mandalay Bay

Mandalay boasts two spas: Spa Mandalay and the Bathhouse, located in THEhotel. The Bathhouse is a bit more intimate, but both facilities are fabulous and you will be satisfied with the quality of treatments. Try something unusual such as the Volcanic Dust Mask body treatment or the Rose Petal Body Wrap.

 STRIP TEASE

Going to Get Lucky?: Get Your Palm Read and Find Out: Located in the Palms Hotel near the Hunt and Harrington tattoo parlor, is a Palm Reader par excellence. Ask her to unveil your future; don't use your time to see which slot machine is due for the next big jackpot.

⌛ SALONS

While spas relax and invigorate you, salons make you look your best. Even the most put-together Vegas Vixen could use a little guidance from the experts before venturing out into the Vegas night.

Reasons to go to a Salon

You Have a Big Night Out

Get all dolled up for a big night out! Everything about the night will be better because you will feel confident knowing you're looking your best.

You Will Feel Like a Princess

Treat yourself to a luxury. It's not often that you have talent of this caliber at your beck and call. It sure beats the assembly line nail parlor in the strip mall back home.

Mend Those Broken Nails
Accidentally break a nail lugging that carry-on onto the plane? Don't despair. Call the salon and let them know you have a nail emergency and they'll do their best to squeeze you in.

Tips on Salons

Book Early
Plan your appointments before you arrive in Vegas to insure you get your desired time and treatment. Otherwise, you might have to roll out of bed at 8 a.m. to get that pedicure you have been looking forward to.

Go for a Package
If you're going to do it, do it right. A mani and pedi followed by a wash and dry will leave you feeling gorgeous and ready to ensnare any lucky guy you choose.

Book Together
It is nice to chitchat with your friends while having your hair and nails done side by side. Talk about total gossip time!

Give Yourself Ample Time
Sometimes an appointment will get off to a late start and take longer than anticipated. Make sure you have plenty of extra time after your appointment to get ready for the next activity on you agenda.

Best Salons for Women
Again, if you're staying at one of the *Red Book*'s "top 10 hotels for women," book your services at the hotel salon, so you can easily whip back up to your room to get ready for the big evening ahead. If the salon is all booked up, try these stellar options:

AMP at the Palms
AMP is known for its celebrities, but the services and facility are

what make it top notch. When you enter from the main entrance of Palms casino, AMP is located on the far back left of the casino floor. On busy weekends, be sure to book well in advance.

Canyon Ranch at The Venetian
The salon is part of Canyon Ranch, so after your massage is over, you can have your nails done without ever changing out of your robe.

Mandalay Bay
Excellent facilities and a salon menu featuring exotic versions of the manicure: Coconut Creme, Peppermint Pleasures, Fijian Sugar Polish, and Orange Peel.

 WHERE THE STARS GET THE ROYAL TREATMENT

The head-turning AMP Salon at Palms, and Canyon Ranch at The Venetian, are both owned and operated by celebrity colorist Michael Boychuck. Blondes by Boychuck include every star that steps foot onto the Strip and every Vegas Vixen that calls Sin City home. For more than ten years, Paris Hilton and her family have summoned Boychuck to help paint them pretty.

Head on Out
As you head back toward your room to prepare for your night on the town, pick up some ingredients to make a pre-night-out cocktail. Once in the room, take a nap, take a shower, get dressed, sip your Cosmo, and get ready to head out for a wondrous evening.

✳ Chapter 8 ✳

Nighttime: Things Really Heat Up When the Sun Goes Down

✳ ....

Once the sun finally creeps down behind the Luxor and the Strip begins to sparkle and buzz, it's time for you and your girls to prepare for your evening of desert decadence. As you embark on your elaborate *toilette*, the question we pose to you is this: In a city where you can be absolutely anybody, *who* will you be, and more importantly, *where* will you be, amidst the blazing neon? Since Sin City is a non-stop 24-hour party, having a good time in Vegas isn't exactly rocket science. But who wants good? You and your posse deserve nothing short of *fabulous*. Your nighttime pleasure trip through Sin City should be sexy, sultry, and most of all . . . magical; that said, you need to plan ahead. Let the *Litttle Red Book* guide you toward an evening that is truly transcendent. Trust us, you'll have juicy stories to tell, a radiant smile gracing your face, and an aching need for sleep, once we're through with you!

Plan Your Night

A detailed plan involves research, prioritizing, and communicating with all of your girls. Sure, it's a bit of work, but damn it's fun — and damn important if you don't want to end up being one of those groups of girls flailing about the Strip looking frustrated and confused, while desperately waiting for the night to somehow take off. And all you alpha girls out there . . . remember:

There's a fine line between strategic planning and over planning. If you plan well, you'll stay in control of your evening, have *several* viable options for raucous fun, and may even find yourself in the same place, at the same time, as your favorite celebrity.

⚷ INSIDER REPORT

When Bad Outfits Happen to Good People: Leave the "Only in Vegas" Threads on the Pages of "Fashion Don'ts"

We beg you to *please*, no matter how tempting, *do not* succumb to the "only in Vegas" outfit. Not only is a slutty outfit a waste of money, but you never know who you may run into on the Strip — your boss, boyfriend's mother, sister-in-law. Don't gamble on style. If you let your hair down and expect to rub elbows with the celebs, make sure your fashion sense is showing: classy, not trashy!

Why Vegas Nightlife is Red Hot

A club's hip appeal is based directly on the number of women walking through its doors. Clubs in Vegas want at least a four-to-one girl-to-guy ratio, with the one guy being financially sound enough to treat all four girls, all night long; so conjure that Vegas Vixen and watch as the club does back flips for you and your girls.

Clubs Define the "Hip Factor" of a Resort

Trendy nightclubs and ultra lounges are the heart and soul of the mega resort; they define the people that visit, and are usually the culmination of a lengthy and thoroughly researched brand and image campaign designed to make the guests feel like stars (or bigger stars than they already are).

Money Makers

Where do the majority of people end up after a night of clubbing? On the gaming floor. Since great nightlife means more people spilling into the casino, each mega resort competes aggressively for you and your hard earned money with fabulous state of the art clubs and lounges. So choose wisely — if you're a girl in Vegas, you'll have a smorgasbord of great possibilities at your fingertips.

Celebrity Factor

Vegas *is* the new celebrity playground and the properties know that without a buzz-worthy nightclub, they have no chance to attract Hollywood A-listers. Casino marketers receive high-fives at every turn when celebrities visit a property, because the public will associate the property with the celebrities for years to come. Sizzling hot nightlife can help put a casino resort on the map. Just think how much you know about Palms as a result of MTV's *Real World: Las Vegas*, Bravo's *Celebrity Poker Showdown*, E!'s *Party at the Palms*, hosted by Jenny McCarthy, and A&E's *Inked*.

 STRIP TEASE

The Manhattanization of Las Vegas: Vegas is fast becoming one of the nation's hottest high-rise condo markets in what is being called the "Manhattanization of Las Vegas." A-listers are discovering Vegas to be a great location for their second home away from home, largely In part to the happening nightlife. Palms Place — soon to be the most coveted address in town — opens its doors in late 2007 to Eminem, Lance Bass, Leonardo DiCaprio, Roger Clemens, Carmen Electra, Dave Navarro, Jessica Simpson, and Pamela Anderson. Onward and upward!

NIGHTCLUBS, BARS, AND ULTRA LOUNGES . . . OH MY!

The Vegas nightlife scene is on a scale that puts every other city to shame. Sure, there are plenty of clubs in Miami or Los Angeles, but they all pale compared to the places the *Little Red Book* will take you to in Sin City. The Vegas club scene is sizzling — with celebrity appearances 24/7. Don't waste your time getting caught up in the hype. Sip Cosmos and dance the night away. Dedicate yourself to the notion that anything can happen in Vegas . . . and probably will. It's time to get *your* party started in a city where the party never really stops. Here's how.

Ladies, Name Your Poison

In Vegas, a club is never just a club. Sin City boasts three different types of nightlife venues, each a perfect fit depending on your mood, the time of night, or the girls you're traveling with. Before swinging into party mode, learn the lingo, chat with your girls, and think through your priorities.

Nightclubs

Typically the largest of the three venue options, nightclubs are all about the dance floor and the music. World famous DJs work dancers into a lather and crowds line up and clamor to get in. If you plan to strut, make sure you practice your moves long before you hit the dance floor. Nightclubs open around 10 in the evening, and close around 4 a.m.

Ultra Lounges

Cozy, hip lounges with music and bottle service, ultra lounges have DJs to set the mood, but without a dance floor, the trendy music tends to recede into the background. Ultra lounges are conducive to actually talking. You can carry on a conversation without shouting, which makes ultra lounges the perfect venue not only for meeting a special guy, but for sharing all your blushingly intimate secrets and desires, should you decide to take the plunge. The dress code is sophisticated because you will most likely be sipping champagne rather than pounding body shots. Ultra Lounges open around 8 p.m. and close around 4 a.m.

Bars

Bars are fun, relaxed and filled with a partying crowd. Come as you are; jeans and a trendy camisole are perfectly acceptable, as is a casual or funky mini dress. Bars usually open from around noon and close around 3 a.m., but some stay open 24 hours.

⚷ INSIDERS REPORT

Estimate How Long it Will Take You to Get Ready — Now Double It: There's only so much space in front of the mirror, and everyone is entitled to her turn, so plan on spending more time on getting ready than you would think. A good way to accelerate the process is to send one group down to the center bar to get a table and order drinks, while a second group finishes the glamour game. No one wants to sit around the room waiting an hour to take a shower. Breaking up into two efficient groups allows everyone to get ready at their own pace.

🎵 NIGHTCLUBS

The *Little Red Book* will point you to only the right places for your group of Vegas Vixens. Plenty of clubs may be terrific, but not the best for a group of girls. The Lucky 7, below, are spectacular venues where you can enjoy a cocktail (okay, several) without waiting in line, while mingling with the best Las Vegas has to offer. Here are a few key factors in determining the best places to unleash your Vegas Vixen.

Four Criteria For a Fabulous Girl's Night Club

1. <u>Easy Entry</u>. As a woman, you deserve to get in for free! A good club whisks you inside without you fighting your way to the front of the line, tipping the doorman, and snagging a stocking.

2. <u>Facility</u>. A fabulous nightclub is pristine and has décor and lighting that make it a special place to party. If the club is big, it needs to have multiple areas with different themes, so in every corner there's another party vying for your attention. In addition, there should be plenty of comfortable seats, ample bars, and a high-energy dance floor.

3. <u>Atmosphere</u>. Seductively luxurious. The music, energy and vibe of the club should make you want to dance, socialize, and let loose, rather than sit around and people watch. It should be full of men and women seeking a great time, infusing the club with a constant flow of energy. Great clubs will boast a certain level of star wattage, and cater to celebrities' wild ways.

4. <u>The Right Men</u>. On any given night, a club must have a large number of men who fit the universally accepted general guidelines for attractiveness. The men need to be guys you will enjoy partying with, even in the daylight. You know 'em when you see 'em.

Night Club	Location	Entry	Facility	Atmosphere	Men	Total
PURE	Caesars Palace	10	10	10	9	39
Tryst	Wynn	9	10	10	9	38
Tao	Venetian	9	10	9	9	37
Moon	Palms	9	10	9	9	37
Rain	Palms	8	10	9	9	36
Body English	Hard Rock	8	9	10	8	35
JET	Mirage	8	9	9	8	34
Light	Bellagio	9	9	8	7	33
The Whiskey	Green Valley Ranch	8	8	9	7	32
Studio 54	MGM Grand	7	8	6	6	27

✓ THE *LITTLE RED BOOK*'S LUCKY 7 NIGHT CLUBS

1) PURE at Caesars Palace: Celebrity Playground

If you're wondering why everyone seems to be talking about PURE Nightclub at Caesars Palace, the answer is simple: It's the hippest hotspot in the nation.

In a special "E! Entertainment" feature, the network named the club the "No. 1 hippest hotspot" in the country for the way it takes nightclubs to a new level and caters to celebrity clientele. Since PURE's opening New Year's Eve 2005, the guest list has read like a *Who's Who* of entertainment and sports. With its reputation for excitement and its prime location at the center of the Las Vegas Strip, PURE is easily the breakout star on the national nightlife scene.

<u>Entry</u>: Pure has an "unescorted women" line that allows you to bypass the huge crowd fighting to get to the front. If you do have guys in your group, be ruthless, split up, and let them buy their way in. Otherwise, expect to wait.

<u>Facility</u>: The two-story 36,000 square-foot club features three distinct areas: the main room features three bars, large, plush beds swathed in white linen for seating, and a raised VIP area that overlooks the dance floor; the sophisticated and sensual VIP ultra lounge Red Room; and the Terrace, a hidden enclave four stories high offering incredible panoramic views of the glowing jewel box that is Sin City at night.

<u>Atmosphere</u>: This is the top club in the country, so only one word describes it: *Alive*. The staff is well trained and cordial, the DJs are world-class, and every person that steps through the door adds to the hip, fun, party atmosphere. All the celebrities love this place, and so will you. PURE is not just a nightclub; it is the Strip's premier nightlife destination.

<u>Men</u>: Most men have to buy a table to get into PURE, which starts at around $300 for only the most basic bottle service. What this tells you is that the men you encounter here will either have money to burn, or the right connections. You will find a lot of slick L.A. types, with the clothes and the pickup lines to match. If you get tired of one group of guys drooling over you, just head to a different section of the club. It's such a big playground that they probably won't be able to find you again. Unless you want them to!

📷 STAR GAZING IN THE DESERT

Jeremy Piven, Ben Affleck, and Ryan Reynolds shot a scene at PURE nightclub for their film *Smokin' Aces*. Set in and around Lake Tahoe, the storyline has Piven playing a coked-up magician-mobster who is being pursued by the Feds, bail bondsmen, and hitmen . . . not the typical PURE Nightclub clientele.

---

2) Tryst at Wynn Las Vegas: A Touch of Class

Steve Wynn got it right with Tryst, a gorgeous club situated on a man-made lake sporting a dramatic man-made waterfall. Tryst, a name invoking an intimate rendezvous for lovers, jumped to the top of Sin City's sexiest clubs after opening its doors New Year's Eve 2006, and boasts the best-looking nightlife crowd on the Vegas scene.

<u>Entry</u>: The entry way is slightly hidden below the sushi restaurant Okada, and by the main valet entrance. You will see many different lines of people in the hallway, but before you choose one, flash a smile and ask a doorman for a little guidance. The door staff is refreshingly friendly and courteous, compared to other clubs where they may seem flustered by the crowd. Once you make it through the line, proceed down a stairway and into the club.

<u>Facility</u>: It's a smaller nightclub, just over 12,000 square feet, but every inch of this luscious hotspot is well done. Less smoky and surprisingly calmer than other clubs, the main room has an open-air ambiance and a sizable dance floor extending into the breathtaking 90-foot waterfall that cascades into a secluded lagoon. There are plenty of tables (all VIP), but also room to stand at the bar on the left side of the club. Avoid the right side of the club unless you have a table or need to use the restroom, as there is no place to stand. If you are with a group of girls, you will have no problem having your drinks paid for all night from the men sitting at the tables.

<u>Atmosphere</u>: Because of its open-air ambiance, Tryst is a refreshing change from the normal boxed-in nightclub. The music is slightly more subdued than other clubs because the sound escapes to the outside, which means you'll be able to carry on a conversation and feel like dancing at the same time. Deep reds, chocolate browns, and resin blacks distinguish the sophisticated interior of Tryst, while the outside patios are enveloped in dramatic white linens and surrounded by palm trees.

<u>Men</u>: The men tend to be older than those at some of the other clubs, but given that Tryst is in Wynn Las Vegas, it's to be expected: Wynn is the most upscale resort in Vegas. At the sexiest club on the Strip, the guys will try to impress you with their money and perceived power. Game on!

👄 IT'S GOOD TO BE A GIRL

The Purse Drawer: For guests seeking ultra-VIP treatment, Tao nightclub offers eight private skyboxes, each featuring European bottle service, a mini-bar, an espresso machine, and banquettes with secured purse drawers. Yes, your very own purse drawer! Use it for your Louis, your lipgloss, or even your collection of cocktail napkins scrawled with phone numbers of the men you've just met on the dance floor.

---

3) Tao at Venetian: The Buddha Parties

New York class meets Vegas flash! A $20 million design-driven dining and entertainment complex, Tao opened in New York City in 2000 and has retained its status as a hotspot, attracting celebrities and sports figures while packing the restaurant each and every night. This winning concept blew into Las Vegas' Venetian, where the Buddha-themed, massive complex has been extremely successful since opening in 2005.

<u>Entry</u>: Entry can get a little hectic. The lines are long and confusing given that the entrance is by the Strip (go across the walkway from Treasure Island if you are on the west side of the Strip). If you are arriving by car, park in valet at Venetian's front entrance for quick access.

<u>Facility</u>: The cozy Tao features three bars in two main rooms, a variety of hip hop, house, and rock 'n' roll music, and state-of-the-art audio and lighting systems. Tao is designed for voyeurs: the nightclub allows you to see the entire venue from almost every point in the room, while sexy performance vi-

gnettes, including dazzling, scantily clad women taking rose petal baths, can be seen nightly.

<u>Atmosphere</u>: Tao is high energy, meaning its DJs simply won't stop until the whole place is rocking. Go-go dancers and a state of the art lighting system add to the exhilarating vibe.

<u>Men</u>: Two words — Eye Candy. The Asian décor brings out the best in everyone. Just remember, your new friend, the club's 20-foot Buddha, is watching your every move.

🍸 VEGAS VIXEN

Accessorize: The Tao crowd is dressed to impress. Your best bets are accessories (like chunky turquoise or chandelier earrings) that add simple trendy touches to your outfit, allowing you to enter a new level of Tao-greatness.

---

4) Moon at Palms: The Sky Is the Limit

Dance among the stars, literally. The retractable roof highlights the new, exclusive penthouse club that sits on top of the Playboy Club in the Fantasy Tower of Palms. The roof is the gateway to the refreshing desert air; pumping oxygen into the club.

<u>Entry</u>: Moon and the Playboy Club are joined at the hip. Get into one, and you are good for the other. The line starts forming around 10 p.m. at the entrance to the Fantasy Tower, and can get very long on weekends. So, while tapping into your Vegas Vixen in order to glide by the less well-informed, be sure to take some time to stop and smell the roses. The Mint High Roller Lounge is located next to the infamous line and has some fabulous eye candy.

<u>Facility</u>: It's not the biggest club, but it makes up for size with character. The key feature is the retractable roof, which opens

periodically throughout the night to expose the night sky. It is a show to see with lots of music, and even more theatrical fog. Only in Vegas! Once the fog clears, you become fully aware there is no longer a roof over your head as you dance 600 feet above the Strip.

<u>Atmosphere</u>: VIP all the way! The VIP room, to the left of the entrance, is decked in a translucent yellow glass mosaic. Platforms for dancing surround plush VIP booths along the perimeter of the club, setting the stage for a sexy, yet laid-back, evening. There is a bar plus two lounge-style rooms almost hidden in the back of the club. Two dramatic steel and glass staircases will lead you upstairs to a VIP balcony with majestic views from what feels like outer space. While there

are plenty of tables to tempt you to sit, the key at Moon is to stay on the dance floor.

<u>Men</u>: The men at Moon are hipper and more sophisticated than those downstairs at Rain Nightclub, partly just because they knew enough to choose Moon instead of the more obvious, former number one Rain. It's easy for men to become overwhelmed by the abundance of VIP services and table options at Moon. Fortunately, to loosen up, they hit the dance floor. And get this . . . the men that come here actually know how to dance (surprise, surprise!), so expect your hottetst moves to be matched.

5) Rain at Palms: Large and In Charge

Rain in the desert? You'd better believe it. The club has multiple levels and environments totaling 25,000 square feet, cool design and special effects, and luxurious private areas for intimate chat and kanoodling.

📷 **STAR GAZING IN THE DESERT**

A tipsy Tara Reid made a splash at a *Stuff* magazine party in August 2004. After a tiff with Lindsay Lohan, Reid leaped into the Skin pool fully clothed. Skin was also the scene of Lohan's threat to kick a fan's backside for asking for an autograph. There was also a very famous lady who went skinny-dipping at 5 a.m. with galpals, but then, as the billboard says, "What happened at Palms, never happened."

<u>Entry</u>: Rain is one of the toughest clubs to get into. Given its huge popularity, the lines form into a mass herd of people backed up into the casino's slot machines. The slow moving main line forms on the right hand side and weaves around Little Buddha and Garduno's restaurant. Those with higher hopes of VIP status are jam-packed at the entrance by the velvet ropes, trying to get the doorman's attention. Some people wait for hours. This is a club that requires you to use your

Vegas Vixen wiles to latch on to a group of guys that have already bought a table or even better, a skybox. If you choose to play by the rules, you'll spend a good deal of the evening in a state of frustration. And that's *so* not what Vegas should be!

Facility: You've never seen anything like this! Rain's entrance, a tunnel of gold-mirrored mosaic with color-changing lights, fog, and sound, prepares you for the energy level inside. When you enter, walk past the crowded bar on your right on to the bar in the center of the room. You will feel tempted to walk up the stairs to the walkways where the VIP cabanas are

---

👄 IT'S GOOD TO BE A Girl

Girls Only: The dance floor has a small stage "for girls only," that is almost like its own secret club. It's a great place to escape that guy who won't leave you alone; even Tommy Lee can't put a leg up on the stage! If you need a break, the women's restroom is its own little girly pad with enough room to primp and chat with your vixens.

---

situated, but only do so if you have a reserved table, because standing room is at a premium. Rain offers multiple VIP skyboxes (accessible by taking elevators with biometric thumbprint scanners to the skybox level), cabana areas and water booths (where the patent leather banquettes are actually filled with water). The stairs leading to the skyboxes are on the far left hand side of the club. Look for guys at the bottom of the stairs. These high rollers have bought a skybox for the evening, and are looking for girls to party with. Get them to give you a wristband: These are as good as gold! If you're lucky enough to get a wristband, you can hang out at the VIP bar upstairs, where it is much easier to get a drink.

Atmosphere: The main scene at the club is the dance floor, with fourteen-foot fireballs shooting across the ceiling and

LUXE LAS VEGAS

The Presidential Martini: Feeling especially thirsty for bling? Up the ante by ordering "The Presidential," a $2,000 martini with real gold flakes.

lighting up your every move. You will feel like you're dancing on water as a computer-generated river runs through the club, complete with dancing jets and fountains struggling to keep up with your moves.

<u>Men</u>: The younger guys tend to congregate on the main floor; from there, it's like moving up in tax brackets. The men get older and richer as you move up each level and make your way past the water booths and then to the cabanas. Once you reach the third floor, it's all in! The skyboxes attract the most select this city has to offer.

STAR GAZING IN THE DESERT

Local porn icon Jenna Jameson didn't spare many details during an interview with Howard Stern about her two Las Vegas trysts with Jenny McCarthy. Jameson says that while at Body English she and McCarthy fogged up the mirrors in a bathroom, and managed to get into some frisky trouble in a VIP booth. Talk about catching an eyeful . . .

6) Body English at Hard Rock: Rock and Roll Decadence

When the Hilton Sisters, Pamela Anderson, Kanye West, or Carmen Electra party the night away in Sin City, they do it at Body English, at the Hard Rock. Since June of 2004, the exclusive club has gained a reputation for throwing Las Vegas' most ridiculous parties that attract the stunningly beautiful and hip Vegas partygoers. As you wait in line in hopes that you will get to descend the staircase leading down into a cavernous underground space of debauchery, keep an eye out for spontaneous celeb appearances.

<u>Entry</u>: Set below the casino floor, the line forms by the hotel check-in area and moves fairly quickly, but as the crowd inside grows to its capacity, only a select few are let in on the action. Most groups of girls will be dressed to kill, making this one of the few venues where being a girl does not guarantee deferential treatment. Get there early, secure a wristband, hit Pink Taco and the Center Bar, then smugly stroll past the late birds.

<u>Facility</u>: Body English boasts a $250,000 Baccarat chandelier above the massive dance floor, black walls with leather booths, mirrors everywhere, and alluring waitresses clad in lingerie, reflecting the club's delicious rock and roll decadence.

<u>Atmosphere</u>: The dance floor is a comfortable size, and leaves you enough room to dance amidst the occasional burst of theatrical smoke. DJs play a variety of hip-hop, house and rock music. Since the place has an elegant presence, the crowd is well dressed and can seem a bit reserved, but look out.

<u>Men</u>: The young guys of the Hard Rock are out to max out their credit cards like true rock stars to impress you. Work it to your advantage. Get some drinks and then hit the dance floor with the girls.

7) JET at Mirage: Modern/Hip

JET Nightclub opened in December 2005 as part of the Mirage's mega-renovation.

<u>Entry</u>: The entrance to JET is located by the hotel check-in. The line can be overwhelming; be sure to talk to a doorman so you don't get stuck with the rookies.

<u>Facility</u>: JET features three distinct rooms, each a unique space, with its own dance floor, DJ booth and sound system. The main room offers the best of rock, hip-hop and popular dance music. The room to your immediate left is dedicated to house music spun by guest and international DJs, while the room on your far right plays an eclectic mix of music ranging from 80s to rock. It is not necessary to secure a table; there is plenty of room along the two bars against the walls of the main room.

<u>Atmosphere</u>: JET has all the bells and whistles to make it cutting-edge. Naturally, the bars serve as a social hang out, but be forewarned that the state of the art lighting system may make the guys look much more fabulous than they really are.

<u>Men</u>: A lot of guys at JET are not traveling solo, and are already with girls when they arrive at the club, so that hot guy you're chatting with may just be filling time until his girl returns from the ladies room. Don't lose hope — if you look hard enough, you just may find a handsome wolf in amongst the sheep.

👄 IT IS GOOD TO BE A GIRL

Don't Pay the Entry Fee: Cover charges? No problem! Long lines and over-the-top cover charges aren't in a girl's vocabulary while in Vegas. Dress for success and carry yourself like a true Vegas Vixen, and you'll have your very own red carpet every step of the way. Girls get in for free at most places in this town, but not everywhere. If you are being hustled for an entry fee, it is not a place you want to go. Paying entry fees is for guys.

> **The N9NE Group: Hip Innovations:** The N9NE Group, founded by entrepreneurs Michael Morton and Scott DeGraff, unveiled several now-legendary venues at Palms when the hotel opened in 2001, including Rain, ghostbar, N9NE Steakhouse, and the boutique Stuff. With the recent resort expansion, N9NE Group once again struts its stuff at Palms Fantasy Tower and the Playboy Club, Moon Nightclub, and Nove Italiano restaurant, some of the hottest new clubs and restaurants in town, cementing Palms reputation as the hippest of the hip.

On the Cusp: Three Runners-Up

These three nightclubs are worth considering once you've burned through the lucky 7.

8) Light at Bellagio: Bottle Service A-Plenty

Light Nightclub started the new wave of nightlife in Vegas and still holds the distinction of being one of Sin City's most opulent destinations. Designed with the dance maniac in mind, Light is distinctively Bellagio, with plush décor and top-notch service.

Entry: Located at the Bellagio's north valet entrance. You will have to fight your way through the crowd just to get the doorman's attention to alert him that you're a group of girls. Don't expect to hear or see a preview of the action inside while you are waiting in line. An escalator will take you up to the party, and when you do finally get through, you can still expect to pay a cover.

Facility: Modeled on the New York nightclub of the same name, Light is decorated in a combination of wood and red-purple drapery, with soft lighting, modern furniture, and a moderate-sized dance floor. A smaller club by Vegas' standards, Light is short on seating, and long on waiting for a drink. The best seat in the house — should you be so lucky — is in the VIP area offering a complete view of the venue.

<u>Atmosphere</u>: Mysterious, posh, exclusive. The furnishings include lush purple couches and curtains. The mysterious vibe stays with you until you leave, as the escalators travel only one way up to the club. You must take an elevator, hidden at the end of another dark corridor, to make your descent back downstairs to reality.

<u>Men</u>: You'll find a good number of women with their own tables here. The in-the-know cocktail waitresses at Light know exactly what they're doing. By filling the tables with their gorgeous and fun-loving girls, they're making their own noble contribution to humanity by helping maintain the eye candy. As the guys watch the parade of enticing gals saunter by, they become even more desperate to get inside the club. The guys that make it in are well worth it and quite tasty we mean, ah, tasteful!

⌇― INSIDER'S REPORT

Got Music?: Any decent club has a sound system that prevents you from carrying on a conversation. Who needs small talk with gorgeous eye candy? If you do need to have a heart-to-heart with your girls, make a trip to the bathroom. The women's bathroom is a peaceful oasis away from the music. The massive mirrors in most nightclub bathrooms allow you to see more angles than you ever knew existed. Need some Advil, a comb, maybe a spritz of Chanel COCO Mademoiselle? It's usually all right before your eyes in nightclub bathrooms. Technically it is free . . . but unless you want your bad karma to outshine your glamorous new MAC lipgloss, be sure to tip the attendant a few dollars.

9) The Whiskey at Green Valley Ranch: Fun Off the Strip

Located off the Strip at Green Valley Ranch, the Whiskey is owned by Rande Gerber, husband of Cindy Crawford. Featuring a lush outdoor area with private cabanas and day beds, flat screen televisions, and a panoramic view of the Las Vegas Strip, The Whiskey is a local hangout perfect for those seeking to avoid the chaos of the Strip, while still indulging in the excitement and action expected from Vegas.

<u>Entry</u>: Entry is free and it's a breeze getting in, even if you have guys in your group. But since The Whiskey is located a good 20 minutes off the Strip, you have to get a ride out there, making it an expensive proposition to get your group there and back.

<u>Facility</u>: A small interior with hip décor; what makes it a hidden gem is that it opens up onto Whiskey Beach, the expansive pool backyard of Green Valley Ranch. The VIP Living Room, located on the left as you enter is a better place to get a table than the exclusive VIP Bedroom, which is hidden behind a wall of mirrors by the dance floor. There is plenty of seating outside, but most people choose to stand and socialize.

<u>Atmosphere</u>: It starts out as a lounge, but turns into a buzz-filled dance club by 11 p.m. The crowd is dressed in casual chic attire, and knows a thing or two about drinking. The club is a magnet for the who's who on the local scene. So, girl-friend, the question is, can you hang with the locals? Keep reading the *Little Red Book* . . . and I'll see you there!

<u>Men</u>: Rande Gerber is close buddies with George Clooney and Brad Pitt so, don't be surprised to bump into a few of *People's* "Sexist Men on Earth" nominees while living it up at this hidden nightspot. But, most of the guys are locals, which means they always have a line about how they can hook you up in Vegas. Ask for a business card, and for a free ride back to your hotel room. We aren't responsible for what happens after that.

We just want you to save some dollars for the late-night sinful shopping sprees!

10) Studio 54 at MGM Grand: Return of the Mega Club

Thankfully, it's not your '70s discotheque. Instead, the nightclub that revolutionized Las Vegas' nightlife scene makes history once again as the hip, ever pulsating, "go to place" for the masses, looking for an all out great time . . . not there's anything wrong with that!

<u>Entry</u>: Studio 54 attracts a huge crowd, so the line can get unmanageable at times. Get there early — around 11 p.m. The entrance is located just off the Strip by the walkway to New York–New York. Management tends to charge everyone at the door, so you might be forced to pay cover here, despite how glamorous you look.

 LUXE LAS VEGAS

The Whiskey Suite: Can't get enough? Make your own after-hours party by checking into the 2,500-square foot Whiskey Suite at Green Valley Ranch. It comes complete with a full bar and bartender, your own personal turntable, a projection wall, and a nightclub quality lighting system. Just be prepared to fork over $5,000 a night!

<u>Facility</u>: It's an enormous venue with multiple levels, so stick close to your friends because it is easy to turn a corner and get lost. This is a true dance nightclub, so expect to get your drinks from the bar (as opposed to table service).

<u>Atmosphere</u>: A three-ring circus. If you're looking for a stereotypical nightclub, then Studio 54 fits the bill with its carefree, festive atmosphere. Confetti cannons and balloon drops contribute to the party vibe, as do dozens of video screens that

show music videos or live action from around the club. This
is one of the few clubs in town that also has male dancers, so
turn the tables and ogle the entertainment! Heads-up — expect to be entertained by acrobats suspended from the ceiling
and by dancers on swings above the dance floor.

<u>Men</u>: The age of the guys may run the gamut, but they do
share one common trait. These guys typically don't want to
spend a lot of money. They come to Studio 54 because it is a
place for the masses, a far cry from the high-end clubs such as
Pure, Tryst and Tao.

📀 ULTRA LOUNGES

Ultra lounges aren't nightclubs and certainly aren't your run of
the mill lounge. Ultra lounges are intimate and swanky bars with
a DJ spinning stiletto-tapping tunes, but without the massive
dance floor to pull your focus — and your body — away from
the hot guy who just cozied up to you on the plush, deco-
inspired settee. Entering a great ultra lounge should make you
feel glamorous, sophisticated, and awash in contemporary elegance like a modern day Audrey Hepburn. Here's the skinny on
ultra lounges, "the new black," in Sin City.

Ultra Lounge	Location	Vibe	Facility	Music	Service	Total
Playboy Club	Palms	10	10	10	10	40
ghostbar	Palms	9	10	10	10	39
MIX	Mandalay Bay	9	10	9	10	38
Tabú	MGM Grand	9	8	10	10	37
Lure	Wynn	10	9	9	8	36
Pussycat Lounge	Caesars	8	8	9	10	35
Tangerine	Treasure Island	9	8	8	9	34
Caramel	Bellagio	8	8	8	9	33
Foundation Room	Mandalay Bay	7	8	6	10	31
Forty Deuce	Mandalay Bay	9	7	7	8	31

The Criteria of a Fabulous Girl's Ultra Lounge

1) <u>Vibe</u>. A cool trendy vibe.

2) <u>Facility</u>. A beautifully decorated room with stylish pods for seating, so you and your group can sit and chat comfortably without others disturbing you.

3) <u>Music</u>. The beats need to be low enough so you can carry on a conversation, but loud enough to keep the energy flowing.

4) <u>Service</u>. Great service is key: You're there to be pampered, not to elbow your way through the writhing masses to get a drink at the bar.

✓ THE *LITTLE RED BOOK*'S LUCKY 7 ULTRA LOUNGES

1) Playboy Club: A Mansion in the Sky

What happens when you mix part ultra lounge, part casino, and a splash of Robert Cavalli-designed Bunny costumes? Playboy Cub: the best ultra lounge for women in Vegas. 50102 may be the room number to the Hugh Hefner suite in the main tower at Palms, but there's a new home away from home for Hef and the *Girls Next Door.* Although the Bunnies have been in hiding for 20 years, when Hef decided to take his famous club out of storage, he looked to Las Vegas and the Palms Casino Resort to create what is currently the only Playboy Club in the World.

Vibe: Upon entering the Playboy Club with its rich, seductive blend of red, black, brown, gold, and chrome, your eyes will be torn between the gorgeous hostess Bunnies and the dramatic Diamond Bar built with 10,000 diamond-shaped crystals. Check out the collage wallpaper in the bathrooms featuring every centerfold from the last twenty-five years

---

📷 STAR GAZING IN THE DESERT

Egged on by ghostbar VIP host Marko Greisen, Kelly Clarkson and her gal pals sang her hit "Since You've Been Gone" when the fireworks show ended, New Year's 2006.

Vanilla Ice, after hearing chants of "Ice, Ice, Ice" at ghostbar, picked up a large bucket of ice cubes and poured it over his head in front of a camera crew filming VH1's "The Surreal World: Fame Games," hosted by Robin Leach. Also partying at Palms was rap mogul Suge Knight. An accidental meeting between Knight and Vanilla Ice might have caused an Ice melt-down in the desert! In the early 1990s, Vanilla Ice accused Knight of dangling him out of a high-rise balcony, forcing him to sign over royalties

---

adorned in glowing jewels. Yearning for an adrenaline high? Playboy Club is the only Vegas ultra lounge where you can revel in a hot streak at blackjack and roulette in between martinis and kanoodling with "Mr.Right Now" on a lush, cushy sofa. You can also choose to sit on low-profile lounge furniture or on higher chairs while gambling thanks to the hydraulic lifts in the leather and granite gaming tables!

Facility: It's like walking into a modern Playboy Mansion in the sky! The top three floors of the Fantasy Tower, which include the Playboy Club, Moon, and Nove, are what one would call a one-stop *sexy* shop; every detail is perfect. Almost the entire south wall of the main room is covered with plasmas displaying Playboy footage, including centerfold shoots, magazine covers, and star-studded events at the Mansion. The east wall, behind a 40-foot bling-bling Bunny Bar, is floor-to-ceiling glass, offering views of the Strip that will wow even the most seasoned Vegas Vixen. To the left of the entrance, you can snuggle with your new best friend by the fireplace in the VIP room. Another ultra-luxe VIP room is outfitted for celebrity poker and contains two nostalgic Playboy pinball machines.

Music: The DJs know how to spin a solid, steady, smooth vibe to keep you energized through the night, but they never overdo it, since there are gamblers on the premises hard at work on making money for themselves.

Service: Bottom line: Expect to be treated even better than an A-lister. And yes, the waitresses *do* do the Bunny Dip when they serve you drinks; think of it as a nice abdominal workout to take home with you!

2) ghostbar at Palms: The Ultra Lounge for Ultra People
High above the glittering expanse of Vegas, the 8,000 square foot ghostbar is a sultry and sophisticated indoor-outdoor lounge and sky deck on the 55th floor of Palms. It is the ultra

lounge for the ultra crowd, so get ready for some unbelievable views of Vegas — and we aren't just referring to the Bellagio fountains. Enough said!

<u>Vibe</u>: ghostbar is where the famous and soon to be famous congregate for relaxation and heavy duty socializing. The sleek, space-age, ultra-chic décor enhances the hipper-than-thou vibe. Don't be surprised to run into every Playmate, pro athlete, and Hollywood A-lister under the sun.

<u>Facility</u>: Sleek, dramatic and exciting. As the chrome elevator doors open, you're ushered into a seductive adult playpen boasting twelve-foot floor-to-ceiling windows, and ultra-contemporary lounging furniture in an ethereal color scheme of silver, white, greens and grays. Outdoors, the sky deck, featuring posh seating areas, provides a nearly 360-degree view of Vegas at its most glittering, with a glass inset in the floor offering a view straight down — not for the vertigo inclined!

<u>Music</u>: A 30-foot ghost-shaped soffit in the ceiling changes colors as a DJ spins an eclectic music mix. The beats get louder as the evening progresses and the crowd from Alize (the sizzling restaurant above) follows the music to a post-meal cocktail.

Service: Service is unbelievably good, even when you find yourself vying with the competition for a comfortable place to sit. The bartenders are on top of their game; you'll be sure to get a cocktail quickly, and with a smile. Specialty cocktails include champagne concoctions and the signature "Ghostini," as well as an extensive champagne selection and a hand-picked wine list, with high-end wines by the glass. But this is your ultimate getaway, so live large and go for the bottle!

3) Mix at Mandalay Bay: The View from the Top

Located on the top floor of THEhotel at Mandalay Bay, Mix is part ultra lounge, part nightclub, and 100 percent hot! The views are spectacular, the vibe just right, and the décor sleek and sexy.

Entry: The entrance is located in the THEhotel tower of Mandalay Bay, past the race and sportsbook and the "Mama Mia" showroom. Lines form at the bottom of the tower by the elevators, but the staff funnels the crowd fairly quickly. They usually charge everyone a cover, so play your cards right.

Facility: Mix is bedecked entirely in dark brown faux leather from floor to ceiling, with aluminum tables lit from beneath with a glowing orange light. A pulsating fiber optic Milky Way streams across the "sky." The effect is arresting: You'll feel warm, seductive, as if bathed in an aphrodisiac, so by all means exhibit caution — or throw that caution to the wind — while functioning under the Mix influence! If you can drag yourself away, there's an outdoor patio that runs almost the entire length of the lounge with large lounge beds perfect for kicking back or gazing at the spectacular views of the Strip.

Atmosphere: Mix is all about sipping that delicious white chocolate martini versus hard partying. This music is not overbearing, but provides an ongoing energy, so you'll be poised to scope out potential friends, make new friends, or invite your new friends over to your lounging area to play.

<u>Men</u>: Fabulous! You'll most likely encounter young to middle-aged businessmen staying at THEhotel. These are the type of guys that enjoy a night out, but don't want to fight for a cocktail at a pedestrian club packed with throngs of people. The Mix scene is mellow and low key, so if you're looking for action and spot an attractive guy, you may have to reapply your MAC lipgloss and make that first move.

4) Tabú at MGM Grand: Model Central

Tabú bills itself as Vegas' first "ultra lounge," and continues to uphold its chic, cosmopolitan vibe — but really, when anyone talks about Tabú they're talking about the models. Yes, gorgeous, sophisticated, whip-lash inducing models, dressed to kill, serve you cocktails as you sit back reveling in beauty in all its shapes and forms. If they weren't all so nice and accommodating, and so deliriously happy to be serving you at Tabú, they could be downright intimidating!

<u>Vibe</u>: Tabú is all about VIPs in an intimate setting. Before midnight, Tabú is a social gathering, with people conversing over their first cocktail of the evening. As the night grows on and libidos loosen, the music gets livelier and girls start dancing on and around the tables. Join in on the fun; you only live once, and anything goes at Tabú. If you choose Tabú for a pre- or post-party cocktail, you will quickly decide to scrap any of your other plans to make an entire evening of it.

<u>Facility</u>: A table is a must at Tabú; it absolutely, unequivocally makes the experience, especially since there isn't much space to sit or stand at the bar. Choose from a couple different seating areas: On the left as you walk in you'll see tables against the wall. These tables are set back from the sound system, so the noise level is not unbearable. In the middle of the room are the groups of tables where the famous active graphics bounce from surface to surface. Trust us: watching the movement is a cool experience. There's also the VIP room, set back on the right hand side of the room, and then again — who are we kidding — just grab a seat with some men that have already purchased a couple of bottles, and make a night out of it!

<u>Music</u>: A comfortable level of European-influenced vocal house music allows guests to carry on conversations while taking in the scene. From classic lounge tunes with a twist, played earlier in the night, to the more progressive vocal blends featured later in the evening, the eclectic music encourages movement, mingling and dancing — despite the fact that there is no dance floor!

<u>Service</u>: Fine bottle service and some of the best signature cocktails in Sin City. Bottles are beautifully presented in a block of carved ice, with a tray of drink garnishes to match your choice of alcohol.

5) Lure at Wynn Las Vegas: Elegance

Ensconced in white gauze and candlelight, Lure is one of the most beautiful ultra lounges on the Strip, and an elegant respite from the frenetic nightclub scene. This is the place to go when you are in need of being catered to like a queen in surroundings that are as sophisticated as any "It" place you'll find gracing the pages of *Travel and Leisure*. The cocktails are pitch-perfect, and the people watching is some of the best you'll find in Vegas.

📷 STAR GAZING IN THE DESERT

Sir, Yes, Sir!: *Desperate Housewives* star Nicollette Sheridan held a red rose and sipped Dom Perignon while kissing boyfriend Michael Bolton during her appearance with the Pussycat Dolls. She wore a military outfit and wished the troops worldwide a Happy Valentine's Day.

<u>Vibe</u>: Lure is all about giving yourself over to cocktails and conversation in the most high end and graceful of surroundings. When you first walk in, you may feel horrifyingly underdressed in your trendiest jeans, halter top and high-heeled sandals. But don't be intimidated. As you nestle your way up to the bar on the left side of the lounge, you'll feel thoroughly at ease amidst the opulence. The fashionable and fun crowd that makes this ultra lounge their home away from home exude such an infectious friendliness that you'll be sitting at a VIP table in no time.

<u>Facility</u>: Gorgeous and sexy. The opalescent décor is sleek and modern; the rectangular room is accented with sleek white curtains, and candlelight emanates from the circular VIP booths and low marble tables. Mahogany wood and mirrors form the backdrop of the long narrow bar. The back of the club opens to a small patio and fire pit outside.

Music: The music is for lounging, not dancing. Modish beats fill the room and serve as a seductive backdrop to your conversation.

Service: The cocktail servers are dressed in gowns and will take care of you in style as they cater to your every whim. Savor signature cocktails such as the Dream, the Lure Martini, and the Vanity. And, if you wish to sip on absolute decadence, indulge in a $12,000 bottle of Courvoisier L'Esprit — an individually numbered, designer bottle containing cognac dating from 1802 to 1910. Bling!

6) Pussycat Lounge at Caesars Palace: Doll Me Up

The Pussycat Dolls bring their world-renowned show to Vegas at the Pussycat Dolls Lounge, located next to PURE. The Dolls climb to the stage, swing from the ceiling, and even pop out of a giant champagne glass to delight crowds with their aggressively sexy blend of song, movement and fashion. If you're lucky, you could catch Pamela Anderson, Fergie, Paris Hilton, Christina Aguilera, Gwen Stefani, and Carmen Electra — all of whom have graced the Pussycat stage as celebrity "Guest Dolls."

💋 IT'S GOOD TO BE A GIRL

Get Your Drinks for Free: Have a VIP Host seat you at a table where the guys have bought a bottle. Just stand around the table area and it won't be long before a host approaches you. (The VIP host gets tips from the guys to bring girls over to join their table.) When you're seated, be nice to the little guys — even if they aren't on your level — and schmooze them up while you're sipping your cocktail, before moving on to the next challenge. Remember: You can always go back to the bar and another host will grab you for a different table filled with a fresh crop of guys. Keep doing this until you find the group of guys that are worthy of your attention.

<u>Vibe</u>: Warm it up or cool it off. The Pussycat Dolls grace the lounge Tuesday thru Saturday beginning at 10:30 p.m. until 4:00 a.m., with shows running every half hour. Take your pen and paper for notes on fashion (fishnets, bustiers, leather accessories, lacey bras) and moves (undulating, hip swinging, breast heaving acrobatics)! Once the show ends, it is time to cool back down and enjoy conversation with your friends.

<u>Facility</u>: The sexy song and dance group performs in a multi million-dollar space designed exclusively for the Dolls. Show up early for a prime table by the swing. (Yes, any doll/doll action you can imagine using a swing as a prop, probably has and will happen!)

<u>Music</u>: In between sets, the DJ plays eclectic music including a few of the original Pussycat Dolls hits, "Don't you wish your boyfriend was hot like me. . . ."

⚷ INSIDER'S REPORT

Play it Smart: Always keep tabs on your drink. It doesn't matter how gorgeous your desert cutie may be; he may have an unwanted surprise for you. Always get a new drink if you've left yours unattended. Never assume that just because a vodka tonic is clear, it's safe.

<u>Service</u>: Expect the PURE crowd to flow in and out of the room, creating a controlled but energized chaos. Take advantage, as everyone is in search of their very own doll!

7) Tangerine at Treasure Island (TI): Sweetening Nightlife

We can't figure out why this ultra lounge is called Tangerine. True, there is an overall orange hue about the place, but the walls behind the table area are draped in white cloth, burlesque dancers prance about, and there's nothing tropical about it. But even with a fruity name, Tangerine is a great place to go with your friends. Bombshell Carmen Electra is the unofficial Tangerine muse; she loves the place and even makes surprise burlesque appearances to tease and tantalize guests.

Vibe: No frat boys here — just a well-heeled crowd out to enjoy the night. Tangerine is one ultra lounge where you don't need a table, as there's plenty of room to mingle, schmooze with the big boys, and check out the scene.

Facility: Overlooking Sirens' Cove and the steamy Sirens of TI performances, this sweet spot is designed with subdued orange, amber and earth-tone hues, and features an indoor lounge and outdoor deck, each with its own DJ. Inside, on top of the bar, burlesque dancers periodically shimmy to a three-piece band, wearing anything from evening attire to lingerie. The indoor lounge gets crowded, so take a break, go outdoors and grab a seat along the bar on the right hand side, where it's easier to get a drink than at the main bar.

Music: Although the club can only handle 500 people, it's one of the few ultra lounges that can still accommodate dancing. The DJs spin tunes between the sensual burlesque revues.

Service: The bartenders are well trained and can usually keep up with the crowd's demands. Since the indoor bar is sunken, it can be a little difficult to get the bartender's attention.

On the Cusp: Three Runners-Up

These two ultra lounges are worth considering once you've burned through the Lucky 7.

8) Carâmel at Bellagio: Step into Classy

A step away from the casino action, Carâmel is a luxurious ultra lounge, perfect for relaxing and unwinding, while offering the best aspects of a high-energy club. Its doors open at 5 p.m., making it the ideal starting point for a night on the town.

Vibe: Smoldering. Carâmel oozes mystery and seduction. The minute you enter, you'll feel your embers slowly burning over the beautiful riches (hot men, stunning women, to-die-for décor) surrounding you. It's the place to see Paris & Nicky Hilton, Ashton Kutcher & Demi Moore, David Arquette, Nicolette Sheridan, and Jamie-Lynn DiScala.

Facility: Like *buttah*: rich and creamy. The caramel-colored leather couches are at a premium because of the intimate size of the lounge.

Music: The music drowns out the noise from the neighboring casino and paves the way for a memorable night.

Service: If you're able to get a seat, you'll find the cocktail service fast, attentive and friendly. If you're left standing, you'll have to fight your way to the bar, which can be more of a challenge than you've bargained for.

📸 STAR GAZING IN THE DESERT

Who said only Tom Cruise can jump on things and make headlines? Jennifer Aniston jumped on the dance stage at Ivan Kane's Forty Deuce and rocked the house with a dance show for boyfriend Vince Vaughn, who earlier performed in his *Wild West Comedy Show* at Mandalay Bay.

9) Foundation Room at Mandalay Bay: Exclusive Relaxation

Foundation Room is a VIP member club, meaning it's exclusive, upscale, and because of its "members only" policy, naturally screens out the riffraff. It also means Foundation Room is a perfect sanctuary for women. The club is only open to non-members on Monday, but for a group of unescorted women, they'll roll out the carpet for you any day of the week!

Vibe: An ultra-exotic, intimate, and high-end hideaway that may feel a bit formidable, but after one drink you'll have taken to the role of pampered princess so well you'll be ready to call the butler for your belongings so you can move right in.

Facility: Think of a richly appointed penthouse apartment with multiple rooms in all shapes and sizes, an intimate dining room, and a main lounge with fireplace, surrounded by comfortable sofas. It's rarely teeming with partyers, so it's unlikely you'll ever have to fight for a drink no matter where you sit.

Music: They only house a DJ on big nights or special occasions. Otherwise, the place is extremely chill, with light house music playing in the background.

Service: They cater to please. Those who do choose Foundation Room spend freely, and the staff fervently devotes attention to its customers.

10) Ivan Kane's Forty Deuce at Mandalay Bay: Burlesque Bombshell

A small burlesque lounge evoking a low tech, retro, striptease feel. Ever see the movie or play, *Gypsy*? Regulars at the Hollywood and Vegas clubs include Uma Thurman, Sandra Bullock, George Clooney, Kate Hudson, Naomi Watts, Courteney and David Arquette, Mick Jagger, Demi Moore, and Sting.

<u>Vibe</u>: Think of the evening as a form of extended foreplay. Continuous sexy burlesque shows are performed nightly, and the women are red hot with moves to keep the crowd turned on. Feel like playing the role of bawdy burlesque babe? A couture costume lingerie collection is available at "Champagne Suzy," the lounge's saucy on-site boutique.

<u>Facility</u>: This sultry spot features a low bar, plush lounge chairs, intimate tiered seating and cocktail tables with small, seductive lamps creating a sexy, "smoky" vibe. Hand picked dancers from around the world strut their stuff, sans nudity, several times a night.

<u>Music</u>: A live three-piece bump and grind combo — stand up bass, drums and a wailing sax — accompanies the ladies as they seduce the crowd. In between each performance, a DJ keeps the crowd on its feet.

<u>Service</u>: The service is great early in the evening when the club is not yet packed. By the time 1 a.m. rolls around, it's tough for the cocktail servers to make their way through the throngs.

Ultra Lounges & Nightclubs: A Fabulous Combination

Many of the top *Little Red Book* ultra lounges are located near our top rated nightclubs. It makes a great night to visit an ultra lounge early in your evening, and then hit the nightclub when you feel like dancing. Some great ultra lounge — nightclub combinations:

✣ Caesars Palace: Shadow Bar or Pussycat Dolls Lounge — PURE

* Bellagio: Carâmel — Light
* Palms: ghostbar — Rain
* MGM Grand: Tabú — Studio 54
* Wynn: Lure — Tryst

 # BARS

A Vegas bar is more relaxed than a nightclub and ultra lounge, but much more fun than your local neighborhood watering hole. Vegas bars are full of young people less concerned with image than with just having a great time.

> ### 🔑 INSIDER REPORT
>
> **Center Bars — What are They?:** Fun, fast and fabulous! Located in the middle of the casino, these bars have video poker and are a quick place to grab a drink for busy women on the go, and a convenient meeting place for your group. If you plan to spend the night gambling, or just gawking, the center bar is a great place to congregate. They're open 24 hours a day.

The Criteria of a Fabulous Girl's Bar

1) Fun Atmosphere. A bar needs to have a lively fun atmosphere with an infectious energy.

2) Entertainment. Entertainment is key to keep the party going.

3) Fun Guys. A good bar needs to have the right guys to keep things animated and interesting — not a bunch of losers sitting around and getting drunk.

4) Layout. A good bar layout has an area for socializing, as well as an area to people watch for sumptuous eye candy.

Bar	Location	Atmosphere	Entertainment	Fun Guys	Layout	Total
Center Bar	Hard Rock Hotel	10	9	8	9	36
Parasol Up/ Parasol Down	Wynn Las Vegas	10	9	8	9	36
Coyote Ugly	NY-NY	10	9	8	6	33
Voodoo Lounge	Rio	9	8	7	8	33
Fontana Bar	Bellagio	8	8	7	9	33
Shadow Bar	Caesars Palace	8	8	7	8	32
The Island Bar	Palms	10	8	6	7	31
Beauty Bar	Downtown	9	8	6	8	31
Rainbow Bar & Grill	Next to Hard Rock	8	8	5	7	29
Ice House	Downtown	8	6	6	6	26

1) Center Bar at Hard Rock: The Social Magnet

The Center Bar is truly the center of the action at Hard Rock. The bar is large enough to fit a couple hundred people, and on any given night it does!

Atmosphere: Hip and hot, with rock and roll music always pumping – but never too loud for conversation.

Entertainment: The characters at the Center Bar *are* the entertainment; it's one big visual fantasy feast. You may also spot some potential on the casino floor from the great, elevated view.

Fun Guys: Lot's of young good-looking guys flock to the Center Bar every night. They're a bit more laid back and not as sophisticated as the men at Body English.

<u>Layout</u>: Easy to access, with four entrances from the casino floor. That means you can also make a quick escape, if needed! The only seats are along the bar, but you don't want to sit down as your back will be against the action.

2) Parasol Up/Parasol Down at Wynn Las Vegas:
Two Bars in One

A fanciful, elegant, dreamlike collection of upside-down parasols mark the location of the hotel's two center bars. You'll find Parasol Down on the Lake Level, embraced by two circular escalators. Take the escalator to the Casino Level for tea or cocktails at Parasol Up.

<u>Atmosphere</u>: Parasol Up is a perfect place to sip a dirty martini and listen to the grand piano; it's elegant yet relaxed. Parasol Down is more casual, with a view of the Wynn water show.

<u>Entertainment</u>: Parasol Up has excellent piano players playing classical and jazz music throughout the night. The music provides a refined backdrop for drinks and dialogue. Parasol Down has no music, but every 15 minutes the water show puts on a cool sensory experience for your eyes and ears.

⌐ INSIDER'S REPORT

Restaurants With Bars: The trendier restaurants in Vegas also have superb bars for grabbing a cocktail. You don't have to dine at these restaurants to be part of their bar scene, but you can snack on an appetizer if you wish.

- N9NE at Palms
- TAO Lounge and Asian Bistro at The Venetian
- FIX at Bellagio
- Nobu at Hard Rock Hotel
- Daniel Boulud Brasserie at Wynn Las Vegas
- Red Square at Mandalay Bay

<u>Fun Guys</u>: Start your evening at Parasol Up. The Wynn crowd tends to enjoy the finer things in life, and the people-watching at Parasol Up will be one of the highlights of your trip. Parasol Down is the place to go once you've met that special someone and want to have an intimate drink, and an even more intimate conversation.

<u>Layout</u>: Since it's at the casino level, a larger crowd congregates at Parasol Up. A hostess will seat you, and even if it takes a few minutes for a table, it's a better alternative then going directly to the bar for a drink. At Parasol Down, you can more easily snag a table without actually being seated, or you can ask the hostess for a table outdoors on the patio, which opens up on the Wynn Lake and water show. These tables are difficult to secure, so expect to tip the hostess.

3) Coyote Ugly at New York New–York: Howl at the Moon

It's a drinking bar . . . and the women have the upper hand! For anyone wishing to dispute that, Coyote Ugly is populated with dozens of beautiful "Coyotes" to entertain guests from behind and on top of the bar — dancing, tough talking and spraying the crowd (and each other) down with water. More than 1,000 applicants competed for these coveted "Coyote" positions, and they are some of the sexiest, sassiest and most talented women Sin City has to offer.

<u>Atmosphere</u>: This wild watering hole offers a raucous party seven days a week. Like the New York City original, Coyote Ugly Las Vegas is designed to look like a southern bar that has weathered years of hard partying, decorated with Southern garage sale finds and well-worn wood.

<u>Entertainment</u>: This is a place where anyone can lose their inhibitions, and where you'll find the most reserved women jumping up and dancing on the bar with the friendly Coyotes. If you're the adventurous type, feel free to offer your bra to be showcased from the rafters. Only women are allowed to

dance on the bar, .and will be cheered on by the guys who seem pretty content to watch the talents of the other species. So, what do you have to lose? Climb up and give it the old college try.

<u>Fun Guys</u>: This is a bar where you may want to go with a group of guys, since most of the guys you'll meet are ogling the dancing bartenders and female customers, or concentrating on drinking.

<u>Layout</u>: There are no seats, just standing room only. It gets packed, so try to get close to the bar or you'll end up pushing your way through the crowd to get a drink, which will take awhile but damn, the wait is fun!

4) Voodoo Lounge at Rio: Getting Down on the Roof
Located on the roof of Rio, Voodoo is a nice mix of lounge party and outside dance floor, high above the Vegas Strip. Voodoo is the one place that offers the look and feel of a nightclub without being one.

<u>Atmosphere</u>: A non-intimidating atmosphere where everyone is out to have a good time. The staircase, which begins on the 51st floor upper level of the Voodoo Lounge, and descends in a wild curve around the dance floor on the 50th floor lower level observation deck outside the Voodoo Café, is the hottest place to make a grand entrance and soak up dramatic views of the city. It's a long and winding way down, so grip that ironwork railing like a life raft, especially if you're wearing stilettos with pencil thin heels, or if you've had a few to many.

<u>Entertainment</u>: The sinuous staircase features platforms for go-go dancers, a DJ booth, and a special seating area directly on the staircase. A house band plays music inside the bar, while outside a DJ spins dance music.

<u>Fun Guys</u>: You will find a mix of businessmen and single younger guys. This is a great place to meet men for a casual evening of fun.

<u>Layout</u>: It's easy to find a seat inside the bar before 11 p.m.; any later, they 're all taken. There are no table reservations here, so if you see something open up, grab it. On the outside patio, most people hang on the railing or stand in groups to socialize.

5) Fontana Bar at Bellagio: Lounge Lizards

Right off the posh casino floor, this lounge has an inside area with lounge singers and an outdoor patio with the best view of the Bellagio Fountains. When looking for a place to dance without going to a nightclub, Fontana Bar is your place to gather the girls.

<u>Atmosphere</u>: High end. The crowd is relaxed and tranquil, and once you get past any needless intimidation about being in the elegant and refined setting of the Bellagio, it's easy to let you hair down.

<u>Entertainment</u>: The best lounge singers in Vegas perform here every night. Their top performer, Dian Diaz, entertains be-

Vegas Vixen

Girls Can Enjoy Gentlemen's Clubs Too: They're not just for the guys anymore. The better gentlemen's clubs are as festive as nightclubs and welcome women as much as they do men. You might even take a few pointers on how to pole dance! Stick with these sure things:

- Seamless
- Spearmint Rhino
- Scores
- Sapphire
- Olympic Garden

tween 10 p.m. and 1 a.m. (She sings like Gloria Estefan, and looks like Shania Twain.) In between the band sets, top-40 dance music pumps through the sound system.

Fun Guys: The men that end up at Fontana usually aren't looking to socialize, but rather are guys looking for an upscale place to drink and enjoy some entertainment. After a couple hours, you will see some mingling between the sexes, and at that point, the dance floor ignites.

Layout: The layout is refreshingly airy and open with plentiful seats inside the bar. Wait in the short line at the hostess stand to be seated, and ask for a table in the back: Those in the front are adjacent to the dance floor, making it difficult to see the singer, due to all the writhing bodies in front of you. When you want to get away from the music, head out to the patio and enjoy the desert air and Bellagio Fountains.

6) Shadow Bar at Caesars Palace: Succulent Silhouettes

To put it simply: Shadow Bar leads the pack of bar destinations because it's located next to PURE, Pussycat Dolls

Lounge, and is adjacent to the Coliseum theatre and Bobby Flay's Mesa Grill.

> ### ⊶ INSIDER"s REPORT
>
> **Don't Let Yourself Be Mistaken for a Working Girl:** Yep — we said it! Vixens such as yourselves complain bitterly that men in Vegas think they're working girls, and offer them money for sex. Don't sit at a bar by yourself after 10 p.m. at night, and *don't* drink hot tea or coffee at a casino bar. These are dead giveaways that a girl is "working."

<u>Atmosphere</u>: Exciting. Sensual naked shadow dancers are silhouetted through sheer backlit screens, and award-winning flair bartenders juggle bottles, toss limes, twirl glasses, pour multiple glasses and do backflips as they prepare your favorite cocktail. Need we say more?

<u>Entertainment</u>: A DJ plays party tunes while the dancers dance and the bartenders put on a show. The entertainment *is* the whole Shadow Bar experience.

<u>Fun Guys</u>: If you're seated at a table, the fun guys won't approach you, but if you're at the bar, expect some conversation. The men at Shadow Bar are more hip and better dressed than those at other Vegas bars because of its location in the epicenter of the action.

<u>Layout</u>: There are plenty of seats early in the evening, but if you have more than four in your group, you could have a hard time finding enough chairs together. By 11 p.m. every seat is taken, but by that time you better be having so much fun hanging out at the bar that it shouldn't matter!

7) Island Bar at Palms: Visual Fantasy Feast

If the lines at ghostbar, Rain, Moon, or the Playboy Club are just too long, hit the Island Bar at Palms. Located in the middle of the table game area, there's always a social scene and a hip crowd eager to grab a drink.

<u>Atmosphere</u>: Although it's a small lively bar, it's still a far cry from other Palms venues. Grabbing a drink or two is fun; just don't make a whole night out of it!

<u>Entertainment</u>: Socialize with the hot bartenders, wait staff, customers and random Vegas characters, and you'll be sure to be entertained!

<u>Fun Guys</u>: There are tons of guys at Palms looking to have a good time, and it may be tough for them to get into the nightclub and ultra lounges, so Center Bar — here they come! Expect catcalls from the touristy guys walking through; only the confident men will actually start a conversation with you.

<u>Layout</u>: A smaller center bar that makes for some close encounters with the opposite sex. It's elevated from the casino floor, of which you have a view if you're parked along the front, as well as a great view of everyone entering and exiting the property. If you camp out along the back wall, you'll have some space for a conversation.

On the Cusp: Three Runners-Up

These three hangouts are worth considering once you've burned through the Lucky 7.

 The Lost-and-Found Tour

Many of these venues are lined up next to one another, making for one large, roving party. You'll find that many groups of guys wander from one place to another, searching for a good time. Use this to your advantage. Say hello to a guy when you leave a venue. When you see him again, use the line "Didn't I see you at ..." It gives you a reason to talk to him, and you're no longer an unknown. As if you ever were!

---

8) Beauty Bar in Downtown Vegas: Manicures and Martinis

Located a block off Fremont Street in Downtown Vegas, Beauty Bar brings a hip vintage scene to downtown. The beauty salon-themed nightspot mixes martinis and manicure "demonstrations" while offering a trendy retro-cool alternative to the endless parade of masculine sports bars.

Atmosphere: Home of the original "martini manicure happy hour," you'll find a mix of Vegas locals, artist types, and young visitors staying downtown. Pretty much everyone fits in here, no matter what the attire.

Entertainment: Opens daily at 5 p.m., but DJs don't start playing until 9 p.m. on most nights. Music is mostly laid-back electro house designed to keep the energy flowing.

Fun Guys: Attracts more of an arty intellectual type than the typical downtown reveler. You might actually engage in a conversation about the latest Woody Allen film, rather than smiling blandly at annoying pick up lines.

Layout: A gaming-free joint outfitted with '50s salon décor —

THREE SAFETY TIPS FOR NIGHTTIME:

Keep one eye on the neon as you throw caution to the desert wind.

1) <u>Hold your purse close to your chest</u>: Never place your purse on the floor in the bathroom or on a highly placed rack. You'll be surprised how fast you sober up when your entire life is stolen from right underneath you.

2) <u>The house always wins</u>: If you open a tab at the bar, don't make the mistake of letting the entire club know. You'll be shocked at how quickly you become everyone's new best friend!

3) <u>Sex, drugs, and rock 'n' roll</u>: We can't say it enough — Always keep an eye on your drink and never accept a drink from a shady guy or a jealous bitch.

including old-school hair dryer seats. The bartenders are well trained, but as the crowd grows, it becomes harder to get a drink. Stick with the easy to make cocktails or wine as the night wears on, or the bartender might look the other way the next time you sidle up to the bar.

9) Rainbow Bar & Grill by Hard Rock: Not Just Bikers

It's rock and roll, and the Rainbow Bar & Grill rocks hard. A landmark on Hollywood's Sunset Strip, the two-level rock spot has come to Vegas, located across the street from the Hard Rock Hotel & Casino.

<u>Atmosphere</u>: The Rainbow provides great service and excellent food and drinks in a casual environment. Rock and roll clientele can be seen slurping mouthfuls of famous chicken soup in between tequila shots.

<u>Entertainment</u>: Steady rock and roll music until the DJs bring on the mash-up and top-40 tunes at 10 p.m.

<u>Fun Guys</u>: Hit or miss crowd. Guys seem to pour into this place at around 2 a.m., when they're drunk, horny, and searching for some late night action. The silver lining is that you can always roll across the street for the some hotties at Hard Rock Hotel.

<u>Layout</u>: Bar seating gets filled quickly, but the patio comes to the rescue and becomes the choice for drinks and socializing.

10) Ice House in Downtown Vegas: Ice Deco

This swanky bar, located in the arts district of downtown Vegas, is a bit removed from the action, but only a short cab ride away from Fremont Street.

Its location works to its advantage, as people consider it a destination, rather than a place to stumble into for no good reason.

THE SEXIER SIDE OF NIGHTLIFE

Seamless in Depth: Vegas' nightclubs have been climbing the sexiness ladder, with many go-go dancers just one bra strap away from revealing their ta-tas. Sin City's strip clubs have upped the ante with more "wow" factors in recent months. Basically, the two nightlife industries have been converging for some time now, which makes this high-tech, high-class, female-friendly gentlemen's club long overdue. From noon to 4 a.m., Seamless functions as an upscale topless cabaret, and then transforms — Cinderella-like — at 4 a.m. into an after-hours ultra lounge that's still sexy but not as overt in its displays of our gender's charms as it is earlier in the evening. This is a high roller lounge, and something you probably can't experience back home. Take advantage of the opportunity to broaden your horizons and enter past a seven-foot tall martini glass with its own bathing beauty, into 10,000 square feet of titillating decadence.

Atmosphere: Ice House has an Art Deco feel with palm trees, white stucco, colored lighting and vintage photographs of Vegas. The bar is made of ice . . . so your drinks stay refreshingly cool.

Entertainment: Local DJs spin downstairs from 9 p.m. to 3 a.m. Before 9 p.m., Ice House is solely an after work spot for the downtown workforce.

<u>Fun Guys</u>: Lots of Vegas locals: mostly businessmen leaving work and looking to tie one on with the boys. When midnight approaches, a new group of men descend: mostly edgy artist types with plenty of tattoos. You know the type!

<u>Layout</u>: If you want to socialize, sit around the bar rather than the large tables on the right. If the weather is nice, be sure to check out the patios on each level.

☾ LATE NIGHT

Want to make sure you fill every last sinful hour? There's something to do, eat or see any time of day or night in Sin City, but knowing the salon that's open past 7 p.m. or where to get a martini, newspaper, and French toast at 4 a.m. is critical information. East coasters: your body clocks have been warned!

Late Night Partying

1) <u>Seamless</u>: A gentlemen's club . . . most of the time. At 4 a.m., they move the strippers to the VIP area, and convert the room into an ultra lounge with top Vegas DJs It's located off the Strip by the Orleans casino, so expect to cab it.

2) <u>Rainbow Bar & Grill</u>: Rainbow has an after hours party where you'll find seven guys for every girl. Expect to be hit on time after time: choose wisely and enjoy!

3) <u>Drai's</u>: Located in the Barbary Coast, DJs play deep house and trance music to a packed dance floor.

4) <u>Peppermill Fireside Lounge</u>: A swanky, old-school lounge, Peppermill is a favorite if you want a drink in a relaxed environment — so relaxed that you'll see couples making out in the back corners.

5) <u>Empire Ballroom</u>: Located next to the MGM Grand and across from the Monte Carlo, the ballroom is really a large club with a stage for bands, that turns into a huge after hours party after 2 a.m.

Sleeping

Vegas is one of the few places in the world where your reality is more exciting than your dreams at night, but if your evening has lost its mojo, then call it a night and get your beauty rest.

1. <u>Don't stay up just to stay up</u>: If you have hit the wall and are just staying up to stay up, then hit the sheets. People tend to make more out of the Vegas "late night" than there really is.

2. <u>Sleeping is free</u>: In Vegas, sleeping is one of the only available blocks of time when you won't be spending any money. Take advantage of it.

Putting It All Together

Remember: women have the power in Vegas; the nightclubs need you more than you need them; always work your magic to bypass the line, get in free, and score some cocktails. These golden rules will help you save some Benjamins for those sinful shopping sprees. We have your back covered . . . literally!

Chapter 9

SHOWS – LIVE FROM LAS VEGAS

✶ ....

Las Vegas is touted the world over as the *entertainment capital* of America, and it proudly lives up to its reputation. As a Mecca for performers and for those seeking to be entertained, Vegas offers more opportunities and more venues for entertainment around the clock. First, know what type of entertainment you are seeking; next, consult The *Little Red Book*; and voilà, fun happens.

 ## SHOWTIME IN VEGAS

Shows make Las Vegas the legend that it is. Vegas has evolved into a fascinating and tempting smorgasbord of delights for the members of your party who are of a mind to see something astounding, spectacular, or unique. Prices, venues, and performers change quickly in a town where today's hottest entertainers are tomorrow's old news, so do your homework before you get on the plane.

Why Go to a Show?

A Vegas show is sheer spectacle, on a scale unimaginable anywhere else. Contrary to myth, shows are not something to do because you have no other plans: Vegas shows are a fabulous ingredient to the ultimate girl's getaway.

Three Reasons to Hit a Show

1. <u>A Show is a Great Diversion</u>: Although everything else you do in Vegas can be done at any hour, most shows are only available at night (a few also offer matinees). A good show is a fabulous way to hit the town and a perfect event to plan your evening around. Follow it up with a late dinner and drinks, dancing at a nightclub, and your evening is a class act.

2. <u>See a Star</u>: While you may not be able to see Paris Hilton at the nightclub later, you are guaranteed to see star performances at the show! Vegas hosts the best entertainers from around the world.

3. <u>Meet Men</u>: You may meet some men at a show, and then unexpectedly (or not) at the nearest bar afterwards. You will have a common experience to share, so chat 'em up. It is a great icebreaker.

Purchasing Show Tickets

Buy Tickets Before You Get to Vegas

To keep the group together, it would be good to go ahead and buy show tickets before you arrive in Vegas. It can be hard to get buy-in from the girls on going to a show once they get a taste of the shopping and nightlife when they hit town. Get them to commit in advance; otherwise, you'll get a handful of naysayers once you touch down in town. Plus, if you wait until the last minute, the only shows you'll be able to get tickets to will be the ones you wouldn't want to see anyway.

Are Shows too Expensive?

Shows seem expensive, but they are worth the experience. $85 might seem like a lot to pony up for a show, but that $85 will provide a lasting memory of your time in Vegas. You can easily blow that much in a fraction of the time shopping, gambling or clubbing.

How to Purchase Tickets

You can go to the show property's Web site, call the property directly or use a Web site such as VEGAS.com.

What to Do if You Didn't Think Ahead

If you didn't think ahead, you have a couple of options to get decent deals on day-of tickets:

- ❖ <u>VEGAS.com Concierge Desks</u>: Located at the Palms, Mandalay Bay, MGM Grand, Paris, Bally's, New York–New York, and other hotels throughout the city, the VEGAS.com concierge desk has easy access to all the shows in town, not just the ones at the property in which you are visiting.

⚷ INSIDER'S REPORT

Get to the Show 30 Minutes Ahead of Time: Give yourself some extra time to get to the show. The show rooms do not let tardy people in until between acts, so you will miss the first 20 minutes of the show. In addition, the pre-show activities, especially of the Cirque de Soleilshows, really build up the anticipation of what is to come. You would not get the same experience if you arrive right when the show starts.

- ❖ <u>Tickets2Nite</u>: This place offers half-price tickets on the day of the show. You'll find this place behind the giant Coke bottle next to the MGM Grand. It opens at noon daily.

- ❖ <u>Tix4Tonight</u>: Also offering half-price tickets, Tix4Tonight has three locations: next to the Harley-Davidson Café; the Strip entrance to the Fashion Show Mall; and across from the Stardust on the Strip.

Unfortunately, since these are always day-of show tickets there's probably not a very good chance that you'll be able to get a large block right next to one another. So your group will most likely have to split up for the show.

Choosing the Right Show

There are many different types of shows in Vegas. Each type varies in cost, length, and production type.

> **☞ INSIDER'S REPORT**
>
> **Avoid the Show Stand-By Line:** Many show box offices have a line for people who don't have tickets but are waiting for others not to show up to get into the show. There are three reasons why you don't want to do this. First, people start lining up hours before the show. You don't want to waste your time standing around when there is so much to do in Vegas. Second, there are very few people who actually get in, so all that time in line was a waste. Finally, they won't let you in until after the first break in the show. So you'll miss a quarter of the show and have to disturb the audience in your row as you get to your seat. Either buy tickets beforehand or find something else to do . . . which won't be a challenge in Sin City . . . keep reading . . .

Types of Shows

1. <u>Production Shows</u>: Full shows with many different types of talent, theatrics and music. The showrooms are extravagant, and have been built specifically for each show. Production shows are typically the most expensive of the shows in Vegas.

2. <u>Headliner Performers</u>: The Elton Johns, Barry Manilows, and Celine Dions of the world singing original music. There are some background effects and dancers, but these shows are centered on the headliners.

3. <u>Comedians & Magic</u>: Comedians and magic shows are smaller productions, but make for a fun and entertaining night. While typically half the ticket price of production shows, these shows feature superb but not overly famous per-

formers. Purchase tickets a week or two in advance for the best seats, otherwise a couple days out will suffice.

4. <u>Adult Shows</u>: Adult themes surround these shows, some being with men and some women. Adult shows are typically the least expensive. Unless it is an extremely popular travel weekend, tickets can be purchased a day or two out.

INSIDER'S REPORT

New Shows Pop Up in Vegas All the Time: It seems like every time you turn around, there is a new show in Vegas. Casinos are building shows rooms as fast as they are installing slot machines. The new show's tickets are hard to come by, so if you can't get them on your trip, then go ahead and book them months in advance. It will give you an another excuse to come to Vegas. As if you need one!

PRODUCTION SHOWS

These are the full scale Vegas shows featuring many performers and unbelievable sets. The tickets for these shows are hard to get, so be sure to plan ahead.

✓ THE *LITTLE RED BOOK*'S LUCKY 7 PRODUCTION SHOWS

1) *Zumanity* at New York–New York: Sexy with a Twist

The number one show for women defines sexiness. A twist on Cirque du Soleil's signature performances, the show tastefully pushes the sexual boundaries by exploring the full spectrum of human sexuality and intimacy to create a mosaic of love in all its brilliant shapes and forms that we can only dream about.

<u>Cost</u>: $65 to $95.

2) "O" at Bellagio: Water Wonder

A true marvel to the abilities of human kind. The performance is set around a massive 1.6 million gallon pool, which the international cast of world-class acrobats, synchronized swimmers, divers and characters (featuring more than a dozen Olympians) fly into and emerge from. The best seats are not in front, but half way up the center section. There is so much going on at once, you need to keep you eyes open as the elegant drama unfolds before your very eyes.

Cost: $92 to $150

3) *Phantom of the Opera* at The Venetian: Broadway at its Finest

An all-new staging of the world's most recognized musical theater masterpiece, and longest–running show in Broadway history, is uniquely presented in a new, $40 million theater featuring never before seen special effects, which make this classic even more dramatic.

Cost: $75 to 150

4) *KA* at MGM Grand: Cirque Storytelling at its Best

This riveting live event is more about storytelling than any previous Cirque du Soleil production. The one-of-a-kind stage transforms into different shapes and sizes and at one point even goes completely vertical. Even more remarkable are the acrobatic performers that balance, swing, and jump along the stage and its fixtures to tell the epic saga of imperial twins.

Cost: $99 to $150

5) *La Rêve* at Wynn Las Vegas: Enter the Dream

With the farthest seat just 42 feet from the action, this theater in the round creates an extremely intimate experience. Many wild things happen during the show, from demons descending from a hole in the theatre ceiling to a platoon of platinum blondes disappearing into the pool, leaving only their legs above water, seducing the audience with their dancing red high heels. If you don't want to ruin that snazzy outfit, don't sit in the first three rows. It is appropriately called the "Splash Zone."

Cost: $88 to $121

🔑 INSIDER'S REPORT

Use the Concierge for Those Hard to Get Tickets: Your hotel's concierge can be your best friend when finding tickets to shows. Shows leave a block of tickets for the casino's high rollers called "the casino block." Concierges have access to get the box office to pull tickets from the block and sell them to you. Just remember, the better the show, the bigger the tip for the concierge.

---

6) The Beatles *LOVE* at Mirage: Only in Vegas, Baby!

Do you love the Beatles? Then you will absolutely LOVE this show. But it does not take a love for the Beatles to enjoy LOVE. Using a combination of dance, extreme sports, aerial performances and 100-foot tall digital moving images, each Beatles song is choreographed to be an onslaught to the mind. You will leave with a new appreciation for the Beatles.

Cost: $69 to $150

7) *Mystère* at TI: The Flower in the Desert Continues to Bloom

Mystère was the first Cirque de Soleil production in Vegas. Its vivid sets are punctuated by colorful costumes and signature Cirque du Soleil acts such as the Taiko (Japanese drums), Chinese Poles, Hand to Hand balancing, Aerial High Bar, Bungee, and Korean Plank acts. The maternal side in you may appear as the jumbo-size baby scalavants around the stage . . . don't worry, she is already a world-class athlete. Good genes.

Cost: $60 to $95

8) *The Producers* at Paris: Mel Brooks Takes on Vegas

The classical musical comedy is a show that everyone must see. If you don't ever get a chance to go to Broadway, then see it in Vegas. It stars David Hasselhoff (yes, from *Baywatch* and *Night Rider* fame) in the lead role.

Cost: $75 to $145

✆ INSIDER'S REPORT

Free Entertainment with Lounge Acts: Looking to listen to a band or singer, but don't want to shell out the big bucks for a headliner show? Make your way to the casino lounge. Most major casino's have a lounge that, at night, have a band playing enjoyable '90s and contemporary music. Some even have a small dance floor that fills up as the night goes on. The best lounges in town for free entertainment:

- ❧ Fontana Lounge at Bellagio
- ❧ Coral Lounge at Mandalay Bay
- ❧ Casbar Lounge at Sahara
- ❧ Big Apple Lounge at New York–New York

9) *Mamma Mia* at Mandalay Bay: Have the Time of Your Life

The first Broadway show on the Strip, *Mamma Mia* is a musical set to the timeless songs of ABBA. By the end of the show, you will be sure to be singing and dancing in the aisles (and yes, it's socially acceptable here and actually encouraged). The theatre is extremely large, and it will really pay off to get seats up close to the action.

Cost: $45 to $110

10) *Blue Man Group* at The Venetian: Experience Bluephoria

You won't understand the concept of this show until you see it with your own two eyes. Three bald, blue, non-speaking characters performing non-stop comedy, percussion, and general wackiness in a blissful, party atmosphere. If you choose the first seven rows, be prepared for the fashion faux pas of a plastic rain coat to protect you from the spray on stage. Here is a hint: it's not water this time!

<u>Cost</u>: $85 to $110

★ HEADLINER SHOWS

Headliner shows center around one amazing musical performer. Usually accompanied by a band, theatrics and possibly dancers, the show is a collection or original songs and tributes. The top headliners are sold out for months, so be sure to purchase tickets well in advance.

Reasons to go to a Headliner Show

Once in a Lifetime
See them while you can because headliners can't perform forever. Unlike production shows where the talent is interchangeable, headliners are the entire show.

More Intimate than a Concert
Headliner shows are more personable than a big concert, where these type of acts usually perform. With typical audience sizes around 1,000, you really feel the intimacy of the performance.

Venues Built for the Talent
Shows used to be in glorified banquet rooms. Now, the venue is part of the show, with amazing sets, lighting and choreography. The special effects bring a whole new dimension to the performance.

⚷→ INSIDER'S REPORT

Tribute Shows: Want to see a performer at a fraction of the price? Or maybe a performer you can't go see at any price because they are, well, dead? Vegas hosts the best tribute shows in the country. These performers look and act like the real thing.

- ⚜ American Superstars: Britney Spears, Christina Aguilera, Michael Jackson
- ⚜ All Shook Up: Elvis
- ⚜ The Fab Four: The Beatles
- ⚜ Legends in Concert: Cher, Elvis, The Temptations
- ⚜ The Tribute to Frank, Sammy, Joey, and Dean: The Rat Pack

✓ THE *LITTLE RED BOOK*'S LUCKY 7 HEADLINER SHOWS

1) Celine Dion at Caesars Palace: Pure Talent and Beauty

With more than 175 million albums worldwide, Celine Dion is the biggest selling female artist of all time. Celine was the inspiration behind the 4,000-seat theatre (designed to resemble the Coliseum in Rome) where she is in front of the largest indoor LED screen in North America displaying real life graphics and a choreographed group of dancers. Each song is a multisensory experience that you will never forget — even if you think Celine Dion is a little, well, *Celine Dion.*

<u>Cost</u>: $85 to $225

2) Elton John: When the Glitter Settles, Elton is Still Standing

Elton shares the Coliseum venue with Celine Dion, performing weeks at a time when Celine's show is dark. Together with photographer David LaChapelle, Elton John has created The Red Piano — a career overview performance with an underlying theme of love. Behind him, the video screen is choreographed to each song including the most buzzed about scene with Pamela Anderson dancing on a stripper pole to his classic "The Bitch is Back."

Cost: $100 to $250

3) Barry Manilow at the Hilton: Music and Passion is Always in Fashion

Manilow's mesmerizing voice and extensive list of songs are clearly the stars of the show that features contemporary hi-tech music and effects mixed with the classic entertainment values of Las Vegas legends such as Sinatra, Presley, Davis, and Martin. Manilow performs his classic such as "Mandy" and "Cococabana," mixed in with some of his newer material. There are a few highly sought-after "on-stage" seats for an up close view of the legend.

Cost: $85 to $225

👄 IT IS GOOD TO BE A GIRL

Become Part of the Show: Magicians always use members of the audience as part of their acts. When they choose people from the stage, who do they always choose? Women! If you get a front aisle seat, be prepared! Don't pass up the opportunity, it will be a story that you will be telling your friends for years to come.

---

4) Wayne Newton at Harrah's: The Classic Vegas Entertainer

Wayne Newton is a Las Vegas icon with over 25,000 performances under his belt. He still knows how to put on a great show. The best seats are the Golden Circle tickets, which give you an up close and personal show, followed by a meet-and-greet with Mr. Las Vegas himself.

Cost: $86, Golden Ticket $117.

 **STRIP TEASE**

7 Days, 7 Showgirls, 1 Magician, No Food or Water: Only in Vegas! Houdini submerged himself while shackled in chains; David Blaine was enclosed in a giant fishbowl; but rising star Nathan Burton concocted a Vegas-style stunt and vaulted himself to legendary status and into the history books by spending seven days in a glass box suspended in the air, with only energy drinks for sustenance, and seven sexy, scantily-clad showgirls for company. So how do you snag a gig like that? Well, Nathan has been a staple performer in Vegas for more than a decade, performing everywhere from Caesars Palace to The Venetian until finding his new home at Aladdin (now Planet Hollywood).

5) Danny Gans at Mirage: The Man of Many Voices

Dan Gans' impressions are extraordinary. Not just the voices, but also the facial expressions and mannerisms of famous artists, which are right on the money. He's famous for his Michael Jackson, who morphs into smooth Nat King Cole and seamlessly into Natalie Cole, then into a classically cool Dean Martin. Or maybe he is Bill Clinton one minute, Elvis the next, and by the time Sammy Davis Jr. shows up onstage, you will be completely enthralled. The show changes each night, so you never know which of the more than 300 characterizations you will see.

Cost: $100

6) Toni Braxton at Flamingo: Unbelievable Voice Revealed

Toni's voice is the star of the show. While she is surrounded by a full-scale production show, the show centers on her amazing talent as a singer. You have a deep appreciation for her music after you experience her live.

Cost: $69–$109

7) Gordie Brown at The Venetian: Impressions Galore

Backed by a live band, Gordie Brown will keep you on your toes with an edgy mix of energetic and engaging comedy, music and mastery of impressions. Gordie writes his own material, which consists of more than 50 voices, original song parodies, jokes and signature impersonations for a one-of-a-kind brand of entertainment.

Cost: $50 to $75

 ## COMEDY AND MAGIC SHOWS

While comedy and magic are clearly two different types of shows, we treat them together here because they both actively involve the audience as participants. The best magicians and comedians perform in Vegas. Tickets should be purchased at least two weeks out, because these smaller venues tend to sell out quickly.

Reasons to go to a Magic or Comedy Show

Less Expensive

Usually about half the price of a production or headliner show, magic and comedy shows are a great value for you entertainment dollar.

Better Seats

Since the venues are about half the size of the production shows, you will be able to get a better seat than at a larger show.

More Personable

Smaller shows are more personable as both comedians and magicians involve the audience in the performance.

THE *LITTLE RED BOOK*'S LUCKY 7 COMEDY AND MAGIC SHOWS

1) David Copperfield at MGM Grand: Anything is Possible

Known around the world for his jaw-dropping illusions, David Copperfield puts on an amazing show. You will be shaking your head afterward trying to figure out how he performs the illusions.

Cost: $97

2) Penn & Teller at Rio: Magic with an Edge

Penn & Teller are the self-proclaimed "Bad Boys of Magic," and their show is an edgy mix of magic, comedy, and cultural commentary. They routinely break the cardinal rule of the magician's art by revealing the myths of some illusions (a magician's no-no), while leaving some to the imagination. Teller (the short one) never utters a word throughout the show, while Penn gives constant commentary on almost everything they do. Hilarious, hip, and happening magic.

Cost: $75

3) Carrot Top at Luxor: A One Man Circus

With a knack for rock 'n' roll gadgets and in-your-face energy, Carrot Top's super imaginative performances and outrageous style have made him a pop culture phenomenon. Known as a genius when it comes to inventive props, Carrot Top has fun lampooning celebrities, pop culture icons, red necks . . . and maybe even you, with his six trunks full of odd inventions.

Cost: $54 to $65

4) Lance Burton at Monte Carlo: Master Magician

From sleight of hand tricks to a flying Corvette, Burton knows what it takes to captivate an audience, sprinkled with a sinfully sweet humor. You can even get up-close and personal as Lance signs autographs after the show in the adjoining magic shop.

Cost: $66 to $73

5) Anthony Cools: Good, Clean, Dirty Fun

Hypnosis has taken over Vegas, and leading the wave is Anthony Cools. He takes hypnosis on the wild side, but never so far over the edge that the audience will be embarrassed. You will find the show hilarious and will want to come back for more.

Cost: $52–$75

6) Scintas at the Sahara: It's All in the Family

The Scintas is an entertaining, light-hearted show where you will follow a Sicilian family as they relate their experiences while growing up in Buffalo, N.Y., and how it has affected their lives. The talented quartet of Joe, Frank, Chrissi and Peter are very personable and by the end of show, you will consider them friends and refer to them by their first names too.

Cost: $69

7) Beacher's Madhouse: You Never Know

The show literally gets its name from your first impression: This place is a MADHOUSE! A mix of comedians and variety acts, each show is outrageous and funny. Get to the show at least an hour early, where camera crews race from table to table projecting it on the big screen as people loosen-up and take chances in this anything-goes atmosphere. If you are feeling brave, sign-up for the Beacher's Madhouse signature audience Karaoke Rock Star and Dance Idol Contests.

Cost: $25

⌐➔ INSIDER'S REPORT

Go Behind the Scenes of *Jubilee!*: You can now discover the secrets and history behind the glitz and glamour of *Jubilee!* with a once-in-a-lifetime opportunity to go behind the scenes of one of the longest running and most popular showgirl productions in Vegas. During the hour-long tour, a *Jubilee!* performer will guide you through the historical and technical aspects of the show and fill you in on many fun facts, from the Bob Mackie designer costumes to the maneuvering of the 6,000-pound sets. Try one of the signature headdresses on for size . . . after 15 short minutes of prancing around, I had a cramp in my neck for days!

X ADULT SHOWS

For a group of Vegas Vixens out on the town nothing says entertainment quite like a stage full of muscular, tanned, oiled, near-naked young men writhing and dancing for your pleasure. Did we mention they sport some of the best bodies you have ever laid eyes on?! Vegas has long been home to the topless show (not to mention the strip club capital of the world), but Sin City now boasts an impressive array of shows for women featuring some of the hottest men in the world. When you see one (and we highly recommend it!) you know that you are really experiencing the true glitz and glam of America's number one adult playground.

And don't forget the topless shows: these women express the true virtues of the Vegas Vixen — displaying utter composure while wearing stilettos, dazzling costumes that cover nothing but weigh 50 lbs., running up and down stairs, all with a genuine smile. One of the only downsides to the adult show is that it usually starts later in the evening, but that's not a problem for you, right?

Reasons to go to a Adult show

Wild Night Out
> It is a chance to see a show that is not just risqué, but loads of fun too.

Readily Available
> Purchase tickets the day before for the adult shows. If you want a seat in the front row for a close up view, purchase at least a week ahead.

Affordable
> See a show while leaving money left over for shopping tomorrow.

√ THE *LITTLE RED BOOK*'S LUCKY 7 ADULT SHOWS

1) *Thunder from Down Under* at Excalibur: Struck by Thundermania

Australia's hottest export helps put the sizzle in the Vegas desert. The internationally acclaimed Australian male revue show is a nonstop, 90-minute, sensual journey. There is a Thunder charm that separates this show from any other male revue, trust us.

<u>Cost</u>: $40 to $55

2) Chippendales at Rio: First Lady Laura Bush Can't be Wrong

If First Lady Laura Bush enjoys a girl's night out with the Chippendales there's nothing wrong with you doing so, too! Think of it as your patriotic duty. The original all-male revue revs things up at the new Chippendales Theater with a Sky Lounge, a Gossip Pit, and the alluring new night spot, Flirt!

Cost: $40 to $55

3) *Jubliee!* At Bally's: 74 Show Girls

A dazzling spectacle filled with stunning showgirls, extravagant costumes and elaborate sets, Donn Arden's *Jubilee!* has set itself apart as the classic Vegas production show for more than 25 years. The visual feast features 74 showgirls dressed in lavish costumes with thousands of jewels covering next to nothing.

Cost: $65 to $82

4) La Femme at MGM Grand: Art of the Nude

You will instantly be transported from Vegas to France, as the La Femme Theater is an exact replica of the famed Parisian Crazy Horse. Whether performing a solo tango, posing inside a rotating hoop or maneuvering high in the air on suspended stools, the women of La Femme lure you into their erotic world, truly a beautiful display in the art of the nude.

Cost: $59

5) Crazy Girls at Riviera: Famous Back Sides

With an arsenal of chains, black leather, and spiked heels, the eight dancers perform in various states of undress, giving you plenty of opportunity to view their famous (and fabulous) behinds that adorn many billboard and taxi tops around the valley. The mastermind behind (no pun intended) the curtain is one of the original Crazy Girls (and wife of famed colorist Michael Boychuck), the lovely Karen Raider. If you are interested in seeing some of the history of the trendsetting show, arrive 10 minutes before the production is unleashed.

Cost: $38 to $66

6) X Girls at Planet Hollywood: The X-citing Show

An adventure full of naughty schoolgirls, red hot cowgirls and mile-high hostesses, set to a soundtrack of today's hottest hits.

Cost: $55 to $65

7) Fantasy at Luxor: Sexy Showgirls

Featuring new choreography by Cris Judd and Eddie Garcia, the FANTASY adult revue features sultry costumes and stimulating fast paced dance numbers that will tempt you throughout the indulgent journey with just the right amount of seduction. Some of the sensual fantasies include the infamous forbidden office romances, sultry secret agents and lusting after a cowboy. You might even pick up a few tips . . .

Cost: $49 to $62

After The Show

You've had drinks at the center bar, eaten a fabulous meal by an award-winning chef, and just seen an amazing show. Is that the end of your night out? Not in Vegas, baby! One or two of your group will be tempted to get their beauty rest, which is why it's important to keep moving, keep partying, and keep enjoying all that Vegas has to offer. Don't let your trip die now. Many of the shows let out just before the nightclubs open, so head in before the lines get long, have a drink, and plan your next adventure.

You've hit the nightclubs, shopped until your Visa card begged for mercy, and rejuvenated in the spa. But have you had the true Vegas experience? You know what we're talking about: the nighttime foray into "what happens here, stays here," territory? A trip to Vegas gives you a chance to get in touch with your more adventurous side in a hedonistic paradise where anything goes. Live it up by partying down.

✶ Chapter 10 ✶

Walk on the Wild Side: Bachelorettes and Party Girls

✶ ....

Bachelorette Parties in Vegas

Bachelorette parties are big business in Vegas, so big that Sin City has been dubbed the "Bachelorette Capital of the World," since it offers all the experiences you would hope to have during your last days as a single woman: great dining, pools, spas, shopping, clubs, entertainment and the opportunity to get wild in an environment where you won't be chastised for pushing your limits.

When to Have the Bachelorette Night

The best evening to have your "wild night out" is the second night of your trip. On your first evening in Vegas, you'll be partying and seeing old friends for the first time — or waiting around for those members of your group who end up arriving late. Planning an "all out" second night allows you to build excitement and gives you something to obsess over and look forward to during your trip.

SECRETS TO A SUCCESSFUL BACHELORETTE PARTY

1. <u>Start Early</u>: You need an early start to the night. This means getting the girls out of the pool at 3 p.m., so everyone can shower, dress and be ready to paint the town by 5 p.m. If you

don't leave your hotel room for dinner until 10 p.m., it's going to be a short and disappointing night.

2. <u>Dress to Impress</u>: You need to look your Vegas Vixen best. Whether you're bride to be, or lady in waiting, there will be a plethora of pictures taken of you throughout the night. Make sure you strike that delicate balance between comfort and style – there's nothing wrong with a perfect little black dress – backless, strapless or with spaghetti straps – and a pair of sexy pumps: After all, it's a classic that still reigns supreme!

3. <u>Travel in Style</u>: A limo is a must and worth every penny! Book it for the night, so you don't have to worry about getting from place to place. Make sure to book it at least a couple weeks ahead of time, because limo companies have been known to run out of cars on busy weekends.

4. <u>Dine at a Hip, Fun Place</u>: Dinner should take place at a fun and lively restaurant where the staff appreciates hosting a group of intoxicated, wild girls. The best places have private dining areas so you can spread out and aren't confined to sitting at a bunch of tables pushed together in the main room. Make sure the restaurant is somewhere you can talk comfortably — not some fancy romantic eatery where words are uttered in hushed tones.

5. <u>Add Some "Risqué" to the Night</u>: You need men, lots of men, lots of hot, sexy men. While you may have just met a really sweet guy in the casino, for a party such as this, you have no choice but to turn to the professionals. Either buy tickets to a Chippendales-style show or plan on hitting a male strip club. This is your opportunity to turn the tables for once and treat the men like slabs of meat . . . and enjoy every minute of it.

6. <u>Hit the Hot Night Club</u>: After getting all worked up over all those hunky men, you need to keep the energy pumping with a quick trip to a happening nightclub. Don't let the group disperse (some of them might want to gamble) because you'll never get them back together, and the night is still brimming with possibility!

7. <u>Dance, Enjoy, and let the Night Unfold</u>: Once you're at the club, immediately hit the dance floor as a group: You'll be sure to grab everyone's attention . . . then let the night unfurl. Let guys buy your group drinks (they love doing this because they actually think they may have a shot with at least one of you), be a strategic Vegas Vixen to get up into the VIP area, and by all means get a little wild and crazy. Remember: This is a girls' night out, so don't venture out on your own or leave by yourself. Even if you're burnt out, suck it up for the sake of the group — you'll be happy you did.

8. <u>Remember the Night Together</u>: One of the best parts about a fun night out is reminiscing about it the morning after. Be sure to plan a late breakfast or early lunch to laugh, share stories and come clean about the night before.

Making the Night Special
Follow these pointers and you'll have an evening that runs seamlessly and sparks a devilish glint in your eye, each time you think of it, for years to come.

⚷— INSIDER'S REPORT

Don't Let Bachelorettes Have all the Fun: If no one in your group is getting married (not counting the fantasy of that quickie nuptial with the bartender from Light), it doesn't mean you can't blow off some serious steam. Remember, Vegas is a town to let it out, party down, and unleash your inhibitions. Who needs an excuse to go wild? If you do, just make one up!

Cameras

Make sure one person brings a good digital camera to document the decadence: Avoid having everyone arrive with their own Walgreens disposable, so you end up taking the same picture 10 times in a row. Who really wants to bother with getting all of that film developed, anyway? Post the suitable pix to an online photo album, and most importantly, discard the embarrassing shots right away.

Games

Don't go overboard on the games. Yes, wearing a veil while you're out and about can be cheesy fun, but in Vegas you have the thrills at your fingertips, and don't need to generate your own excitement with games like "pin the garter on the bride." Besides, aside from being embarrassing, can anyone honestly say bachelorette games are fun?

Penile Paraphernalia

Yes, maybe one or two plastic penis trinkets will bring a laugh for the night; but don't go overboard. The "wearing a bunch of items shaped like a penis joke," gets old fast. So, tell your wacky friend who wants to buy the inflatable penis balloon to save her money and buy the bride another martini.

Costumes

During many bachelorette parties in Vegas, the group will all wear the same costume. Yes, this actually happens! Usually there are a few women in the group who consider this "oodles of fun," while the rest of the group is flushed with embarrassment. While dressing in identical little schoolgirl skirts may draw attention to your group, instead try wearing similar accessories such as feathered boas or killer fishnet stockings, rather than donning the exact same outfit.

Double Check Your Guest List.

Remember, you're looking for controlled chaos — not scary, horrifying chaos. Make sure you know what to expect from your friends when they party it up; there's no fun in awkwardly looking on as one of your girls acts like she's auditioning for the next *"Girls Gone Wild"* DVD. Make sure no one in your crew will get you ejected, arrested or deported. There *is* such a thing as too much of a good time.

 ## SAMPLE ITENERARY OF A BACHELORETTE PARTY

> ### ⌇ INSIDER'S REPORT
>
> **Don't Get the Bride-to-Be Too Drunk:** Don't start feeding your sweet bride-to-be shots at 6 p.m. If she gets too drunk, you'll end up carrying her around all night, or even worse, you might find her making out with some guy in a dark corner with her shirt off. Then she'll blame *you* for getting her drunk.

3:00 p.m.   Double check the whereabouts of your friends. Make sure everyone is aware of the time.

4:00 p.m.   Get ready for the evening (nothing too fancy or casual allowed).

5:00 p.m.   Enjoy the first celebratory drinks at the casino's center bar . . . courtesy of the lucky guys sitting next to you.

5:30 p.m.	Pile into the awaiting limo for a joy ride up the Strip.
6:00 p.m.	Dine in the private dining area of N9NE at the Palms.
7:30 p.m.	Limo to Rio for a drink in the Flirt Lounge.
8:00 p.m.	Hoot and holler as the guys strip it off at Chippendales.

⚷ INSIDER'S REPORT

Your Bachelorette Party Will Not Get Special Treatment:
In your hometown, Susan's bachelorette party may be a big deal with every neighborhood bar and restaurant doing their share to make it a special occasion. Not so in Vegas, which is home to hundreds of bachelorette parties on any given weekend. If you're visiting Olympic Gardens to ogle the male dancers (or for your first lap dance), don't think you'll get special treatment just because you're part of a bachelorette party.

10:00 p.m.	Grab a round of drinks for the limo ride to PURE, Caesars Palace.
10:30 p.m.	Down a celebratory shot in Shadow Bar while en route to the nightclub . . . coerce some eager guys to do the buying.
11:00 p.m.	Dance and flirt heavily at PURE nightclub; anything is possible.
4:00 a.m.	Gossip and laugh over omelettes or quesadillas in the coffee shop (if any of you can still walk).

Otherwise, make plans for lunch after you hit the sheets.

5:00 a.m.   Sleep like a happy baby.

STRIP CLUBS

You may think that strip clubs are just for sleazy, hard-up guys looking for action while out of town at a middle management sales conference. You're probably right . . . except that strip clubs in Vegas are actually for intelligent, spirited, open-minded women like yourself, and every type of guy imaginable, from the low-life, to the brilliant entrepreneur, to the ethical (or not so ethical) family man. Vegas strip clubs are high-end, entertaining carnivals of pleasure for men *and women*. Don't miss out on an "only in Vegas experience": sense of humor and smile required.

Dancers: Male vs. Female

Male Dancers

When you enter a club featuring male performers, you'll probably need a little time to adjust to the spectacle surrounding you: a small stage surrounded by screaming women throwing money on a buff stud wearing the smallest g-string you have every seen. The front of the g-string is "form fitting" to the guy's member, in a way that puts a Speedo to shame. You have to see it to believe it!

These men are very muscular, very endowed and very aggressive. Expect them to be all over you the second you walk in, pressuring you to pay $20 for a private dance. If you agree, they'll take you to an intimate corner and flex and thrust for you. It's basically a male version of a lap dance.

While your idea of "fun," may not include having a sexy yet sweaty stranger humping you in public, when you feel the energy pulsing through the room, you will most likely — and quite happily — get swept into the action. Bring at least $100, because you're going to go though it quickly . . . and we're not joking!

Female Dancers

The vibe at a strip club showcasing female dancers is much more laid back than what you'll find when the men are center stage. While girls *will be* dancing on stage, they are not the focus, and function more like visual background music. Most of the attention is centered on the girls wandering around the room, engaging people in conversation and using their charms to convince them to buy a lap dance.

Female dancers usually love giving lap dances to women. Rocking back and forth on a lovely woman smelling faintly of perfume and body lotion is a refreshing change from grinding away on some perverted guy reeking of alcohol, garlic and body odor. Plus, the dancers can relate to women much better. Expect them to engage you in deep conversation about their life.

The Best Strip Clubs for Groups of Girls

Not all strip clubs are created equal. Stick with these four to insure your group has a dandy time.

Olympic Gardens

Olympic Gardens or "OGs" features the best male strippers in the business. Located a few blocks north of the Stratosphere, you'll definitely need a cab, as the surrounding area is a bit sketchy. Female dancers are located on the first floor of the club, and male dancers are located upstairs.

When entering the club, turn right when you get through the doorman. Everyone pays a cover, so save your breath with the "let me in for free" line. The stairs to the second floor are located on the wall to your left, about half way down the room. As you climb the stairs, you may think you're not in the right place: no wrap around line of eager women pushing and clawing their way to get upstairs. Once entering the room, you'll be surrounded by male entertainers *extraordinaire*. Every seat has a view of the stage, but if you sit up front, expect the environment to get the best of you, as the dollars will flow from your purse into the hunk's g-string.

Sapphires
Known as the world's largest strip club, Sapphires has both male and female entertainers. The very large main room houses many beautiful female strippers. If you want their company, try to get a table on the floor, instead of at the two bars located on either side of the room. In a separate area of the club, dubbed the "Playgirl Lounge," the men of Sapphires start out with an exotic dance revue at 10 p.m., but it's after the show when things really heat up. The men change out of their theatrical costumes and strut around, just like the male entertainers at Olympic Gardens.

Scores
Made famous by Howard Stern, who compulsively extols the virtues of the New York City Scores, this pristine and upscale club features female entertainers, a high-end clientele, and a friendly and courteous staff that makes sure women feel welcome and comfortable. While you won't be the center of attention, the stunning dancers will flock to your group to see if there's anything they can do to help contribute to your evening of decadence. The club is large and there are plenty of places to sit, but it's best to get a table in the main room facing the stage. Other areas of the club may be less packed, but offer obstructed views of the action.

Seamless
Seamless is located by the Orelans Hotel, a couple of miles off the Strip. It's perfect for a group of girls when looking for a non-intimidating adult atmosphere. The V-shaped bar is a great spot to grab a seat, or ask for a table close to the state. The girls are friendly, attractive, and love to dance for other girls. As the night moves on, the entire facility transforms into a late-night club dedicated to dancing and mingling.

> ## 🍸 VEGAS VIXEN
>
> **Stripper 101:** So, you like what you see? Did you ever wish that you could dance like that? For a mere $30, you can learn from the professionals at the Stripper Studio in the Miracle Mile shops. The hour-long class is for women only, so you can learn the ropes without feeling embarrassed by the watchful eyes of lurking guys. The instructor will take you through 25 different dance moves, including how to use the stripper pole. While you may not be ready to perform at a Las Vegas strip club, you will be able to wow your man back home with your new sultry moves!

 REALLY WILD

Ok, ready girls? You've watched gorgeous men strip down, stuffed dollar bills down their tiny g-strings, and delighted in your first girl/girl lap dance. While we don't recommend it, if you want to take it up another notch, Vegas can fulfill that fantasy.

Swinger Clubs

Vegas has its share of swingers clubs, and they openly advertise everywhere. All of them let single girls in for free; they are the most coveted commodity in the world of swinging. Just fore-warned, if you go this route you'll probably feel pressure, as you'll be seen as the fulfillment of every couple's fantasy involving a frisky threesome. And what about *your* fantasy? If it entails an erotic "play date" with a handsome man and a sexy woman, you might be disappointed. While some gorgeous couples are active in "the lifestyle," the typical swinger is probably much older than you, doesn't work out, and has eaten one too many bags of chips.

Brothels

If you think brothels are for men only, then think again. Pay for sex? Yes. Worth it? Probably not. Not only are the brothels ridiculously expensive (around $1,000 for an hour), they're located a good hour and a half from the Vegas Strip. If you have ever watched the HBO series *Cat House* then you know what you're getting into.

 Coming Soon

The Heidi Fleiss Stud Farm: The Hollywood Madam is building something truly unique in the Nevada desert. Currently in development is the world's first "stud farm," where all the prostitutes are men. It sounds crazy, but the buzz in Vegas has been big — very big. She's in the process of hiring some of the most gorgeous men around, each one a true Fabio type.

Get Back to Reality

You've dined, shopped, danced, and squeezed every ounce of pleasure out of your Vegas getaway. Now it's time to merge back into reality and re-enter your normal life back home. Sigh . . .

PART III

Leaving Las Vegas

Chapter 11

Departure: All Good Things . . .

✳ ....

Good night, good night! Parting is such sweet sorrow,
That I shall say good night till it be morrow.

— Romeo and Juliet

A sort of sadness lingers in the air when your getaway to Vegas winds down to its final, inevitable conclusion. You've had a memorable, magical few days and nights, reconnecting with your old friends, and maybe making some new ones. But trust us, the only thing worse than not getting enough Las Vegas is getting *way too much* Las Vegas. It is time to leave, and part of your melancholy can be assuaged by planning for your departure the same way you planned for your arrival: well in advance. At the very least, your sadness won't be leavened with panic if you set up your return reservations before you hail your taxi to the airport or hit the road home.

Assume that when it's time to leave, you'll be exhausted. Even a laid-back weekend reunion with your friends is going to wear you out. Face it: Las Vegas is intense. So, be prepared, set up your departure so that you have plenty of time to recoup and re-focus for your world of work when you return.

IMPORTANT CONSIDERATIONS FOR DEPARTURE

Can You Wrangle an Extra Day Off?

It's the best of all possible worlds: fly home Sunday night — take Monday off from work. Wouldn't it be lovely to have the luxury of adding one day to your getaway as a reality check after being lulled into a weekend of self-indulgent pleasure seeking?

Of course, this is easier said than done, and if you can't get an extra day, make sure you don't have a major presentation or, even worse, your annual review the day you return. For something that important, you want to be sharp, not walking around with your head still in the clouds.

Stay-Over Rates

If you're able to swing the day off, most hotels offer cut-rate stay-over room rates. The idea is that you leave on Monday morning when the lines are shorter, or keep the room, but don't stay overnight, and instead take a red-eye flight and give yourself some time to relax before the hustle and bustle of the airport or highway. It may be worth it to you to pay for an extra night to have the luxury of keeping your room until you have to leave for the airport.

Leave Together

While it's more fun to arrive together, it can also be a great time leaving together. Take care of this detail before you and your girls even book your flights. Being the last one to go home is lonely. You'll probably end up heading over to the airport with the rest of the girls, see them all off, and have nothing to do. You'll only have a few options, play away some dollars at the airport slots (they have the worst return rates in Vegas), or sit at the bar and sip on one last cocktail. Either way, you'll be thoroughly bummed out in no time.

Check Out the Right Way

Check-out times are not carved in stone. If your hotel states that check-out time is 10 a.m., don't worry if is it 11 a.m. before you get out the door. There is a built in time buffer at work. If you want to wrangle a late check out, and think you'd like to return to that hotel, work with a guest relations manager; note the name, and follow-up with a complimentary letter to the Hotel Director upon your return. Vegas is all about the return guest. Your contact will want you to book another visit.

The Late Checkout
Perhaps you can get a late checkout, allowing you to sleep in, eat a casual breakfast, shower, and taxi leisurely to the airport. Ask in advance, Vegas hotels are mega resorts with ample rooms so chances are on a Sunday there isn't anyone waiting around to get your room for the night.

Check out by the Hotel's Television
Avoid a rushed, hectic, last minute check out at the front desk by using the hotel's television check out system. It's simple and easy to use.

Split the Cost of the Room
It's really important to figure out how you're going to pay for the room in advance. Best suggestion is to pick one person in your room who wants lots of airline miles, check-in by putting the room on her mileage credit card, and have everyone else write her a check or pay her cash for their portion of the bill when you checkout.

Check Your Bags with the Bellhop
Don't lug your bags around with you; check them in with the Bell Desk. If you are going to spend the rest of your time at a different hotel before you leave, bring your bags with you and check them in with the bell desk at that hotel. You don't have to be a guest there to check your bags, and anything is better than carting them up and down the Strip all day.

✈ TRANSPORTATION

Leaving Las Vegas creates a mixture of emotions and a separation anxiety.

The departure crowds at the airport are a mix of the physically over-partied, the financially overextended, and the emotionally withdrawn. Everyone in the airport either wants to leave ASAP and get back to their own bed, or doesn't want to leave at all and reality bites.

⚷ INSIDER'S REPORT

You Don't Need a Limo for Your Ride to the Airport: Limos are perfect for your arrival to Vegas, but by the time you are leaving, you just won't appreciate the extra luxury. Plus, you have probably blown more money gambling and done more shopping then anticipated. Now is the time to save. It might take a little longer to get a taxi, but pass on the limo to the airport: your bankroll will appreciate it.

Make Sure You Know How You're Getting to the Airport

Airports tend to cycle their flights to better utilize their resources on the ground by scheduling flights to arrive and depart in chunks of busy time. As a result, the taxi lines can be a little long at certain times of the day as everyone is going to or coming from the airport at the same time. So if you're planning on taking a taxi, allow plenty of time even if the airport is only minutes away from your hotel.

Check Bags

You did more shopping then expected and now your luggage is overly packed and you *still* have new clothes and souvenirs that you can't fit in to your bags. While you may be able to get through security with more than one bag, avoid the hassle. With the new airport check in system, you can use the express electronic kiosks and still check your bags with ease. Do you really want to drag them all across the airport and do calisthenics to pack them into the non-existent overhead storage? Sure, you'll have to wait a bit for your baggage when you arrive at your destination, but it's much better than lugging them around only to be told by the flight attendant that the overhead storage space is full. Our advice is: *don't* check your bags flying in to Vegas; *do* check them flying out.

Leave Early, Leave Late

If you want to avoid some of the airport congestion, leave early or late. Early is sometimes the best way to go. By leaving early you may just snag that nap in your own bed the day before you have to go back to work. On the late side, red eye flights are becoming increasingly popular, and therefore more crowded. They are generally less expensive because they are no-frills flights in the middle of the night to the wee hours of the morning.

⚷━ INSIDER'S REPORT

Avoid the Slots at the Airport: You might be tempted to use your last dollar on a couple of pulls of the Megabucks machine. Save your money. Not only will you be bored with gambling by this time, it is important to note that the airport's slot machines are the tightest machines in Vegas, meaning they pay out to the player less frequently.

Don't Loiter at the Airport

Whatever you do, don't head over to the airport with your friends if their flights depart hours before yours. This is a popular, miserable mistake. You'll be stuck in an overcrowded airport just trying to kill time and no really comfortable place to relax.

No Food or Drinks

Allow time to eat before you get to the airport. Not only are the lines at the fast food stands really long but the food is bad and overpriced. Eat that final meal at your hotel, don't be reduced to pushing and shoving for the last bag of Cheetos at the airport.

 **STRIP TEASE: O₂ Recharge**

There's an Oxygen Bar located in the C Terminal at McCarran International Airport in Vegas. We can't vouch for its effects, but they claim that the O_2 boost will help clean out all the secondhand cigarette smoke that you have been taking in at the casinos. Just a thought if you have a few extra minutes and ten bucks to spend on breathing deeply.

Hit the Road

If you're driving home, make sure you leave extra early. The traffic out of Vegas, especially heading south on I-15 toward L.A., becomes congested by about 11am. The last thing you want is to be stuck in a five-hour traffic jam. Of course that's probably what you'll be facing for Monday's commute if you live in L.A., but that's a story for another day.

STRESS FREE TRAVEL

Looking for a stress-free way to get back to reality? Here are a few golden rules:

Leave on Monday

There are no lines on a Monday. You can breeze right through to your gate, and with the flights being relatively empty, perhaps even have some extra elbow room or a place to stretch out.

Dress Comfortably

On your way into Vegas, you want to be dressed ready to go out. On your way out of Vegas, dress in the most comfortable clothes that you have. No dresses, no high heels, no expensive jewelry . . . you get the point. Plus, it will be easier to get through the airport security without a belt, rings, watches and lace up shoes.

Massage Before You Board

Unwind before you return, book a massage the morning before your flight. You'll feel rested, recharged and ready to return. Schedule a massage for *after* you check out, and spend a couple of hours detoxifying. Take your time in the steam room, soak in the hot tub, and get a massage. Eat the complimentary fresh fruit and drink as much water as possible. Not only will your body be recuperating, but you will be able to a take a nice long hot shower and change your clothes just before you leave for the airport.

✳ Chapter 12 ✳

Rekindle Your Vegas Spirit

✳ ....

This is my story and I'm sticking to it . . .

Think before you speak. Organize your thoughts. If you kept a
journal and entered your Vegas getaway adventures you can easily determine what you will share and what stays in Vegas. Even
if you happen to be a journalist, chances are that you were too
delightfully busy following the *Little Red Book* to pen your fabulous experiences. No worries - Just remember that you are now
the new *it girl* to your friends and family back home. This title
carries with it the responsibility to share your version of the best
hotel . . . the best entertainment . . . the best restaurant . . . the
best nightlife . . . the best of Vegas according to *you*!

Stories Are Expected and Anticipated

Taking a Vegas vacation is different from any other vacation. You
might come back from any other vacation and people will ask,
"How was it?" and you will say "Great." But if you come back
from a Vegas vacation, people will say "Tell me *everything* that
happened."

You can't come home without a few fabulous tales to tell. If you
followed anything at all in the preceding pages, you will have a
ton of jaw-dropping experiences to share with the girls at the
nail salon. While you were vacationing, the friends and family

that you left back home were living an everyday life running errands, working overtime, cleaning the kitchen and fantasizing about what *you* are doing, at that moment, in Vegas. They may be envious of you living it up in Sin City. So, as you return to reality, an over-shopped, liberated, partied-out girl with a smirk on your face, you owe them some secrets. If you come home without something to say, these envious ones will probably wish you just didn't bother to come home at all. They are dying to hear your stories of sin and excess, so don't disappoint them.

 INSIDER'S REPORT

Think Before You Speak: You made it home and you're so excited to relay true tales of misadventure that you neglect to incorporate some basic storytelling structure. Remember, the stories need to have a beginning, middle, and end. If you don't think about what you're going to say and how you're going to say it, you'll lose your audience. Think before you speak, and take notes if you have to. If you spend a minute beforehand focusing in on what you want to say, you'll have them hanging on your every word.

Be Ready for the Standard Vegas Questions

Everyone who has been to Vegas loves to talk about Vegas. Be prepared for this set of ten standard questions when you return home.

- ❖ Did you spot any celebrities?
- ❖ Did you get lucky in the casino?
- ❖ Did you see the Bellagio Fountains? What about the Mirage Volcano?
- ❖ Did you go to Wynn Resort?
- ❖ Did you meet any interesting guys? *Tell me everything!*
- ❖ Did you go shopping in Rome (The Forum Shops) and

Venice (Grand Canal Shoppes)?
- ✤ Did you dine at any of the celebrity chefs restaurants?
- ✤ Did you indulge in the luxurious spas?
- ✤ Did you go to any shows?
- ✤ Did you party at the Palms and the Hard Rock Hotel?

It is better to make sure you see these places then have to deal with people asking you "How could you not see the Bellagio Fountains? They are right in the middle of the strip. What did you do?"

YOUR DUTY

Once you've been back for several days, you'll probably tell the story about how you partied with Tobey Maguire at PURE every night. Not that it's not a great story — I mean, come on, it's not every day that you meet Spider-Man himself. Once that initial euphoria has worn off, it's time to own up to your responsibilities to reality and to your integrity.

Come Clean

Why do so many people spend half a day in line trying to get to the top of Stratosphere? Why do so many girls go to the Beach Nightclub, only to spend a whole night trying to figure out how to get a table? Because someone, somewhere told them it was the *it* thing to do. Just because you may have been misled prior to using the *Little Red Book* as your guide to the perfect Vegas getaway doesn't mean that you should let a friend, acquaintance, or perfect stranger suffer the same fate. If something was subpar, admit it. If you had a dreadful experience, help others avoid it.

Don't Spread Vegas Hype

"Vegas Hype" is a particular category of untruth arising, like Vegas itself, out of the need to mythologize, glamorize, and celebrate beyond all bounds of reason and taste. It's Vegas, Baby! Bigger than life, faster, hipper, richer, more frenetic than any city on earth. How could it possibly all be true? It's not — so be honest, and admit, when pressed, the venues in Vegas that didn't work for you, that felt like a rip-off or a complete waste of time.

Spread the Truth

In retrospect, you overpaid for dinner and one of your over-intoxicated girls convinced you to meet up with a group of guys for an evening that turned out badly. You have to tell others. Some of the lamest things in Vegas thrive solely because no one is willing to admit the truth, so get real. *Don't* confess your deepest, darkest secrets or share them with everyone you know: *Do* admit when your head was turned by some over-hyped club, restaurant, show or event. You went against the advice of the *Red Book*, and you got burned. It happens. Just help make sure it doesn't happen to others.

HOW TO TELL A VEGAS STORY

Vegas stories tend to be unique. If you tell it well, a Vegas story will play much better than your daily, idle, reality-show recap, chitchat at the water cooler.

Think About the Little Things

While the action is big and often dramatic, as with any good story, the success of a Vegas exposé lies in the details. Maybe an Elvis impersonator cut in front of you at the buffet? Or a celebrity invited you to join him at his VIP table? Or a high roller gave you money to gamble with him? Maybe in a moment of passionate bliss one of you almost got married at a wedding chapel? (This never happens, by the way, unless your name is Britney) Maybe you hit a jackpot and were able to buy the Louie Vuitton purse you spotted at the Forum Shops at Caesars Palace? Or you were pulled on stage by a Chippendale? Or you got on the bar and danced with the crowd at Coyote Ugly? Or you were invited to an exclusive party in one of the Palms' Fantasy Suites? Or you made a bold gambling wager that paid for your trip or broke you? The more unusual the details, the better your story will play to your audience when it comes to Vegas.

Start from the Beginning

The story begins at the airport, on the plane, and getting to your hotel. You need a casual buildup before you knock them out with a big punch.

Hit the Key Points

If you followed the advice of the *Little Red Book*, then your trip was action-packed with many different events. When you tell the story, people won't believe that you were able to experience so many over-the-top adventures in such a short amount of time. You planned properly, though, and you eliminated the aimless wandering, sitting in taxis, and waiting around that waste the time and suck the excitement out of everybody else's Vegas getaway.

Finish with a Bang

End your story with the highlight of your getaway that shows you living large with all your new friends — not with you sitting in the airport for a couple of hours trying to get back. People love visiting Vegas, and once you have shared your adventure you will have a whole new set of girls that will want to do Vegas with you the *Little Red Book* way.

PLAN YOUR NEXT TRIP

Now that you have experienced Vegas in *Little Red Book* style, it's time to take some time to insure that your next trip will start where you left off.

Put it in Writing

Whether or not you're used to keeping a journal, take notes on your Vegas Vixen getaway, as this will be evidence that you can pass along to your friends or refer to for yourself. Take time on your way home to jot down what worked and what requires re-working. As you know, there are so many adventures waiting for you in Vegas that it virtually demands a return trip. Or many. Your detailed descriptions could save someone you know time and money . . . that someone may be you.

Help Us Help You

If you experienced a new venue with *WOW FACTOR* share it with the *Little Red Book* by logging on to www.vegaslittleredbook.com and tell us your story. We'll get the word out and make sure others benefit from your new find or your unfortunate mistake. If you had a great time (of course you did, if you followed our advice) we want to know about that, too. Sign up for our newsletter. We will share up to the minute details on all the hits and misses in Sin City.

Tell the Guys: *Las Vegas Little Black Book*

Vegas vacations are not the same for guys and for girls. Share with your favorite guy friends who are planning a getaway to Sin City. The *Las Vegas Little Black Book: A Guy's Guide to the Perfect Vegas Weekend* provides groups of guys with a step by step through Vegas, just like the girl's book did for you and your girls.

RETURN!

Start planning your next trip to Las Vegas before you leave. It's easier that way and gives you something to look forward to. Learn from what went right and wrong on your trip. Trust us, now that you are a Vegas Vixen and know how to do Vegas right, the next trip will be even better. As Frank Sinatra once said, "The best is yet to come."

Itineraries: Follow the Plan

✳ ....

LITTLE RED BOOK ITINERARIES

With so many choices in Vegas, it is difficult to make a plan for the entire trip. These six itineraries are designed for you to follow or use as your base for your Vegas weekend.

Alpha Babes

An alpha babe is a woman who knows what she wants and when she wants it. She is high powered and creates her own destiny.
<u>Accommodations</u>: The Venetian
<u>Group Size</u>: 3–5

Day 1: Get in the Flow

7:00 p.m.	Arrival into Vegas
8:00 p.m.	Limo to the hotel and check into two adjoining suites
9:00 p.m.	Get settled and have a glass of Chardonnay
9:30 p.m.	Drinks at the Tao Lounge
10:00 p.m.	Dinner at the Tao Restaurant
12:00 a.m.	Dance at the Tao Nightclub
2:00 a.m.	Late night snack and gossip at the Grand Lux Café
3:00 a.m.	Sleep

Day 2: Take Care of Number One

10:00 a.m.	Wake Up
11:00 a.m.	Coffee and a scone at Coffee Bean & Tea Leaf
12:00 p.m.	Walk up the Strip to Wynn
1:00 p.m.	Stroll the Wynn Esplanade shops
2:00 p.m.	Test your luck on the slots
3:30 p.m.	Take group photo by Lake of Dreams
4:00 p.m.	Snack at ZooZa Crackers
5:00 p.m.	High Tea at Wynn's Parasol Up
6:00 p.m.	Shower and change clothes.
7:00 p.m.	Meet up at the V Bar for a cocktail
8:00 p.m.	*Phantom of the Opera*
10:00 p.m.	Late Dinner at Aquaknox
11:30 p.m.	Pussycat Lounge at Caesars
12:30 a.m.	PURE Nightclub
3:00 a.m.	Late night at Drai's
5:00 a.m.	Sleep

Day 3: Relax

10:00 a.m.	Have room service bring breakfast to room
11:00 a.m.	Check out
12:00 p.m.	Deep tissue massage at Canyon Ranch
2:00 p.m.	Stroll the Grand Canal Shoppes
3:00 p.m.	Late sushi lunch at Tsunami Asian Grill
4:00 p.m.	Airport and depart

Party Girls

The party girl wants a non-stop wild weekend with some good stories to tell when she gets back home.

<u>Accommodations</u>: Palms

<u>Group Size</u>: 4–8

Day 1: Start off with a Bang

5:00 p.m.	Arrival into Vegas
6:00 p.m.	Check into hotel
6:30 p.m.	Cocktail at the center bar

7:30 p.m.	Sushi at Little Budda
9:00 p.m.	Take in the view at the ghostbar
11:00 p.m.	Rain Nightclub
3:00 a.m.	After hours at Seamless
5:00 a.m.	Sleep

Day 2: Make your Move

12:00 p.m.	Wake up
1:00 p.m.	Enjoy a Bloody Mary by the pool
2:00 p.m.	Late lunch poolside
3:00 p.m.	Try on some outfits at the Playboy store
4:00 p.m.	Play roulette as a group and enjoy some free drinks
5:00 p.m.	Rest and shower back at the room
6:30 p.m.	Meet up at N9NE bar for drinks
7:00 p.m.	Dinner at N9NE including a sampling of the champagne and caviar menu
9:00 p.m.	Limo to Sapphires for the Men of Sapphires show
11:00 p.m.	Cocktails at Lure at Wynn
12:00 p.m.	Dance at Tryst
3:00 a.m.	After hours at Drai's
5:00 a.m.	Sleep

Day 3: Party by the Pool

10:00 a.m.	Breakfast from room service
1:00 a.m.	Hard Rock's Rehab Pool Party
4:00 p.m.	Early dinner at Pink Taco
6:00 p.m.	Late Check Out
7:00 p.m.	Airport and departure

Fashionistas

Your life is centered on shopping . . . so is your vacation. Do it right.

<u>Accommodations</u>: Caesars Palace

<u>Group Size</u>: 3–6

Day 1: Roll in Style

6:00 p.m.	Arrival into Vegas
6:30 p.m.	Limo ride to Caesars
7:00 p.m.	Check into big suite in the Augusta Tower
8:00 p.m.	Dinner at Spago in the Forum Shops
9:30 p.m.	Pick out an accessory to compliment your outfit
10:30 p.m.	Shadow Bar for a drink
11:30 pm.	PURE nightclub
2:00 a.m.	Sleep

Day 2: Shop 'til You Drop

10:00 a.m.	Wake up
11:00 a.m.	Grab a coffee and walk up the Strip to Fashion Show Hall
1:00 p.m.	Lunch on the patio of Café Ba Ba Reeb.
2:00 p.m.	Stroll the high-end shops at the Wynn Esplanade
4:00 p.m.	Walk down the Strip toward The Venetian and visit the Grand Canal Shoppes
5:00 p.m.	Stop for a snack and a margarita at Taqueria Cononita
5:30 p.m.	Head back to Caesars to rest and change
7:00 p.m.	Pre-dinner Cosmo at the Seahorse Lounge
7:30 p.m.	Walk next door to Bellagio to browse Via Bellagio
8:00 p.m.	Dinner at FIX
10:00 p.m.	The late show of "O"
12:00 a.m.	Dance and mingle at Light
2:00 a.m.	Sleep

Day 3: Head Out

10:00 a.m.	Have room service bring coffee to room
12:00 p.m.	Check out and have a sushi lunch
2:00 p.m.	Stop by a chintzy souvenir shop on the way to the airport
3:00 p.m.	Airport and departure

Chill Girls

You came to Vegas not to party but to relax and spend time with your friends. Vegas has just the ticket.

<u>Accommodations</u>: Mandalay Bay

<u>Group Size</u>: 4–8

Day 1: Dinner and a Show

6:00 p.m.	Arrival into Vegas
7:00 p.m.	Check into Mandalay Bay
8:00 p.m.	Dinner at Red Square
10:00 p.m.	*Mama Mia* show
12:00 p.m.	Cocktail at Mix to enjoy the view
2:00 a.m.	Sleep

Day 2: Spa and Shop

10:00 a.m.	Wake up with breakfast delivered to the room
11:00 a.m.	Steam and sauna at the Spa
12:00 p.m.	Body wrap
1:00 p.m.	Swedish massage
2:00 p.m.	Manicure and pedicure
3:00 p.m.	Relax pool side with a cocktail and a late lunch
4:00 p.m.	Shower and get ready for the night
5:00 p.m.	Window shop at Mandalay Place
7:00 p.m.	Limo to the Mirage
8:00 p.m.	Take in the Beatles' *Love* show
10:00 p.m.	Dinner at Stack
12:00 a.m.	Dance at JET
2:00 a.m.	Taxi back to Mandalay to sleep

Day 3: A Little More Pool

10:00 a.m.	Breakfast at the coffee shop
12:00 p.m.	Check out
1:00 p.m.	Poolside for sun and relaxation
3:30 p.m.	Spa for sauna and shower
5:00 p.m.	Airport and departure

On The Prowl

You are looking to find "Mr. Right Now." Las Vegas has plenty of options, but you need to hit the right places that give you the best chance to meet successful, available men.

Accommodations: Hard Rock

Group Size: 4–8

Day 1: Rock It Hard

5:00 p.m.	Arrival into Vegas
6:00 p.m.	Check into Hard Rock
7:00 p.m.	Cocktails at the Center Bar
8:00 p.m.	Sushi & sake from the chef's special at Nobu
10:00 p.m.	Check out the guys playing blackjack
12:00 p.m.	Hit Body English and join some men at their table
2:00 a.m.	After hours at Rainbow Bar & Grill
4:00 a.m.	Sleep

Day 2: Mix It Up

10:00 a.m.	Breakfast at Mr. Lucky's
11:00 a.m.	Taxi to Caesars
11:30 a.m.	Find that perfect outfit for the night at the Forum Shops
1:00 p.m.	Lunch at Spago
2:30 p.m.	Taxi back to Hard Rock
3:00 p.m.	Check out the pool for a cocktail and some hard bodies
5:00 p.m.	Shower and change clothes
6:00 p.m.	Taxi over to New York–New York
6:30 p.m.	Cocktails at the Dueling Piano Bar
7:30 p.m.	Survey the table games for men
8:00 p.m.	Enjoy *Zumanity*
10:00 p.m.	Late dinner at STACK at the Mirage
11:30 p.m.	JET Nightclub
1:00 a.m.	Convince the guys to let you gamble with their money

2:00 a.m.	Taxi back to Hard Rock
2:30 a.m.	One last try at the Center Bar
3:00 a.m.	Sleep

Day 3: Try the Pool

10:00 a.m.	Have room service bring coffee to room
11:00 a.m.	Pool side mingling and cocktails
2:00 p.m.	Late lunch pool side
3:00 p.m.	Late check out
4:00 p.m.	Airport and departure

Hot Mamas on a Budget

It is the only time that these hot moms can breakaway from their kids and husbands. But they know that they can't blow their bank account doing it.

Accommodations: MGM Grand

Group Size: 3–6

Day 1: Dinner and Dancing

5:00 p.m.	Arrival into Vegas
6:00 p.m.	Check into MGM Grand
7:00 p.m.	Cocktails at the Centrifuge Bar
8:00 p.m.	Dinner at Emeril's Fish House
10:00 p.m.	Cocktail at the Zuri Center Bar
11:00 p.m.	Enjoy the scene and have a cocktail at Tabú
12:30 p.m.	Dance at Studio 54
3:00 a.m.	Sleep

Day 2: See the Strip

11:00 a.m.	Wake up
12:00 p.m.	Lunch at the Café
1:00 p.m.	The Margarita March for some sightseeing along the Strip
4:00 p.m.	Rest and shower back at the room
5:30 p.m.	Taxi over to the Rio
6:00 p.m.	Dinner at the Rio Buffet

7:00 p.m.	Gamble at the nickel slots
8:00 p.m.	Penn & Teller Show
10:00 p.m.	Voodoo Lounge for cocktails and a view of the city
12:00 p.m.	Taxi to Olympic Gardens for some male strippers
2:30 a.m.	Late night snack back at the hotel
4:00 a.m.	Sleep

Day 3: Shop and Enjoy

11:00 a.m.	Have room service bring coffee to room
12:00 p.m.	Check out of room
12:30 p.m.	Stroll the Miracle Mile Shops at Planet Hollywood
1:30 p.m.	Light lunch at Tacone
3:00 p.m.	Take in the water show at the Bellagio
5:00 p.m.	Airport and departure

Little Red Book Lists: Your Reference Guide

★ ....

These lists are based on the top places for groups of girls. Other places in Vegas may be just as good or even better for other purposes, but are omitted here because they don't fit the special needs of groups of women. Use these lists as your reference when arranging plans and making reservations.

Best Accommodations

Palms	866-725-6773
	www.palms.com
Hard Rock	800-473-7625
	www.hardrockhotel.com
Wynn	888-320-9966
	www.wynnlasvegas.com
Caesars Palace	800-634-6661
	www.caesars.com
Venetian	888-283-6423
	www.venetian.com
Mandalay Bay	877-832-7800
	www.mandalaybay.com
Bellagio	888-987-6667
	www.bellagiolasvegas.com
MGM Grand	800-929-1111
	www.mgmgrand.com

Mirage	800-627-6667
	www.themirage.com
Planet Hollywood	877-333-9474
	www.aladdincasino.com

Best Nightclubs

PURE at Caesars Palace	702-731-7873
Tryst at Wynn	702-770-7100
Tao at Venetian	702-388-8588
Rain at the Palms	702-924-7777
Body English at Hard Rock	702-693-5000
JET at Mirage	702-792-7900
Light at Bellagio	702-693-8300
Whiskey at Green Valley Ranch	702-617-7560
Studio 54 at MGM Grand	702-891-7254
rumjungle at Mandalay Bay	702-632-7777
Moon at the Palms	702-924-7777

Best Ultra Lounges

ghostbar at the Palms	702-938-2666
MIX at Mandalay Bay	702-632-7777
Tabú at MGM Grand	702-891-7254
LURE at Wynn	702-770-7100
Pussycat Dolls Lounge at Caesars	702-731-7873
Tangerine at TI	702-894-7444
Caramel at Bellagio	702-639-7444
Foundation Room at Mandalay Bay	702-632-7600
Forty Deuce at Mandalay Bay	702-632-9442
Playboy Club at the Palms	702-924-7777

Best Bars

The Center Bar at Hard Rock	702-639-5000
Parasol Up/Parasol Down at Wynn	702-770-7100
Coyote Ugly at NY–NY	702-740-6330
Voodoo Lounge at Rio	702-777-7923
Fontana Bar at Bellagio	702-693-7111

Shadow Bar at Caesars	702-731-7110
The Island Bar at the Palms	702-942-7777
Beauty Bar in Downtown	702-598-7965
Rainbow Bar & Grill	702-898-3525
next to the Hard Rock	
Ice House in Downtown	702-315-2570

Best Places to Shop

Forum Shops at Caesars	702-893-4800
Grand Canal Shoppes at Venetian	702-414-4500
Miracle Mile at Planet Hollywood	702-866-0710
Fashion Show	702-369-8382
Mandalay Place	702-632-9333
Wynn Esplanade	702-770-7000
Via Bellagio	702-639-7111

Best Pools

Mandalay Bay	877-832-7800
Palms	866-725-6773
Hard Rock	800-473-7625
Wynn	888-320-9966
Caesars	800-634-6661
Bellagio	888-987-6667
MGM Grand	800-929-1111
Mirage	800-627-6667
Venetian	888-283-6423
Flamingo	800-732-2111

Best Buffets

The Buffet at Wynn	888-320-9966
Dishes at TI	702-894-7444
Cravings at Mirage	702-791-7111
Bay Side Buffet at Mandalay Bay	702-632-7777
Carnival World Buffet at Rio	702-777-7923
Bellagio Buffet	702-639-7223

Best 24-hour Coffee Shops

Mr. Lucky's at Hard Rock	702-693-5000
Grand Lux at the Venetian	702-731-5015
Café Bellagio	702-693-7223
Peppermill	702-735-4177
Café Lago at Caesars	702-731-7731
Sao Paulo at Rio	702-777-7923
Terrace Pointe Café at Wynn	702-770-7100
Raffles Café at Mandalay Bay	702-632-7777

Best Steak and Seafood Restaurants

N9NE at the Palms	702-933-9900
FIX at Bellagio	702-693-7223
Delmonico at the Venetian	702-414-3737
STACK at Mirage	702-791-7111
Aquaknox at Venetian	702-414-3772

Best International Restaurants

Mon Ami Gabi at Paris (French)	702-967-7999
Red Square at Mandalay Bay (Russian)	702-632-7407
Okada at Wynn (Sushi)	702-770-3320
Nove at Palms (Italian)	702-942-6800
Tao at Venetian (Asian)	702-388-8338
Spago at Caesars (California)	702-369-6300

Best Places to Have a Diva Dinner

Joël Robuchon at MGM Mansion	702-891-7925
Mesa Grill at Caesars Palace	702-731-7110
Nobu at Hard Rock	702-693-5090
Aureole at Mandalay Bar	702-632-7401

Best Grab and Go Restaurants

La Creperie at Paris	702-946-7000
Jean Philippe Patrisserie at Bellagio	702-693-7444
ZoozaCrackers at Wynn	702-770-7100

Snacks at Bellagio   702-693-7444
Starbucks

Best Places to Gamble
Hard Rock   800-473-7625
MGM Grand   800-929-1111
Palms   866-725-6773
Wynn   888-320-9966
Rio   800-752-9746
Hooters   866-584-6687

Best Production Shows
Zumanity at New York–New York   800-693-6763
"*O*" at Bellagio   888-987-6667
Phantom of the Opera at Venetian   888-283-6423
KÀ at MGM Grand   800-929-1111
La Rêve at Wynn   888-320-9966
The Beatles *LOVE* at Mirage   800-627-6667
Mystère at TI   800-944-7444
Mama Mia at Mandalay Bay   877-632-7700
Blue Man Group at Venetian   888-283-6423

Best Headliner Shows
Celine Dion at Caesars   800-634-6661
Elton John at Caesars   800-634-6661
Barry Manilow at Hilton   800-732-7117
Wayne Newton at Harrah's   702-369-5222
Danny Gans at Mirage   800-627-6667
Toni Braxton at Flamino   800-221-7299
Gordie Brown at Venetian   888-283-6423

Best Comedy and Magic Shows
David Copperfield at MGM Grand   800-929-1111
Penn & Teller at Rio   800-752-9746
Carrot Top at Luxor   800-288-1000
Lance Burton at Monte Carlo   800-822-8652

Anthony Cools at Paris	877-374-7469
Scintas at Sahara	888-696-2121
Beacher's Madhouse	702-699-7844

Best Adult Shows

Thunder from Down Under at Excalibur	800-937-7777
Chippendales at Rio	800-752-9746
Jubilee! at Bally's	800-634-3434
La Femme at MGM Grand	800-929-1111
Crazy Girls at Riviera	800-634-6753
X Girls at Planet Hollywood	877-333-9474
Fantasy at Luxor	800-288-1000

Best Strip Clubs

Olympic Gardens	702-385-8987
	www.ogvegas.com
Sapphires	702-796-6000
	www.sapphirelasvegas.com
Scores	702-367-4000
	www.scoreslasvegas.com
Seamless	702-227-5200
	www.seamlessclublv.com
Spearmint Rhino	702-796-3600
	www.spearmintrhino.com
Club Paradise	702-734-7990
	www.clubparadise.net

Best Helicopter Companies

Maverick Helicopters	888-261-4411
	www.maverickhelicopters.com
Las Vegas Helicopters	888-779-0800
	www.lasvegashelicopters.com
Sundance Helicopters	800-653-1881
	www.sundancehelicopters.com

Best Limo Companies

AWG	702-792-8000
	www.awgcs.com
Bell Trans	702-739-7990
	www.bell-trans.com
CLS Transportation	702-740-4545
	www.lasvegaslimo.com
24–7 Limousines	702-616-0077
	www.24-7limousines.com